Nevertheless

Nevertheless

A Memoir

Alec Baldwin

HARPER LUXE

An Imprint of HarperCollins*Publishers*

This book is dedicated to my future, the only place
where any possibilities lie.
To my wife, my children, and all our moments together,
which are a dream come true.

HarperCollins books may be purchased for educational, business, or
sales promotional use. For information please e-mail the Special Markets
Department at SPsales@harpercollins.com.

FIRST HARPERLUXE EDITION

ISBN: 978-0-06-249693-5

HarperLuxe™ is a trademark of HarperCollins Publishers.

Library of Congress Cataloging-in-Publication Data is available upon
request.

17 18 19 20 21   ID/LSC   10 9 8 7 6 5 4 3 2 1

Preface

I like to daydream about having a different kind of life. I've wanted to open a stationery store because I was obsessed with fine writing paper, boxed note cards with images of fine art from museums, and exquisite pens. That was on Monday. Or a store that sold antique clocks. Specifically, alarm clocks or mantel clocks. I had a fetish for antique travel alarm clocks, where the clock folded itself, turtle-like, into a pretty case from Hermès or Jaeger-LeCoultre. That was on Tuesday. On Wednesday, I'd be the warden of a prison because I thought that was a powerful way to reach some of the most forgotten people. I'd help those who had done wrong and were actually caught and put away by those of us who, by God's grace, were neither caught nor punished. Come Thursday, I was sure it was an art gallery in Chelsea, one of those places in the West 20s.

I'd live in London Terrace and walk to work every day. I'd travel to Europe, buying and selling acclaimed art. But on Friday, I wanted to be a teacher. I'd hide away behind ivy walls and teach literature or film studies. Or I'd become a lawyer and prosecute those who abuse power, making the bad guys tremble at the sound of my name. Then Saturday forced me to admit that I wanted to relax and have fun, so I'd open a nightclub. Like Rick Blaine, I'd surround myself with a cast of lovably quirky characters. All men would envy me. Women, against their better judgment, would throw themselves at me nightly. But I would demur. I would wait for Ilsa to show up and prove to me that love is real.

I spent Sunday looking over this list, and I realized, after a while, that none of these occupations involved being famous. People who do these jobs may touch many lives, but they are not sports figures or movie stars or potentates. They go about their business and are immune, presumably, to the whims of the public's praise and the scorn of the media.

I didn't end up choosing any of those careers and fell into a completely different line of work. I fell into a rabbit hole, which is defined as "a bizarre, confusing, or nonsensical situation or environment, typically one from which it is difficult to extricate oneself."

I never imagined I would do what I've done for a

living or see what I've seen. Acting can satisfy some of the desires and curiosities found in those imagined careers. Over time, I realized that, through acting, I could touch every station of the cross, as I perceived them (humility, service, loyalty), that might earn my late father's approval. I never wanted to be an actor because it seemed so trite. But as I moved along the game board and thought I might be invited to play a bit longer, much of that cynicism fell away. Opportunities arrived to appreciate life's beauty, mysteries, truths, and heartbreak, to understand life on a higher plane. All of this while you play like a child again. And try to become immortal, like Marilyn Monroe or Elvis. This is what most people in the entertainment business want, I believe. Just as much as they want money and power and adulation, they want a certain kind of immortality.

My own relationship to the entertainment business was much simpler. Acting was a way to ease, though never eliminate, the financial anxieties of the boy from South Shore Long Island who remains inside me today. I'm not actually writing this book to discuss my work, my opinions, or my life. I'm not writing it to explain some of the painful situations I've either landed in or thrown myself into. I'm writing it because I was paid to write it. And as we go along, you'll know that the mercenary force is strong in this one. You might want to stop there and put the book down, knowing that its theme is that I did a lot of things for money. Anything truly worthwhile that emerged was just a bit of luck or wonderful alchemy. I once read that Richard Burton made some choices in his film career so he could buy Elizabeth Taylor a diamond ring or whatnot. That's my excuse, too. Except there was no Liz and there were no diamonds.

However, just as the challenges and charms of performing in public for many years won me over, writing this book also became its own reward. To look at one's life, to stare at all of those joys and mistakes, all of those moments and emotions—you'd be dead, in some sense, if it didn't change you. As was so often the case during my career as an actor, money prompted this memoir until the moment something else took over. Now, I want you to know that my name is Xander Baldwin. (The x sounds like a z.) I'm from 25 Greatwater Avenue in Massapequa, New York, and my siblings, including Beth, Daniel, Billy, Jane, and Stephen, didn't turn out all bad, and that is due to my parents: my mother, who lived to grow and change in remarkable ways, and my father, who sacrificed his life caring for and giving to his children and others.

I'm also writing this book to share the truth, as well as my remorse, about some of the incautious choices I've made and subsequent difficult times I've lived through in public. The worst mistakes I've made in this life live forever on the Internet. Online, people remind me of them every day. I've endured and invited a level of scrutiny that has pushed me to the brink of self-destruction or simply a self-imposed anonymity. I cannot lie to you on that point. The media gauntlet we are either contracted or compelled to run can be soul-crushing. But the boy who first wanted to run for president in the fourth grade still lives in me. I dreamed of doing some kind of work that would make a difference in the lives of the people I cared about. I love my country. My way of loving it meant urging it toward being better. I believe we make it better when we are fully informed and engaged. Informing people, engaging them, that's what I wanted to do. I ended up in the rabbit hole, however, where sometimes we play silly games, and other times we examine life as deeply as novelists, doctors, and judges. And the one difference is that our job is not only to play all the parts and to understand everyone onstage, but also to become them. When we're done, we reacquaint ourselves with who we really are, perhaps the most difficult part of all.

Every day, I'm filled with doubt about my choices. Every day. Writing this book presented a thousand such choices and, thus, has been both painful and therapeutic. Nevertheless, I am grateful to those who will read it and allow me to share some of what I've seen, what I've learned, and who I believe I truly am.

Nevertheless

1
Lie Still

The woman lying next to me was a large woman. I will always remember her that way. Only five feet seven, she seemed taller. Her forearms were like blades, broad and flat, and packed with rippling tendons from endlessly carrying around children and groceries and whatnot. She was strong and had fast hands, gunfighter fast. When she struck you, her right arm sprang toward you . . . snap! . . . like Navratilova's backhand.

Even in sleep, she seemed frightened or wracked, her face slightly contorted, sweat beading around her neck. Her dyed hair, thin and damaged, was matted around her forehead and temples, a brownish tint on a cotton candy fineness of texture. If I turned slightly in any direction, the arm whipped. "Lie still," she ordered, as if she was at sleep's portal until my slightest movement had intervened. I froze. What was I there for? Was it to ease her mind? Was it to protect me from whatever danger she envisioned I'd face if I went out and joined the other children I could hear playing outside in the afternoon? Was I there to keep her company?

The room was as still as the moon. On a bureau against one wall was a television. Along another wall was another bureau, on top of which sat cheap plastic baskets of clothing, some tangled, some already folded. The arrangement of these baskets tumbled down onto the floor, where baskets were piled on top of baskets. One might think that the residents of this house were operating a laundry business. There was laundry, in baskets, everywhere: clothes from previous seasons; clothes passed along from friends as hand-me-downs; clothes purchased, still tagged and new, that were lost under the mountain and never worn. All of it was piled in a multicolored tangle of cotton and synthetics. Years later, it might have been a hit at some contemporary art gallery. Then, it was just a mess.

The furniture in this room was chipped and marred. There were dark rings from wet glasses here, a handle or knob missing there. Go into another room, and it was more of the same. Threadbare chairs, some covered with bedsheets to hide escaping tufts of stuffing, sat in a living room no one used. A dining room held a table requisitioned for folding even more laundry. There was a den, with a TV, that was the center of the home, for all practical purposes. A small kitchen resembled a New York City subway car in the mid-1970s, in terms of traffic, wear and tear.

Doors came off hinges, and windowpanes were cracked or broken. You might wait a year for them to be fixed. Appliances were often in need of repair. Nearly everything in the house was a donation from a relative or friend. Thus our gratitude flowed while they simply expunged their old stuff: sofas and chairs, beds and bedding, inexpensive dishes and mismatched collections of forks and knives. One exception was a beautifully carved bookcase with beveled glass doors, bequeathed by my grandparents, that sat incongruously in the living room, the books inside worth more, perhaps, than the other contents of the house combined.

The woman, half asleep, now breathed heavily, in and out. On the bedside table was a small wicker basket nearly overflowing with a haphazard pile of prescription vials: sleeping pills, blood pressure pills, antianxiety pills, perhaps eight or ten small bottles. Even at my young age, I wondered if the active ingredients of these drugs were constantly rolling around inside her head. She stirred and reached over to sip from a raspberry-colored metallic tumbler, filled with Tab, which sat on the night table near Pill Hill. Beads of sweat ran down its side, making new rings on what was left of the table's finish. The woman, believing that it held magical weight-loss potential, drank rivers of Tab. If slimming was her goal, it was to no effect. Each successive choice to have six kids in eleven years left her body wracked. From the bottom of her rib cage to the top of her pelvis, any muscular fiber was gone. When she coughed or laughed, her stomach, beneath her sheer bedclothes, seemed to ripple like water. I lay there and looked toward the window and wondered if the kids' shouts and whoops accompanied throwing snowballs at cars.

Why did she never want to go outside? Why didn't she want to take a walk or get some fresh air or get out of this room? Slightly stoned and immobile, she might end up like some suburban version of the Collyer brothers, buried by an avalanche of unfolded laundry, I feared. What could I do to help her? "This is my mother," I thought. "Whatever that means."

In the earliest days, she tried. She was alone in her tiny house with six kids and no help. (Sometimes, I repeat that to myself, over and over: "Six kids and no help, six kids and no help.") So she baked, constantly: cookies, brownies, cakes. Popcorn and Kool-Aid were served on a picnic table in summertime. Back then, you controlled your kids, perhaps told them you loved them, by serving them their favorite sweets. Today, love means withholding much of that.

Our previous house, where I had lived until I was nine, was a small ranch that had only two bedrooms. My sister Beth shared a bedroom with two of my brothers and me. The room had had two bunk beds. My younger sister slept in the living room in a playpen-like enclosure. My brother Stephen, then a baby, slept in a crib in my parents' room. At the old house, a clothesline ran across much of the yard, packed tight with children's clothes, sheets, and towels. In a two-bedroom, one-bathroom house with six young children, the absence of a working washing machine or dryer was enough to wear my mother's patience raw. By 1967, my parents realized that these conditions were ridiculous and moved to a nearby dilapidated house with four bedrooms.

Lying next to my mother, I forged a lifetime of conversation with myself. Other children talk to themselves, whispering intently to someone who isn't there. However, I went all out here: not merely repeating lines from films, TV shows, and commercials, but attempting dialects and ethnicities and singing songs. While my mother was next to me "napping," I was channeling Steve Allen, Frank Gorshin, and the Beatles, Allan

Sherman, Dick Shawn, and Paul Lynde. All of them might appear in a single afternoon, all in that bed.

Eventually, my mother would stir. Her fitful nap ended, she headed to the kitchen to grapple with what to make for dinner. She would tell me we needed milk or bread or butter. She would tell me to hike up to the local delicatessen, perhaps a mile away, to get the supplies. I'd be more than willing to go. "I'm out!" I'd think. I was nine years old and addicted to solitude.

If you went out the door of our house and looked west, there was a block of middle-class South Shore Long Island "white flight" homes. In them lived businessmen, contractors, a fireman. It was a mix of education levels and tastes. On their 120-by-100-foot lots, these properties seemed generous and appealing to Brooklynites like my dad. Whereas our neighbors' homes were covered in antiseptic aluminum siding or traditional shingles, our house featured the more urban-style asphalt siding, in a dulled and cracked forest green. The house seemed to sag, a slight bulge here and swelling there, perhaps from dampness or some compromise in the framing underneath. All of the white-painted trim was peeling. The windows were dressed with cheap curtains on tension rods, all graying for need of washing. The pitted driveway was stained from unintentionally expelled automotive fluids. Some neighbors parked a small boat in their yard or planted a garden. Looking at our house, though, you got the feeling that Marjorie Main might come out on the porch and slap Humphrey Bogart across the face.

Directly across the street from our house was a public nine-hole golf course. I walked through a hole that had been cut into the fence and stepped out onto the snowy plain. My lifelong worship of winter and snow was born on these walks. Heavy snowfall is a great homogenizer in making everything pretty. Even our uncared-for house looked slightly more charming, if only for that day.

The golf course divided the neighborhood essentially in half. Streets with Native American names like Pocahontas, Seneca, and Seminole were labeled east and west. The course was called Peninsula and sat directly across Sunset Road from our house on West Iroquois Street. Before any talk of climate change, you'd swear it snowed more on Long Island then. The sun would come out after a big storm and shine on the frozen surface, creating a crème brûlée–like crust on top of acres of powdery snow. Walking across the golf course property after a grand snowfall was like stepping in and out of a series of buckets. Lift your leg straight out, extend, then punch your boot through the icy veneer. Up, out, down. Repeat, repeat. A walk that might have taken ten minutes across grass took thirty. However, a walk that took me along a plowed street was neither as adventurous nor as beautiful. I wanted to feel piercing wind lashing my face. I wanted to walk across this field because it was pristine and white and no one was there. I could talk to myself all I wanted.

In summertime, the golf course was our Hole-in-the-Wall, a sanctuary within which neighborhood kids drank their first beer, smoked their first joint, or had their first fumbling romantic consummation. And, above all, we played ball here for hours and only the darkness could send us home. We played baseball and football games in their seasons. We held the occasional pitch-and-putt golf matches in July and August, when the days were longest and we were guaranteed an hour of fading light after the staff of the club had gone home. The men who ran the place had names like Ferdie and Tiger and Frenchie. If we jumped the gun and attempted, too early, to whack a seven iron toward the third green that ran by our house, one of these guys would come rattling toward us in a golf cart, screaming and cursing. As we got older, they got older and their protests grew to sound more like pleas. When my brother Daniel eventually grabbed a bag of clubs and entered the modest clubhouse to play the course as an eighteen-year-old legitimate, paying customer, it was as if Butch Cassidy had walked into a bank to open a checking account.

The town of Massapequa had a couple of thumbs of land that pointed out into the Great South Bay. Like on much of Long Island's South Shore, canals had been dug to create more waterfront property. They were 1950s developments with names like Bar Harbor, Harbor Green, and Old Harbor Green. Our area was called Nassau Shores, or just "the Shores" by the locals, and it was the least of these areas, in terms of real estate value. The other waterfront communities were zoned so that their kids attended the town's original high school, Massapequa High School, giving them a small but discernible boost of prestige. Older residents called it "The High School," placing it above its crosstown counterpart, Berner High School, which my siblings and I attended.

My dad taught at The High School, and there had been a suggestion that we could go to the school where my dad taught, as other teachers' children had done. But my dad thought it might be too much for us (and I'm sure for him) if we all spent day and night under the same roof. So my dad taught at The High School, and we went to Berner, the more working-class and, in some ways, less desirable of the two. When I looked over my dad's school yearbook every spring, I noticed that The High School seemed to have more of a polish to its efforts. Berner had a Drama Club. The High School had "Masque and Muse." The High School had an "It's Academic" team, aimed at scoring an appearance on the old TV game show. Its faculty adviser, my dad's best friend, Arnie Herman, often laid out his own money to pay for supplies so that the kids had a shot to get on television. The High School's sports teams dominated their league, until eventually Berner's football team beat them in a game that was the final word in their crosstown rivalry that I was there to witness during my junior and senior years. Whereas Massapequa High School looked like a postcard suburban public school, Berner looked like a hastily financed annex, built to handle the overflow of a rapidly growing community. Berner was a concrete battleship of a building, with very few trees and little character.

Our neighborhood was kids and more kids. The Jewish families had one or two kids. The Protestant families had two and three kids. The Catholic families averaged around five kids. This was an era when working-class parents still had large families built on faith, believing that Providence would see them through. Sports and games were the glue that held our neighborhood together. Nearly all of our neighboring families brought talent, if not greatness, to whatever games they were drafted to play. At least that's what we told ourselves. With names like Fat Tony, Buff, and Steiner Forty-Niner, the kids could throw, run, hit, and tackle. They could drive, pitch, and putt. They were fast, tough, and had good hands. They would stand in T-shirts in forty-degree weather, ignoring the cries of their siblings or mothers. With a never-say-die glint in their eyes, they were focused only on the current, last-ditch effort to score another touchdown. Day after day, sunset after sunset, we never, ever wanted to go home.

Our Winter Games were limited by topography. With no hills to speak of, our sledding runs lasted for only seconds down modest inclines. Snow meant snowballs as missiles, used in games that involved the risk we sought more as we got older. One winter you are building a snowman, the next you're crouched down behind a fence inside the sanctuary of Hole-in-the-Wall, flinging snowballs at cars as they slowly curved around the Unqua Circle, the snowball thrower's Dealey Plaza. The game was simple. Hit the car with a snowball, ten points; hit the windshield, twenty points; put the snowball into any open window, fifty points; hit the driver of the vehicle who has leapt from the car in order to scream at or threaten you, one hundred points. The Hall of Famer, the legend, the Sandy Koufax of this contest, was my brother Daniel. Many adult men, unwilling to leave their cars stopped in the relatively busy traffic circle, were gunned down by Daniel. Some were hit more than once. Imagine a car drives by and you hit it with a snowball. The driver gets out and BANG! You hit him. The driver spots you through the fence and he charges after you. But like Namath in the pocket, waiting that extra second for Maynard or Sauer to gain another step, you hang in. You go at them like the Pittsburgh defense, and BANG, you fire again. In the Winter Games, in our contests in every season, Daniel was the champion.

Another even more frowned-upon activity was "skitching." This involved waiting behind a parked car, a tree, or some other blind that was adjacent to a stop sign. Cars usually came to a full stop on those icy roads. The skitcher would get down low and scurry in behind the car, grab onto the bumper, and get pulled along streets that had yet to be plowed, salted, or sanded. You didn't want to be spotted by other drivers, so our block, with the golf course lined with hedges and its stop sign, was prime. Few people went out for a drive right after a big snowfall, so there wasn't a lot of traffic coming up behind you. If you grew up near a lake, in winter, I suppose, you ice fished. In the mountains out West, you skied. In Nassau Shores we threw snowballs at cars or grabbed onto their bumpers for a few minutes of thrills. This was our calling.

2
Squirrels

Perhaps the most consistent bond I had with my dad was watching movies on TV at night. At around 10 p.m., just before she went to sleep, my mother would turn down the heat in our home to fifty-five degrees to save on fuel oil. Some nights, I actually thought I could see my own breath. I had devised some lame excuse that enabled me to end up in front of the TV most nights after 11 p.m. "I'm gonna wait up for dad," I'd tell her, as if he had to be let into his own house, like it was some military base. My mother would moan some reply, lacking the energy to question me. Around 10 or 10:30, my father would walk in. Even when I was ten or eleven, still a young child, he showed me little affection. He had few kind words or gestures. But I persisted, asking him about his day. Tired and distracted as always, he went to the refrigerator to eat whatever was left over, and then lay on the couch with his newspapers and watched the 11 o'clock news.

At 11:30 the local CBS station aired the Late Show, a movie broadcast that ran until around one. At 1 a.m., they showed the Late, Late Show, playing another classic movie. Some nights, they actually had the Late, Late, Late Show at around 3 a.m. Network movie programming at that time relied entirely on old studio libraries. Weekdays brought the 4:30 Movie on the local ABC station, which, for a period of time, showed the same film the entire week. A precursor of the VCR, this was for viewers who could not watch a movie in one sitting. (While home sick one week, I watched *Inherit the Wind* five times and memorized every line.) CBS had Picture for a Sunday Afternoon. There was Chiller Theatre, showing horror. On our TV, the Late Show broadcast movies like *How Green Was My Valley*, *Five Graves to Cairo*, or *Passage to Marseille*. At night, the pattern was always the same. My dad would say, "You'd better get up to bed." Then he would read the old capsule movie reviews from the *New York Times* TV section. These were pithy, often funny one-liners that described the film. (Example: "*Ball of Fire*: Barbara Stanwyck tells Gary Cooper where he can go.") My father would let out a low whistle; then he would say, "*Witness for the Prosecution.* Now that's a good one." I'd ask if I could watch some of it, and he would say, "OK, but just a few minutes." He'd smile at the opening credits, and within fifteen minutes, he was out. The first film I ever stayed up to watch with him was *Sorry, Wrong Number* with Barbara Stanwyck and Burt Lancaster. It made me a die-hard fan of both stars, and I would go on to watch that movie again perhaps twenty or thirty times. That film and *A Christmas Carol* with Alastair Sim are movies I still watch regularly, and although my dad has been gone for many years, when I put them on, I feel as if he is in the room with me again.

I watched hundreds of movies on TV. Before VCRs and DVDs, you had to pay attention. There was no rewind button. I learned every line. "That'll get you in real good with your boss," Bogart intones to Elisha Cook Jr. "Whaddya hear, whaddya say," Cagney chirps in his signature style. "Fasten your seat belts, it's gonna be a bumpy night," Bette Davis sneers at her dinner guests. "Whatever you do, don't leave him lyin' here like this," Brando implores Eva Marie Saint. I watched every movie I could and memorized as many lines as I could, which was actually easier than you'd think because actors back then had a style you don't often see anymore. To watch Kirk Douglas or Elizabeth Taylor or Gregory Peck is to see film acting at its apex, because it was newer then. It was more important and mysterious. Even a battalion of stars who were not necessarily leading men and women but rather pure and wonderful supporting actors could enter your consciousness and never leave. From Franklin Pangborn to Thelma Ritter, from Slim Pickens to Maureen Stapleton, from Lou Costello to Hermione Gingold, I ate them up. My first acting lessons were in that room, with my dad, and they were the best I'd ever have. Gable taught me how to act. Peter O'Toole taught me. William Holden taught me as much, if not more, than any other. Orson Welles, Teresa Wright, Vera Miles, Jerry Lewis, Rock Hudson. There are more acting lessons, real lessons, in watching *To Kill a Mockingbird* than in an entire year in most drama school classrooms. When Brando shouts to Lee J. Cobb, "I'm glad what I done to you," a lump comes up inside me every time. These films are treasures to me. And every emotion I could not express passed through me whenever I watched them.

Massapequa sits in the southeast corner of Nassau County on Long Island. The next town over, Amityville, had a significant black population, particularly in the working-class area north of the Long Island Rail Road. The man who ran everything in the Massapequa school district was a New York lawyer named

Lew Ames who also owned a local real estate company called Big Chief Lewis. The Massapequa High
School football team is called the Chiefs, and Lewis
had an enormous version of an old cigar store Native
American in front of his office. Ames, who was bald
and brusque and resembled the actor William Fraw-
ley, eventually became president of the school board.
My father told me that Ames had kept Massapequa a
"lily-white" town by making sure that brokers never
showed their listings to black families. To do so would
have cost them dearly.

Ames ran the school board, and he handpicked the
superintendent of schools. That superintendent was
handed a list of Ames's "enemies" who were to be
sidestepped for promotion within their departments
and throughout the system. My father was beloved
by his students, and this resulted in an almost Billy
Budd–like resentment on the part of some higher-ups.
He was never offered a position as department chair,
vice-principal, or principal. Those teachers who played
the game and kissed Ames's ass moved ahead. Many
of them were skilled and respectable educators; others,
not so much.

This political bossism came into sharper focus when
I walked into my tenth grade French class and noticed

that my teacher had a distinctly odd attitude toward me. My father told me that this teacher had been an organizer for Ames's school board campaigns and had once contacted my father, trying to cajole him into finally coming around to support Ames. My dad told her where to go.

When I was a child of perhaps eleven or twelve, my father asked me a simple question in order to, hopefully, set my moral compass. My dad had attended Boys High in Brooklyn and had played football at a championship level with many black teammates. He deplored racism, which wasn't necessarily common for a white man of his generation reared in Brooklyn. "What do you think you would do if you were black?' he asked me. "Would you choose the route of Martin Luther King, the patient, nonviolent route? Or would you emulate Eldridge Cleaver and fight for your rights using violence, if necessary?" I recall saying something like, "I'm not sure how long I could be patient and nonviolent." My father let out a little laugh and said, "I thought so."

My father taught in Massapequa for twenty-eight years, spending his entire career in the classroom and with no advancement. As the provider for a large family, and one who sought to make his career in education his sole source of income, he might have played that one hand cautiously, but he was someone who let his stubborn sense of personal integrity overtake his common sense.

My childhood is divided into two parts, the line being the death of my father's parents. Part one is up until I was ten years old, and during that time, my father seemed happy. He was always present, and we spent a lot of time together as a family. At school, my father took on many tasks. He taught classes in American history and economics. He coached football and riflery. He chaperoned dances, supervised weekend recreation programs, and served as the director of one of the school district's summer camp programs. For him, it was one-stop shopping, a synergy between his commitment to education and community. Some years he was a Little League coach or Cub Scout master. His energy seemed inexhaustible. Other teachers, however, had second jobs to supplement their modest incomes. Some owned businesses that cleaned carpets or polished floors. Others spent the summer working construction to bring in cash. With six children at home, my mother probably hoped he would join them. However, my father received nearly all his income from a single employer, and as his friend Arnie Herman told me, he needed to be somewhere that people valued him and what he had to offer. Arnie said, "The students in your father's classes weren't relying on him to paint the house or pay the bills. In his classes, they simply wanted him to teach them." Herman was right. My father's relationship to his students defined him. They rewarded him by making him the first teacher they dedicated the school's yearbook to while he was alive and active, a distinction normally given to one who was retired or deceased. They dedicated it to him twice.

As a man with so many balls in the air at the school, my father had a key ring rivaled only by the custodial staff themselves. He could get into the rifle range, the gymnasium, equipment lockers, storage rooms, locker rooms, A/V storage, you name it. This key ring offered us pretty unlimited access to the trove of athletic equipment that characterized a significant period of our childhoods, especially for the few weeks in summer that my father was free from work. He would load bats, balls, gloves, rubber bases, and even a volleyball net into the back of our old, beat-up station wagon, which was covered in dents and dings, with bald tires and a worn paint finish. My parents would fill a cooler with eggs, bacon, bread, orange juice, tuna salad, bologna, and cheese, and pack paper plates, silverware, frying pans, a cheap grill and charcoal briquettes, and anything else needed to prepare and serve both breakfast and lunch to eight people. The image of us hauling all of this from the parking field to the shore of Jones Beach would later make me think of what it must have been like to film *Lawrence of Arabia*. We'd set up, cook, eat, and then swim and play some kind of ball game until around four o'clock, while my parents alternately watched us or read—the Sunday *Times* for my father, the latest from Sidney Sheldon for my mother. We baked brown in the sun. My sister Beth, the eldest, not one for sports, was usually overwhelmed or fatigued by her four brothers' incessant activity. She typically sat and read magazines, or would elect not to come and would go off and visit friends instead. On the way home, we'd stop at Marjorie Post Park, one of two spacious community parks in Massapequa. My father would herd us through a quick shower in the pool-area locker room. "I'm not gonna have six children backing up my septic tank when they can shower here," he would toss at my mother, who always seemed to sigh at all the corners we had to cut.

My mother grew up in Syracuse, New York, as one of seven children: six girls and one boy. Her father was a relatively successful businessman, and they lived in a nice home in downtown Syracuse. They weren't wealthy in the sense that they spent all of his money, but they lived well, with maids and nannies. I never knew my grandfather, who died when I was one year old, but I'm told that he was a generous and loving father, always coming home from business trips with gifts for his children. My maternal grandmother was ill during my earliest childhood and I never knew her either, as she lived out her last years in a nursing home, spending any money her husband had left behind for her nursing home care. Many of my mother's siblings and their families, a large group, lived in the Syracuse area, and we visited them many summers when I was a small child. We rented a moldy house adjacent to Lake Ontario in a spot called Sandy Pond, where the houses had names like Camp Rendezvous. We swam in Lake Ontario or rowed a boat in the small pond for a couple of weeks, during which time the grown-ups drank, gossiped, and traded war stories about raising children with little money. These were the only family vacations we ever took. Not to Manhattan or Disneyland. We went to Pulaski, New York.

My father had two brothers, one of whom retired from the NYPD and convinced my father to cosign a loan for him to buy a small inn on Lake Wallenpaupack in Pennsylvania. He defaulted on the loan, and my father was hit with a judgment to pay a few thousand dollars. The bank threatened to garnishee his salary to collect. I think that was the financial hit that my father never quite recovered from. My uncle essentially vanished after that. My father's youngest brother, Charles, was a figure out of either a Ken Kesey novel or a Wes Anderson film, depending on the circumstances. Family legend was that Charles had a remarkably high score on his army IQ test. He enrolled briefly at Syracuse University, where both my parents went, and met and married my mother's sister. That was my family: two brothers married two sisters. Within a few years, my uncle Charles left his wife, my aunt Becky. She arrived on our doorstep with her three girls, Ruth, Marion, and Louise. My father was her ex-husband's brother. My mother was her sister. These girls were my double first cousins, the blood in their veins nearly identical to mine. My father, whose Christ complex would surface at the most inopportune times, let them move in. He enrolled them in school. He fed them and clothed them. They stayed with us for almost a year. My father, who had one hand tied behind his back with the loan default from one brother, was now raising the other brother's three kids. I look back and realize that this is not the recipe for a long life—an honorable one, maybe, but not a long one.

My father had grown up in Brooklyn. As children, we visited my grandparents often on St. James Place, in the Fort Greene area. In the 1960s, the neighborhood was blighted. Unemployed men, nearly all Hispanic or

African-American, sat on stoops or sofas that had been left on the sidewalk while drinking beer or liquor from paper bags. I'd walk with my grandfather to the newspaper stand to get all of the daily New York papers, perhaps six or seven of them. Next he'd pick up a carton of Chesterfields and a few quart bottles of Ballantine or Schaefer beer. Once he was stocked, he went inside and hit the sofa and, exactly like the guys outside, smoked and drank all day. The only thing separating them was a law degree and a navy pension.

My father would bring us to his parents' house on a Sunday afternoon, and my grandmother would cook dinner. She was a world-class cook who spent the better part of the afternoon preparing the perfect turkey, the perfect mashed potatoes, and the perfect cookies. My grandparents had no money, but they made sure we felt special by buying us Cokes in the old glass bottles. I have countless memories of watching television in their living room. There was *The Jackie Gleason Show* ("Live, from the fun and sun capital of the world, Miami Beach, Florida!"), *Candid Camera*, and *The Ed Sullivan Show*. I met Paul McCartney on that couch in Brooklyn in August of 1965, during one of his later appearances on the Sullivan show. Around 9 p.m., my father would gather up my siblings and begin to load them into his station wagon. In summertime, with no school the next day, my grandfather would mouth to my father, "Let him stay," pointing at me. As my grandfather's namesake, I was the Dauphin. My father would roll his eyes and sigh. Granting this request meant he'd have to drive back to Brooklyn the next day, but he'd agree, and everyone would trudge off except me. "Why do you and I get along so well, Grandpa?" I'd ask. "Because we have a common enemy," he'd reply.

My grandmother wore a hearing aid and would enter the living room to say good night after she had cleaned the kitchen, my grandfather having never left the couch. "I'm signing off for the evening," she would announce, and head toward a bedroom down the hall from where my grandfather slept. The walls of her room were lined with massive stacks of books and other personal effects belonging to my peripatetic uncle Charles, who used this as a storage room. My grandfather slept in the other bedroom, and those nights with him created the most indelible images of my life. There was a window looking down an alley along the rear of the building. A cat my grandfather had named Two-Eyed Tilly, with eyes of different colors, would cry, and he would put food for her on the windowsill. I lay next to my grandfather in silence, while classical music or some talk show played on the radio. He was on my left, smoking. As he raised a Chesterfield to his mouth, a long ash extended from the bright orange cherry. When he drew from the cigarette, the glow would illuminate his prominent nose. The room was filled with beautiful antique furniture: an enormous armoire, a marble-topped console, a full-length dressing mirror in a handsome hand-carved frame. My father's family had a future once, and lost it under unusual circumstances. On a table near the sill were two busts, one of Shakespeare, another of Jefferson. Shakespeare stared at me. Jefferson stared at Shakespeare. In the air filled with the voice of Barry Gray and a cloud of smoke, the cat went off to bed. My grandfather would extinguish his last cigarette and swing his legs to the floor. The bathroom was fifteen feet down the hallway, but he'd reach for a chamber pot and piss into it, something he'd do two or three more times during the night. I lay there, frozen. If I tried to break that granitic silence, my grandfather would simply yawn and say, "Sleep now, my boy." He always called me "my boy."

Lean, tall, bald, and always with a twinkle in his eye, my grandfather was Alexander Rae Baldwin Sr. My father was junior. I was the third. But three Alecs were one too many, so I was called Xander Baldwin, or Xan for short. The oldest son of an oldest son in an Irish Catholic family is often slotted to become a priest. (I actually considered it, but one look at Miss

Cebu, who taught sixth grade in Unqua Elementary School, and I realized I wasn't cut out for celibacy.) One day, my grandfather and I were entering his apartment when his neighbor passed by us in the hallway. He was a rummy-Irish, forty-year-old bachelor who lived with his mother upstairs. "This your grandson?" he croaked, his face thick with whiskers and missing a few of his teeth. "Yes, Joe," my grandfather said, managing a smile and quickening his search for the keys. Joe handed me a sweet, and I took it. "Here's a penny candy for the boy," he said. My grandfather closed his hand tight around mine that held the candy. "Very kind of you, Joe. Give my best to your mother." We entered the apartment, and my grandfather closed the door and suddenly spun me around. He yanked the candy out of my hand. I was flabbergasted, searching for an explanation. "Taking candy from a man like that? Never been married! No children!" As I did with most things my grandfather said, I walked around muttering it again and again for the rest of the day, like it was a line from one of the classic films I loved. "Never been married! No children!" All the while, I never quite understood what it meant.

In the years I knew him, my grandpa was a bright if somewhat typically racist white New Yorker of his day. He was both a philatelist and a numismatist to the limited degree that he could afford. Traveling across the United States, either gambling at racetracks or pursuing a job offer, he would enclose a note to me and post it with a First Day of Issue stamp. Or, from Brooklyn, he would find out where a First Day Cover was being issued and, like all everyday stamp collectors, he'd send the post office there a self-addressed envelope, with a note to me inside and the money to buy the stamp. The envelope arrived in, for example, Independence, Missouri, prior to the issuance. To his home was mailed the canceled stamp, marked "First Day of Issue." These "First Day Covers" were collectors' items.

He collected coins and placed them in numismatic books, each one a case with individual sleeves. They held liberty dollars, buffalo nickels, Mercury dimes, and the "wheat penny," as we called it, which was replaced with the Lincoln Memorial after that monument was constructed. To this day, when I handle pennies, I search for "wheats" and collect any I find. I could never speak to what the value of the coin collection was, but one would assume that each book, filled with only the finest quality of these collectibles and arranged so carefully, had to be worth a significant amount.

One summer day when I was around thirteen, a couple of years after my grandfather died, I went to the home of a friend and colleague of my dad, Joe McPartlin. Joe was a teacher who did things differently from my father, meaning he had other income, outside of his teaching position, and he took his wife and family on what I imagined were fancy vacations. While they were away, I gathered their mail and cut the grass. One Saturday, I finished late and headed home as the sun was going down. As I pushed my mower along the road, I caught an older man staring at me. He yelled, "You cut grass, sonny?" I told him that I did, and as he approached, he asked my name and if I was from the neighborhood. "Alexander Baldwin," I said. He stared at me and said, "You related to Alex Baldwin, the Brooklyn DA who was indicted in the fur rackets case?" I went white. After I muttered something to him, I ran home, and my father and mother were there. When I explained what had happened, my father became very quiet.

"Get the box," he told her. Down from a shelf in the back of her bedroom closet came a small cardboard box from which my father removed a stack of newspaper clippings, mostly from the old *Brooklyn Eagle*. The story they told explained how my grandfather had been an assistant DA in Brooklyn when he was indicted for taking a bribe. He was acquitted, but during the trial and the subsequent commission hearings conducted by John Harlan Amen, my grandfather was disbarred.

What had been a comfortable home and lifestyle for his family was washed away. They moved from a better area of Brooklyn to the more racially mixed and run-down Fort Greene. He became an income tax preparer. He began to drink heavily, drinking his way down to Florida, where he ran a parking concession at the Hialeah racetrack. Apparently my grandmother soldiered on and raised her three sons on her earnings as a nurse, without a husband around much of the time.

According to the mythology of my family, my father's mother was canonized. In everyone's heart, my grandmother was a saint, thoughtful, loving, kind. These two people were more important to me and created more warm memories during my childhood than almost anyone. And then, the next big change came.

Death comes into children's lives in dramatic ways, or quiet, more ordinary ones. The first important death in my home came in hushed tones and shadows. One night my mother gathered us up, maybe all six of us, and dropped us at the home of my neighbor and best friend, Kevin Cornelius. I was ten. In the other room, my parents spoke quietly and gravely. Then my dad was gone. My grandfather had gone into a hospital in New York for an angioplasty, and my grandmother had fallen down on the stone steps at the hospital's entrance while visiting him. She fractured her skull, was in a coma, and died four days later. The hospital advised that my grandfather not be informed right away, as he was in a cardiac recovery unit. After the first two days, it became unbearable and my father told him.

When Theodore Roosevelt's mother died, he wrote, "The light has gone out of my life," and that's what happened to my dad, too. Years later, a therapist outlined something essential to me by piecing together my father's history. He asked me to examine the period from the fall of 1967 to the fall of 1968. "In one year, your father turned forty and with that came all of the self-appraisals about what he had and had not achieved; as a progressive, he watched Martin Luther King and RFK get killed; next, his political nemesis, Richard Nixon, rises from the dead and is elected president; his mother is killed in a horrible, freak accident." I saw my dad in a clearer light, one that explained why, up until his death in 1983 at the age of only fifty-five, my father was never the same again.

My grandfather was hospitalized in May of the following year. After another angioplasty to overcome the effects of all those Chesterfields and Ballantines, corruption hearings and general shiftlessness, my uncle Charles reported that his father, Alexander Rae Baldwin Sr., had died after eating a pint of maple walnut ice cream in his hospital bed, in direct violation of his doctor's orders. He took an afternoon nap, moaned in midsleep, and died at age sixty-nine. My father sighed and said to me, "When both your parents are gone, you are an orphan."

Without this cozy, albeit urban-blighted, sanctuary to retreat to, without his mother available to support him or comfort him or simply to parent him, my father grew more and more withdrawn. Add to that the fact that he had six kids, all growing, all needing, all costing, and he chose to be around less and less during my early teens, taking any job at the school that would lengthen his day. Often my brothers and I would go up to the school and hang out with him during Saturday recreation programs, or "rec." Rec was big with my father and especially Daniel and Billy, who could each play basketball six hours on end, against older kids, as if it were nothing. My dad volunteered for these assignments, which paid him next to nothing, to avoid going home. My parents' marriage was pretty much done by the time I entered junior high school at age twelve.

My mother was lonely. Without a comfortable home or money to go out and meet friends for lunch, without her own siblings nearby or any real connection to her husband, and, most important, without much spirit or vitality left after raising her large family, her social existence was confined to the telephone or my sister Beth and me. So I exploited that. An early acting assignment for me was to come to the kitchen table in the morning and confide in my mother that I was sick. She would scowl at me, in a perfunctory way. Then a strange thing would happen. A quick review of the day ahead would lead her to say, "Don't ever ask me to do this again." Knowing the drill, I would sit at the kitchen table, dressed for school. My father would enter, mutter some gruff good-bye, and go. Once we heard him driving down the street, it was straight to the couch, where we'd spend the day watching *The Dinah Shore Show*, Art Linkletter, *Match Game*, *Divorce Court*, Virginia Graham, Graham Kerr, *The Outer Limits*, Mike Douglas, just acre after acre of this stuff. This bizarre retreat lasted, off and on, for the three or four years from seventh through tenth grade. Eventually, isolating myself at home watching these meaningless programs presented a problem. I missed more school than I should have, to say the least. However, in the meantime, my lonely, virtually homebound mother only required that I join her on a trip to the laundromat, so that I might carry the seven or eight plastic baskets of laundry to be washed and dried, only to be added to the Great Laundry Mountain in her room. If it was Friday, my sister and I would drive with my mother up to the school where my dad worked, pick up his paycheck from the office, and then head to Jade East, a mock pagoda-style restaurant. Eating eggrolls with my sister and my mother while playing hooky from school was the greatest extravagance of my young life. My sister and my mother developed an unbreakable relationship, forging an emotionally incestuous bond that pulled me, or at least attempted to, into its wake.

I could say that it was puberty that stifled my memory. However, I think it was just the deadness of my home and the loss of my dad's attention. I can't summon up a single memory of school from those two years. The seventh and eighth grade classes were held in a school far across town, which meant an interminable bus ride of forty-five minutes each way. The school bus was a rolling jailhouse of twelve- and thirteen-year-olds shouting tedious, vulgar dialogue. There wasn't a well-delivered, witty line to be heard.

My three brothers and younger sister were still kids, and thus either invisible or annoying. Beth was just beginning to run around with boys, though maintaining her innocence. The six of us were lost souls washed up on the shores of 32 West Iroquois Street, Massapequa, New York. Beth, Xander, Danny, Billy, Jane, and Stephen. Six pieces of driftwood, just bobbing through our neighborhood, without a current to carry us in any particular direction, passing time, trying to pass our classes, avoiding trouble, courting trouble, scoring points, telling jokes, drinking, smoking, always mindful of how little we had.

One day, I was walking out of my house, headed to see some friends or ride my bike by myself, and I saw my brother Stephen up the road, bent over something. As I got closer, I could see he had a stick from a tree branch in his hand and was poking at a squirrel that had been crushed by a car. He looked incredibly moved for a kid who was eight years old. He just stared at the dead squirrel and ran the stick, gently, up and down its fur. "We have to bury it," he said, still fixed on the dead animal. Then, he looked up and said, "Will you help me bury it?"

And as he looked at me, I thought, "He's that squirrel. So am I. And all we have is today and the hope that we don't get crushed by something. We have nothing. And everything seems so fragile." We picked up the dead squirrel using two other branches like chopsticks. We dug the hole and buried it. I always remember how Stephen was very sensitive in that way when he was a kid.

My father had no money to buy things, and thus no power to manipulate us by withholding those same things. The parents of other kids owned boats or second homes in some Connecticut woods ("Who the hell has the money for two homes?!"). There were finished basements with pool tables and jukeboxes and popcorn machines. Some parents also provided cash for skating, to go out to eat, to go to a movie or bowling, you name it. We had none of that. Deprived of these more effective means of disciplining a child, my father had only one card to play: the Fear Program. "What time are you going to be home?" he would say, smoldering in a way that I had never seen in a person, before or since. "Ten thirty," I'd reply, my body stiffening slightly in a half wince. "You better be home by ten thirty or you know what's gonna happen to you, don't you?" In came the iron finger. This was his index finger (and you'd swear he had a thimble on the end of it) driven into your chest muscle. That was it: the stare, the iron finger, the genuine threat in his voice. We would reenter the house by 10:30. This was a man who had failed to broker or outright win the respect he wanted outside this door. He would be damned if he were denied it here.

Even at a very young age, I already had a suspicion about how desperate my parents were financially. They were always receiving notices about the electricity or phone being shut off. The garbage carters would drive down our block on Monday mornings and skip our house, leaving a nonpayment slip in the mailbox: "Your service has been halted . . ." By the time I was twelve, a significant realization dawned on me. I understood that if I wanted money, if I needed money for anything, I'd have to go out and get it. Given the ever-looming shadow of the iron finger, selling marijuana or other drugs, as some enterprising kids in the neighborhood had resorted to, was clearly out of the question. At twelve years old, I'm walking the streets of my neighborhood with a bucket, an oversized sponge, and a bottle of dishwashing liquid. I'm soliciting people in their driveways and offering to wash their car for five bucks. (Or four. Make it three.)

I'm the first squeegee man to hit Nassau Shores. My father saw that I needed a backer, so he bought me a lawn mower. God knows how. The deal was I had to give him a cut of my earnings till he was paid back. I cut eight lawns per weekend. That came out to forty bucks gross. Subtract half for my dad, plus gas and oil, and in the first summer I netted fifteen bucks a week. I was rich. By the following summer, the lawn mower was paid off and I was pocketing thirty a week. The more money I netted, however, the more these funds were subject to another form of taxation, which was my mother.

These were times when it was like we were in a Cagney movie. I would come into our kitchen to find my mother staring out the window. I'd ask her what was wrong and she'd answer with a muffled "Nothing . . . nothing." Then she'd cry. My favorite such scenario was when she would say that she had spent my sister Jane's Girl Scout cookie money. The forty or fifty dollars she was short was, uncannily, the amount of money I had in my pocket at that moment. And whoosh, out it came, she took it, no more tears. This happened countless times, and a powerful die was cast in these moments. For the rest of my life, I was enslaved by the belief that there were few problems that could not be solved by applying money or even more money.

When my grandfather died, he left me boxes of the coins he had collected in, perhaps, fifty books. I was also given a simple gold signet ring that bore our common initials, ARB. One day, my sister asked if I would lend her my ring to wear on a date. I might have thought that request was strange, but I just handed it over, refusing to see anything odd. The next morning, she wasn't home and I didn't see her again until that night, when she looked at me strangely and said, in a matter-of-fact way, "I lost your ring. I'm sorry, but it must have fallen off my hand during the night and I've looked everywhere and it's gone." Her words and tone deflected any serious inquiry. Eventually, I learned it had been sold in some pawnshop. I went into my closet, which was filled with my clothes and sneakers. There I kept the coin collection, in boxes, under my guard. I had never assumed it needed protection, but some of the boxes were now nearly empty. No one had ever said a word.

My father, with an almost haunting sense of timing, called me into the den of our house, a room my mother rarely entered. "What's the situation with the coin collection?" he asked.

I will never forget the look in his eye. "Here it is," he seemed to say. "Here's your chance to get a whiff of what I've been dealing with all these years. Go ahead, lie to me. Tell me that it's all intact up in your closet. You won't throw your mother under the bus, but just look me in the eye and know that I know you're lying."

"Yes," I said. "It's all there." He stared at me for a long beat. I thought I heard a blood vessel of his rupture. He sagged a bit more than usual. He couldn't win. Some of this was his fault, he must have known. But he was just so fucking tired of all of it.

Everyone in my home seemed to be moving apart. My younger siblings had their friends and sports or other activities. Beth seemed overwhelmed from always helping my mother around the house, and would run off with her boyfriend, who could buy her little things and give her some much-needed attention. Meanwhile,

I wandered between three groups of people, none of which completely satisfied me. One was the group of rock-and-roll-worshipping, drug-and-alcohol-abusing, street-fighting tough guys. My way into this pack was my friend's older brother. Most of these guys were older, some around eighteen or nineteen and a few in their early twenties. Almost none were in college, and most still lived at home, waiting for a shot at some type of job. My group, the younger siblings and their friends, buzzed around them like apprentices, begging them to buy cigarettes and beer. The owner of the local delicatessen announced that anyone passing beer on to minors would be reported to the police. Thus, we got a lot of "Get fucked" from our elders, until finally one of them relented, recalling his own desperate pleas on many such cold nights. He told us to walk way down the block, where he would hand us the bag. Every night that I spent with them in this way, I knew at that very moment, was wrong.

Standing on the corner of Unqua and Suffolk Roads, the temperature freezing, bundled up and begging someone I hardly knew to buy me beer and cigarettes, I thought, "I don't know what I want, but I know it's not this. I'm acting as if I'm happy, as if I belong. But this is just like the black guys on the couch on St. James Place. Or more like my grandfather, inside the walls of his apartment—now the suburbs themselves were the wall. And these guys are my grandpa-in-training: white, getting by, unfulfilled, bitter."

Next to Berner High School was a vacant wooded lot through which ran a modest stream whose source no one knew. The hideaway was nicknamed Zappa-land, or just Zappa for short. Frank Zappa's songs, and especially his lyrics, were favorites of the crowd who gathered there to smoke pot at 7:15 a.m., right before the assembly bell. These were the most dedicated of pot smokers. Long before the advent of medical marijuana, they smoked it like it was medicine. They smoked pot like they were on the U.S. Olympic Pot Smoking Team. I wondered what these youths might have achieved if they put as much energy into other, more constructive activities as they did into smoking pot. They lived on a kind of academic sideline. They didn't care about Gian Carlo Menotti or the Sykes-Picot Agreement or even where the stream originated. They just wanted to kill time and get numb. Eventually, I smoked a handful of times with that crew, but I couldn't keep up. I ended up sitting in calculus class, stoned, wondering if calculus could help me fly out of the window, away from calculus class.

In high school I played football and lacrosse, neither of them well. I was skinny and had no desire to physically pummel other people, so my choice of athletic pursuits was a poor one. By the time I was in ninth grade, however, I began to think I wanted a girlfriend, and that being on these teams might facilitate that. But everything was filtered through the realities of our house. I remember my parents arguing in another room, my mother yelling something about my father giving up his pretensions about living among professional men. In our neighborhood, there were doctors and lawyers and businessmen. Their waterfront homes were well kept, with boats lolling in canals in their backyards. It was easier to attract someone if you had a giant TV or a boat or a swimming pool with a gleaming barbecue nearby. Getting laid, I suppose, would have been easier if someone, anyone, had folded the laundry and cleaned the kitchen after baking a pile of chocolate chip cookies for my friends before we headed out on my boat. But that wasn't my situation.

The mood in our house was tense. It seemed, at times, to be every man for himself. Trudging my lawn mower from house to house, cutting grass and all alone, didn't seem appealing anymore. Also, I needed more money. Someone hooked me up with Steve, a tough guy who ran gangs of kids who cut grass and charged more money by calling it landscaping. Steve wanted to get this work over with as fast as possible, get his money and go party. So he'd drive us to a house, we'd leap out of the trailer, and hit the sidewalk. Steve would start his stopwatch. We had fifteen minutes, give or take with the size of the yard, to cut, edge, and blow before rolling on to the next house. Two or three guys handled mowers, and two guys worked with edging tools and blowers. I think he paid us by the house, not the hour. Perhaps I did it to be with the "squad," as opposed to being by myself all summer while working.

There is an image I retain from high school, perfect in that it matches sight with sound, touch with smell. After football practice, my teammates went home to places where their uniforms were tossed into washers and dryers and came out clean and ready to be bundled into a gym bag and toted off to school the next morning. I often put my uniform, damp and soiled, back into my locker, unable to bring it home because our washing machine was broken and the following day was not one of the two days a week when we drove to the laundromat.

The image I can't erase is of me standing along a curb, waiting for my mother to arrive with my clean uniform in time for afternoon practice. Behind me, my teammates walked from the locker room to the playing field. A perimeter roadway separated the building from the field area, and as they crossed it, I could hear their metal cleats striking the concrete. The procession went on for two minutes or so. I kept my back to them, straining to see my mother's car, knowing I was late, convinced that each of these guys behind me knew I had no washing machine in my house. The team marched up a concrete staircase to the field level. By the time the sound stopped, they had all hit the grass, ready for warfare. I was still in my street clothes. When my mother came, she handed me the clothes, sometimes actually wet, moaned her excuse, and left.

After playing football in ninth grade, I came to my sophomore year with a very big chip on my shoulder. I began to wonder, had I not bothered to suit up, would they have even noticed. I felt like I didn't want to be there and they didn't care either way. My sophomore year, I walked off the field and quit the team. The coach was an acquaintance of my dad and, unbeknownst to me, the strings were pulled to get me back on the team. My father drove me to the school himself on a Saturday, which was rare and a clear sign of how much this all meant to him. I went in, sat and listened, and walked out. When I got in the car, my father seemed anxious. A father wants to believe, particularly as a child grows up and is no longer a baby in the arms of its mother, that he will help guide and advise his children. This is his time, when he wants to teach them how to make difficult decisions, especially his sons. He wants them to listen and heed his advice. I told him that I had not taken the coach up on his offer and that I would not rejoin the team. And although he accepted that it was useless to make me do it, I could feel something change between us. My father, pretty reticent to begin with, didn't speak to me for a month.

I had been hanging out with guys whose parents didn't want them around. We shared a need to temporarily run away, for different reasons, all wanting somewhere to go that wasn't home. Sometimes we would pop into someone's house to take liquor or money. But what mattered was that we were outdoors, cracking jokes, smoking cigarettes, or drinking beer year-round. In the dead of winter, we were outside, keeping the flame burning, literally. This crowd didn't drink or smoke pot more than the football team, who were among the more degenerate drinkers and partyers I'd ever known but whose athletic status gave them a legitimacy that the street kids lacked. I didn't fit in either place, but this gang seemed easier at the time. I didn't feel that I was better than them, although many of them struggled greatly in school. But at least I didn't feel like I was less than them either.

Eventually, the handwriting was on the wall and, sure enough, my mother found a bag of pot in my room. My father, who had moved to the suburbs to give his kids a better life, seemed to sink lower under the gathering evidence that white-flight suburbia had its own set of problems. As a public high school teacher, he was exposed to a parade of troubled kids who were being pulled under by drugs and petty crime. Thus, he came down on me hard. Maybe more so than he would have on any other kid in my home, if they'd been caught doing something similar. He threatened to send me away to a military school and painted a picture of the years of hard labor ahead. I assumed they must have a washer/dryer at military school, so I pondered the idea for just a moment. It is, I believe, uncommon for parents to love all of their children equivalently. And I feel that my father cared for me in a different way, maybe even more than he did for my siblings, because he believed that I might get ahead somehow. He wanted that so badly. He was obsessed with it. As he laid into me about military school, his voice quiet yet filled with angst and threat, I got it. I rejoined the football team, and though, at 172 pounds, I held a tackling dummy most of the time, I suited up for my junior and senior years. Our school beat my father's school in a legendary crosstown rivalry, and although I made no contribution whatsoever to those two victories, I think he was glad I was there.

Throughout high school, I coveted other people's

girlfriends and fantasized constantly about what it would be like to have one of my own. I ran for class president and lost. I wondered if I could improve my chances if I was a genuine football hero or if I cultivated the Jesus look and played the guitar. I wanted to be the Treat Williams character in *Hair*, a dancing Dionysian god. High school was a blur of wanting things I couldn't have and missing the wonderful moments right in front of me.

All of the tedium and anxieties of high school life played out over where you sat and with whom in the cafeteria. The most popular kids tended to just bask in the warmth of their sycophants, a table that reveled in their status by passing around one of the old pebble-jacketed notebooks. The pages of it were headed with the names of random people who were deemed worthy of inclusion and not always for the most flattering of reasons. This was called a "slam book," a primitive form of the *TMZ*-style tabloid garbage of today. A given page would say "Suzy J" across the top, and below people would write "Luv ya" or "You are the best friend anyone could ever have." Others, however, might write "whore," "bitch," "skank," and the like. Some people actually took this seriously. The publishers of the book wanted to hurt people. The fact that this happened with such openness and viciousness struck me as odd. When the one gay boy in our school killed himself, it was rumored to be the result of what he'd read about himself in the book. Berner High School: not a place to be gay. Some teachers vowed to confiscate the notebooks, but I once saw a teacher sitting in the cafeteria reading one, a slight smile on his face. I had teachers who were smart, kind, and who were true role models. Others were almost inconceivably limited. One teacher announced to his class that the best thing JFK ever did for his country was to get shot. I approached this man and asked him if he actually said that. He snarled at me. "Yeah, that's right," he said. "What's it to you?"

And then, like a ball game called on account of rain, high school was suddenly over. Just as I had daydreamed away many classes until the bell rang; just as in football practice I'd be staring off, watching the sunset, when my coach would tell me to gather the equipment and I couldn't remember what the hell we had been doing for the past ninety minutes; just as I had walked these halls for four years, wondering who I was and what the hell I was supposed to do here, it just ended, and too abruptly for me. I hadn't figured it out. Everyone else had, or so I thought. I was supposed to go to college. My grades were good, but not what they might have been if I . . . What? Worked harder? Lived under different circumstances? Oddly, all this talk of bright futures and college plans made me homesick for this house I vowed to escape.

My home had provided several resounding reasons why I should get the hell out of there. But there was a strange barrier between me and any dreams of the future. I looked at my family and thought, "These are the only people who really know me? Or care about me? Be it ever so humble, wouldn't it just be worse elsewhere?"

At graduation, all around me my classmates were hugging each other and crying and marking the end of something that they were fully engaged in. For them, high school was truly the best of times, providing a basket of memories to hold on to. But who were they to me? Saying good-bye seemed perfunctory with some, downright false with the rest. I was in the drama club one year, but I couldn't find any of them in this morass to say good-bye to. I played football, but without distinction. The great athletes in our graduating class were embracing each other, confident that one more summer of raucous debauchery lay ahead. No one called me over to enter that circle.

I stood there thinking of Tom Wingfield:

For sixty-five dollars a month I give up all that I dream of doing and being ever! And you say self—

self's all I ever think of! Why, listen, if self is what I thought of, Mother, I'd be where he is—GONE! [He points to his father's picture.] As far as the system of transportation reaches!

I was scared and I had no idea what I was going to do. Maybe that's exactly how it had to be.

3

Not a Drop of Boy

When my family lived in the little two-bedroom house with eight people stuffed inside, we were on what were called "the water streets," near the canals and the bay. After years of riding my bike in and around those streets, I can never forget their progression, alphabetical from west to east: Atwater, Brightwater, Clearwater, Deepwater, Edgewater, Fairwater, Greatwater, Highwater, Leewater, Nearwater, Ripplewater, Stillwater, Tidewater, Waterview. South Bay Drive, which was the spine that connected all of these roads, was my Shaftesbury Avenue, my Via Margutta, and my Bleecker Street rolled into one. I had a Stingray bike, but I might as well have been driving an Aston Martin, because in this land, your bike was everything.

There were certain neighbors of ours who always struck me as very sophisticated people and whose homes and daily lives were completely foreign to mine. One such family lived just around the corner, but I felt like I needed a passport when I entered their house. The father was a successful ad man in Manhattan, the mother an executive at a renowned psychiatric hospital in a nearby town. They had those framed Toulouse-Lautrec prints (Aristide Bruant, the Divan Japonais) on their walls before anyone else did. Miles Davis or bossa nova or Erik Satie played on a turntable. The mother was known as Big Lynn, a misnomer, as she was lithe and extremely stylish, always in black cashmere turtlenecks and slacks. They had three daughters, all of whom were blonde. Little Lynn, the eldest, was a stunning young woman who caused every boy in the neighborhood to gawk each time she left her house, as if she were Kate Middleton. My mother would stop by there, and Big Lynn would give her a box filled with last month's magazines: *Time, Look, Life, New York, Playboy, Penthouse, Cosmo, Psychology Today.* Once home, my mother would skim through an odd copy here and there, normally falling asleep with the magazine at her side. I, however, took the box and read the issues cover to cover. Big Lynn got me hooked on reading.

I read a lot from seventh through tenth grades. Sitting in my bed at night, waiting for my dad to come home, or on weekend afternoons, there was a period when I simply could not stop reading. I liked Nick Pileggi's crime reporting in *New York* magazine, and I laughed and winced reading John Simon's theater reviews. My dad pointed me toward Hugh Sidey at *Time* and William Safire in the *Times.* I actually read *Penthouse* and its forum. I got hooked on Chris Miller's writing in *National Lampoon* after reading crazy pieces like "Night of the Seven Fires." Big Lynn included a lot of books in these boxes as well. I read *The Godfather, Johnny Got His Gun,* Salinger, *To Kill a Mockingbird, The Exorcist,* Leon Uris, Michener, Mailer, *Ball Four, North Dallas Forty, The Valachi Papers.* I read William Goldman's screenplay for *Butch Cassidy.* I fell in love with Dickens and Twain and Poe. I loved biographies and the *Playboy* interview. In a 7-Eleven near my house, they displayed copies of Robert Sam Anson's *"They've Killed the President."* Staring in fascination and slight horror at Oswald's autopsy photos gave me a lifelong obsession with the JFK assassination at the age of thirteen.

In high school I loved any subject that involved reading and barely tolerated everything else. I wanted to read what I wanted when I wanted to, which wasn't the best recipe for academic success. I planned to go to law school eventually, because I was most comfortable with texts and I suppose I wanted to finish something my father had started. My dad had attended Syracuse Law School for one year but dropped out because my mother's father was paying the bill. My dad's pride got the better of him, and he walked away to begin his teaching career the moment he was offered a job.

In my senior year, my parents' discussion of my college plans was one of the more difficult ones they ever had. My mother's well-worn argument that my father had to face reality and limit my options to what they could truly afford was restated ad infinitum. My father, however, continued to dream. I applied to the better state schools—Albany, Buffalo, Binghamton—and sent letters to a small list of good private colleges that appeared, on paper, to offer decent financial aid opportunities, like Muhlenberg and Colgate. My father's goal, however, was for me to attend Columbia. He was still clinging to the hope that I would join a football team and actually play football. Columbia was part of an Ivy League "lightweight" program where the 158-pound limit had been raised to 165. The coaches in this league paired opposing players by weight, so that those over the limit were matched with someone their size. It was essentially a league populated by smaller athletes, some of them very quick, who weren't big enough to play elsewhere. The skinnier version of me fell into this category. Once again, my father knew someone who knew someone, but it was to no avail. My grades were good but not good enough. Columbia made few, if any, allowances for athletes. You were either competitive academically, or not. My father tried to lessen the blow by telling me that the end of the Vietnam War in August of 1975 meant a flood of applicants and thus a more competitive field, but I nonetheless was frustrated and sad that a great opportunity had disappeared.

At that point, I thought about going ROTC. I could join the air force after graduation and learn to fly. Or work my way into the judge advocate general's office of one of the branches and have the military put me through law school. However, once again, the end of the war cast its shadow. "They'll probably train fewer pilots now that it's winding down," my dad volunteered. "The competition will get tougher and you won't be guaranteed a seat in pilot training. You either earn that or you don't." I thought about how I would gladly give years of my life to the air force if it meant I would be trained as a pilot or get my law degree. But without either of those guarantees, I didn't want to go into the military. When thick packages arrived from the schools that accepted me, my parents and I naturally went right to the financial aid section. If I left New York, I would lose some state-funded grants. But one school, which looked good on paper, seemed to make a mix of Pell Grants and TAP loans all add up to yes: George Washington University in DC.

I never visited the school before committing. I just drove down with my dad in August of 1976 and showed up. I was more than overwhelmed. Washington would be the first city I lived in, and I do believe that had I moved straight to Morningside Heights to attend Columbia instead, I might have packed up and gone home to Massapequa. When I arrived in DC, Foggy Bottom was still a sleepy corner of the northwest quadrant, with dingy row houses and pubs, sandwich shops, and laundry facilities catering to college kids. Washington in the 1970s was a quaint town. In the orientation course offered to entering freshmen, entitled "DC Culture and Politics," I was introduced to JFK's witticism that Washington was a city "of Northern hospitality and Southern efficiency." This was before the city sprawled outward, and areas like Herndon and Reston were still covered with farmland. This was a post-1960s and pre-9/11 DC. Iranian students protesting the Shah of Iran burned him in effigy in Lafayette Square directly across from the White House. Mr. Capriotti patrolled in front of the White House fence,

encased in his sandwich board sign, its illegible chicken
scratch pleading with you to understand that the government was controlling his mind through his TV. If
you attempted these kinds of things today you might be
shot by the Secret Service.

Back then, GW was a school where many students
went to make first-year grades that enabled them to
transfer to their first-choice school: Stanford or Harvard or the University of Chicago. But regardless of
GW's lack of status in the 70s, a college campus can
be a social equalizer, and it provided me with an opportunity for the great reinvention. My parents' house,
along with whatever else I had or didn't have, was irrelevant now. Although clothes, jewelry, cars, and stereos clearly indicated levels of wealth and status, and
rich kids from an area of Long Island unknown to me
worked overtime to advertise their privileged upbring-
ings, everyone walked through the same entrance to the
same freshman dormitory, which was called "the Zoo."
I felt right at home. College is the beginning of the
merit-based period of most people's lives. The cachet
of gold chains and Nakamichi stereos was eclipsed by
true mastery of an academic subject. This was especially so if your parents didn't own some company that
was holding a seat for you upon graduation.

At college, one thing remained a constant for me:

fear was the invisible leash that largely controlled my behavior. There was a faint whisper that followed me everywhere, telling me that I shouldn't disappoint my dad. I had to focus on taking full advantage of attending the private university that was an enormous financial sacrifice for my family. Throughout much of college, I practiced a caution that often resembled passivity. Also, I hadn't yet learned that trying to be liked and succeeding were often mutually exclusive. When I played football in high school, like some gridiron Billy Pilgrim, coaches would grab my face mask and scream, "Why didn't you hit Bob when you had a shot?" I thought to myself that I liked Bob and didn't want to smash him. The idea that you tried to destroy some opponent for a couple of hours and afterward hugged him seemed odd to me. The nature of competition, which sometimes led to violent confrontation with someone, became clear later.

Other essential things changed for me in Washington. I fell in love for the first time. In one of the very last days of my freshman year, I walked down a dormitory hall late one night, looking to say good-bye to someone. Suddenly, there was Love, lying on the floor of the hallway, a taut telephone cord stretched out of her doorway to its maximum. In a pale silk dress, her face turned completely toward the wall, she looked as if she was in this position as some form of punishment. Her muffled crying and hushed pleadings, I later found out, were offered to her on-again, off-again boyfriend. Scenes like this are common in college dorms, where vanity is sacrificed for lack of privacy. I stood, frozen. I had never heard anyone speak that way. I had never witnessed such genuine passion. Who was this guy who elicited this behavior in her? I eventually dated her, though not seriously, and by that I mean I only saw her a handful of times, but talked to her on the phone at every opportunity and thought about her every moment of the day. She lived in Virginia and I went home to Long Island for the summer. I think she liked me, but her heart was still with someone else, and there was no getting around that. Nonetheless, she opened up that part of my life. Eventually, chasing that high of intense emotional intimacy with someone, being possessed by them, would become an addiction for me as well.

Many of my fellow students were there to party, as their performance in school had little bearing on where they would land when they finished. Instead of drinking and getting high, I walked into the offices of the student government and something just clicked for me. It's been said that politics is show business for less attractive people, and the offices of the GW Student Association, for the most part, bore that out. But

I was drawn to these kids, who were more like me and needed to extend themselves in order to compete. They had bought into the idea, not entirely wrong, that these school activities would tell other admissions offices and employers what they were made of. I volunteered one year at the office of student programming, booking and coordinating movies, speakers, parties, and concerts. At the end of my sophomore year, I ran for and won the position of chairperson of that board, which paid a tuition stipend. My father was genuinely happy about that. I did fairly well in college, majoring in political science while working at an internship at my congressman's office and later at a law firm specializing in FCC filings.

But no matter how hard I tried to keep my costs low and tap my father's wallet as little as possible, I would slam into the wall of reality. Colleges want you to pay your housing deposit in the spring for the following fall semester. As I stood in the waiting room of the housing office on a beautiful April day, the cherry blossoms outside every window, the lady behind the desk said, at full volume and within earshot of everyone around me, "Your parents' check bounced, so we can only accept a money order from you from now on." At that moment, I lost my spot in the dorm, as that bounced check was all I had. I scrambled to secure a space in an apartment in Arlington, Virginia, with some friends, all of whom would also eventually lose their patience with me because of my insolvency.

In the spring of 1979, my girlfriend, Alison, who was Jewish, was told by her parents to dump me, which she did. I was devastated. This was my first serious relationship. It had basically consisted of lying around on weekends doing nothing, which felt like everything. Convinced that someone cared about me, I was determined to hold on to that feeling. I begged a lot, as I recall. At the same time, I was running for president of the student government. People who worked on my "candidacy" urged me to come into DC from Arlington to campaign. Instead, I stayed home and felt sorry for myself. I was consumed by my need for nearly any kind of achievement on one hand and for the love of a woman on the other. I lost the election and the girl and ended up both defeated and insecure.

My girlfriend's roommate, Shari, had transferred from GW to NYU. On a trip back home, I went to visit her and whine about the loss of Alison. Then, based solely on Shari's playful provocation, I auditioned for the theater program at NYU. Suddenly, this was an idea that was both crazy and necessary. Admitting that I didn't actually want to be a K Street lawyer, I felt a powerful urge to leave DC and burn a bridge again. I needed to win something. It almost didn't matter where that need led me. City Hall or Wall Street or Madison Avenue, I didn't care. I just wanted some taste of success.

My audition was probably the thousandth recitation of Edmund from *Long Day's Journey* that they had heard that week. I had taken an "Acting for Non-Drama Majors" course at GW, where I performed scenes for *Cat on a Hot Tin Roof* with a girl from Long Island who was the scion of a hardware store empire. Raised far from the Pollitts of Mississippi, her accented pronunciation came out "Bah-rick! Bah-rick!" This was an idiotic idea, all things considered. When I eventually pitched it to my parents on the phone, my mother shrieked about what a mistake I was making. My dad just listened. When I told them that I was being offered a need-based scholarship and that NYU, the more expensive school, would actually cost him less money, he said to my mother, "Let's hear him out." I knew something other than money was behind that. Here was a man who had short-circuited his own dreams in order to provide for his family. "You'll never be young enough to do this again," he said.

I decided to stay in DC that summer of 1979, as I had grown fond of city living in general and Washington in particular. It also gave me some time to anguish over whether I had made the right move. In May, after my loss in the election, I sat at a local bar with a professor of mine, whose class I'd enjoyed. He was around fifty, but looked older. He liked to drink and smoke. He wore the uniform of the Washington educator: khakis, a Brooks Brothers button-down, a repp tie, and a navy blazer from either Paul Stuart or Jos. A. Bank. Over our drinks, he attempted to console me with a good deal of "GW's loss is NYU's gain," and so forth. I had little skill then in detecting if a guy was hitting on me, as people were so much more cautious then. But it soon became clear that he was interested. Playing off both my passion for politics and my newfound interest in acting, he laid it on thick, suggesting I was a blend of Robert Redford and JFK. His compliments were delivered affectingly. He was a very smart man, and lonely in the extreme. He asked if we could have dinner, and when I declined, the mood changed. As we sat for another fifteen or twenty minutes, he shifted. When he grilled me about what I expected to achieve by going to acting school, I told him I'd give it a year and if I didn't make it in showbiz to some degree, I would likely head to law school after all. He stared at me, sensing the conversation was coming to an end, and said, "You don't really want to be an actor, do you? When you talk about your goals, there's never any mention of happiness or joy, just some vague desire to 'make it.' Where's the dream? Do you have a dream? There's not a drop of boy in you. That must be tough."

Once classes ended, I got a job at a restaurant called Luigi's Famous, a glorified pizza joint. The owner was a native Italian named Corrado Bruzzo, a remarkably good-looking man, as if Mastroianni owned a DC pizza palace. His wife had just died of cancer in her forties, leaving behind their two children. Bruzzo was a mess, and he sat at his desk most days and just stared at papers. The real boss of the place was an African-American woman named Mrs. Mix, a tall, powerfully built force of nature with a hair net and a colossal bosom stuffed into a white kitchen uniform. She wore glasses and squinted at you as she shouted over the clanging of the large kitchen. "Tell that Alan Ballman to come in here!" she'd bellow. "Alan Ballman" was a name I enjoyed resurrecting years later, using it to check into hotels or with maître d's. Here was my summer love affair, a sixty-year-old, three-hundred-pound black woman from Georgia running a kitchen line with a ragtag staff, mostly from South America. I ran my ass off to please Mrs. Mix, sensing that it didn't take much to rise in the ranks of that outfit. I quickly realized that she needed a sergeant, as she was forever passing her orders through me on to the dining room staff.

I quietly told Mr. Bruzzo that the waitstaff was hopeless. Mrs. Mix needed an adjunct "out front." Mr. Bruzzo smiled wanly, and said, "OK, Alexa. OK." (Bruzzo's accented pronunciation of "Alex" came out as "Alexa.") The name Xander was left in George Barimo's office at 30 Rock. The next day, he lined up the waitresses, waiters, and busboys. They were around fifteen in number, and the grizzled men resembled Alfonso Bedoya's crew from *The Treasure of Sierra Madre*. Mr. Bruzzo said, "Today, I have asked Alexa here to be the *direttore* of the dining room. He will make the schedule, and if you have any questions, please bring them to Alexa. Thank you." That was it. Two sentences, and then he turned and left to stare at a pile of photos of his late wife. Bruzzo had everyone's love and respect, so they simply nodded. After he walked out, however, I thought they might stab me. Now some twenty-one-year-old, white college punk was going to be telling them what to do. The one Italian on the crew, a tough woman who resembled Patti LuPone, muttered, "What the fuck is this?" I spent my farewell-to-DC summer teaching grown men to polish silverware and setting rodent traps at closing time. I really didn't need the added responsibility. I wasn't paid significantly more money. But Bruzzo needed help and his response to my suggestions confirmed what I already knew. By sensing and responding to his grief, I realized I had an above-average empathy for other people's feelings, likely due to growing up with my mother. I could understand other people, get inside them, better than most. I began to think that maybe this acting idea wasn't such a bad decision after all.

I left DC, which was the first place I had ever lived away from home and where I had grown so much. I headed for the one place that seemed to make sense. Like Montgomery Clift leaving Shelley Winters for Elizabeth Taylor in *A Place in the Sun*, I was headed for the Angela Vickers of cities. Driving from Washington to New York at the end of the summer, my father and I rode along in endless silence. I felt I was disappointing him. Yet here was the man with whom I had digested countless movies. Eventually, I asked him what he thought it took to be a good actor. He paused, as he nearly always did before answering a question, and said, "I think you need to be intelligent. And you're pretty intelligent. So, you have a good chance."

NYU was a difficult adjustment. I was back in a dorm. And I didn't know New York well, in any sense. Plopped into the middle of a world of "student actors," I had little in common with anyone else. At GW, people followed the herd into, usually, some rather compelling courses or off-campus internships. I remember the cutthroat competition to get into Stephen Wayne's lectures on the American presidency, a truly great class. These acting class types at NYU, just like boys who had played football in peewee leagues since they were eight, or girls who had taken ballet class nearly their whole lives, had been at this long before college. Their bubbly chatter went something like "I spent the summer at the Blah-Blah theater camp doing *Guys and Dolls.*" Turning to me, they asked, "Have you ever played Sky?" No, I would reply. "Have you ever played Hamlet? Val? Edmund? Billy Bigelow? Chance? Mercutio? Ensign Pulver?" My answer was no, across the board. Other than high school productions of *Teahouse of the August Moon* and *The Spiral Staircase,* as well as scene work from *Cat on a Hot Tin Roof* with my Long Island Maggie the Cat, I had no acting training or experience. I thought that I might have gotten in on my appearance as much as anything else. I was the only blue-eyed "young male ingénue" type in a class filled with pretty female dancers and budding male character actors. The more intense and serious members of the class wore black clothes, drank coffee, and smoked a lot, their faces buried in copies of *Balm in Gilead* or *In the Boom Boom Room.*

I began to worry. I asked myself, "Did you pass up law school for this?" Why was I spending hours at the Lee Strasberg Institute weeping or directing scenes wherein we staged our dreams or shouting into a corner at some unseen source of my anxieties? I walked to class through the old Union Square (before the developer William Zeckendorf cut a deal to clean up the park in exchange for constructing a hideous apartment building that blocked New Yorkers' views of the gorgeous Con Ed clock tower). Drug dealers greeted me at eight a.m. with their whimsical pitches. "Loose joints here! T's and V's! I got the herb superb, the weed you need. The smoke you love to toke! Seconal! Valium!"

I had no time to relax, let alone get high. During my last full-time year of school, my father stressed about money more than ever. I worked throughout the year, first as a busboy at the twilight of Studio 54, then selling men's shirts in a discount apparel store on lower Fifth Avenue. The older clerks glared at me when the place slowed down, as if I had brought a curse through the door. I waited tables at a bistro called Café Bruce Waite, named after a sometime actor and the brother of Ralph Waite. Some of the female staff flirted with me, and Bruce fumed. Bruce had a full-length oil painting of himself in the restaurant's entry hall, posed as if he were Lord Mountbatten. In this *Billy Budd* tableau, he fired me, accusing me of stealing from him by giving my friends free food. After that, I was a chaperone for a tour bus company, escorting older African-American women from Baptist church groups in the Bronx to the Corning Glass Works and then to wine tastings in the Hudson Valley. Driving back with these proper ladies in hats and lace gloves was a kick. Slightly buzzed, we sang gospel songs all the way home. Back at the dorm, I would sneak into the dining hall to pilfer a meal. The manager was a kind, discreet guy. Nonetheless, he had a job to do, and would sidle up next to me and whisper, "You know I gotta ask you to leave. Now finish your slice and get gone."

I studied acting with Geoffrey Horne and Marcia Haufrecht, both outstanding teachers for young actors. I took a fantastic History of Dramatic Lit course with Bill Bly, one that everyone professed was their favorite. Jim Brown taught a survey on the history of comic performance that I loved. Everyone loved Jim. I slowly began to see that there was a pretty substantial chasm between those who delighted the teachers and those who would actually leave there and work, between those for whom acting was a craft and those for whom it was a potential occupation. "Look in a magazine," a teacher once said. "Do you see yourself there? Then, maybe you'll work. Or, if you don't see yourself there, then the business is simply waiting for you to show up." I finished my first year at NYU and in the summer of 1980 found myself living as a boarder in the unair-conditioned Yorkville apartment of a friend of Jim Brown, herself a teacher of anthropology with several children. My six-by-six-foot room came with a lot of rules. "You are to confine yourself to your room and the bathroom. Your rent does not include use of the kitchen or living room or any other area of the apartment," said Mrs. Gleason, who looked like a cross between Eleanor Roosevelt and Rose Sayer, the Katharine Hepburn character in *The African Queen*. The only thing missing was Noah Claypole calling me "Work'us" as I came in. I suspected that my tiny room had originally been a luggage compartment for storing trunks and suitcases.

Back home, my parents were spent. They hardly said a word to each other. The financial stress had crushed my dad. My brothers and sisters seemed to be gone whenever I visited. While I basted in this cell in Manhattan in August, I did some simple math. The looming dissolution of my parents' marriage meant I wouldn't be able to afford the remaining single semester to finish NYU. I couldn't go home, and I couldn't swing the remaining credits to graduate. And then something strange happened.

4

Patchogue by Nightfall

During the summer of 1979, I got a job at a private health club/restaurant at the top of an apartment building near Lincoln Center. I waited tables at the café during lunch, where a couple of dozen women would snap, gesturing toward their cups, "My cawfee is cold," every fifteen minutes. They barely ate. They just stirred "cawfee." In the evening, I lifeguarded at the club's indoor pool. I was in no hurry to rush back to Mrs. Gleason's stifling apartment in between shifts, so I headed to the Drama Book Shop, where I rolled the most famous lines of the greatest playwrights in my mouth. "O, pardon me, thou bleeding piece of earth, that I am meek and gentle with these butchers." "It was a great mistake, my being born a man." And "You ever heard of the Napoleonic code?"

One day at the café, a woman who was there as a guest asked me, "Do you have an agent? My friend is casting a soap opera and you seem like just what she's looking for." In a moment that would become a pattern in my career, I didn't bother to ask exactly what that was. I just wanted to work. The role was on a daytime show called *The Doctors*.

It was eventually explained to me by the show's resident historians that *The Doctors*'s golden years predated the "youth revolution" in daytime drama, when soaps were launched featuring stars and storylines that were younger and the change in demographics pushed more mature actors into the background, into supporting roles. So our cast was an anomaly. The colorful casting director, Roger Sturtevant, along with his partner Pat McCorkle, eschewed hiring models in favor of trained actors for whom the TV gig meant a steady paycheck and medical insurance that allowed them to do theater. Valerie Mahaffey, John Pankow, and Tuck Milligan were among the actors given favorable shooting schedules that allowed them to appear onstage at a Wednesday matinee, and Elizabeth Hubbard and Jim Pritchett, principal players who had been with the show for years, took theater roles during their hiatus from the show. The theater was all they talked about. Hollywood might as well have been the Kimberley diamond mines in terms of their familiarity with or interest in it. Before I had arrived, Kathleen Turner left the show and went to Hollywood to shoot *Body Heat.* Upon hearing the title, someone in the cast of the soap asked if she had starred in a porn film.

The show taped at 30 Rockefeller Plaza in a small studio that seemed as if NBC had forgotten it was even there. Some of the aging, battle-weary crew dated back to the days of Dave Garroway and Carson's early stint in New York. *Saturday Night Live* was a television sensation that was about to undergo a fallow period coinciding with the brief absence of Lorne Michaels. The building housed the *Today* show and Tom Snyder and not much else. Each day after work, I walked out of 30 Rock knowing that there were elevator operators who were better known at NBC than I was. No one was watching the show. The scripts were anemic, but David O'Brien, who played my father, explained that it was hard to expect much more from the writers, who had to churn out fresh pages every day. He said it was our job to try our best to bring something to it.

O'Brien was the first person to greet me and embrace me. He served as my invaluable guide and dear friend during my debut in the business. As elegant as Cary Grant, as witty as Noël Coward, and as quick as Johnny Carson, O'Brien was one of the kindest, most intelligent and urbane men I've ever known. Unlike some of the veterans, who seemed wary of the young additions to the cast, as the show became less and less about them, O'Brien loved actors of all ages and extended himself easily. He was playful one moment and instructive the next. He was kind, patient, and funny every day, and his sense of humor about the job, and the business in general, helped me handle what was often a frustrating introduction to acting in front of a camera.

The show was shot "live to tape," so we were asked to perform it almost like theater: don't stop, unless absolutely necessary, as to do so required extra time and money. No wonder theater actors tended to thrive in this venue. The pressure could be tough. Recalling line after line of often trite and repetitive dialogue wasn't easy. Giving a real performance was elusive. Early on, every day ended with the thought "Better luck tomorrow." But O'Brien knew every trick in the book and didn't hesitate to share them with me. His one overarching note? "When you don't know what to play, I recommend 'Someone in this room farted and I intend to find out who,'" he cracked.

As a few months passed, I was given more to do. The producers wanted me to play a self-involved, semiruthless, amoral cad. It didn't matter if I possessed the personal character of Abraham Lincoln or John Glenn. The audience liked characters who were bad. That's what the producers wanted me to be. O'Brien would tell me acting is about making the audience believe what I'm saying. Some choose to go to the gym every day, dye their hair, whiten their teeth, and hope they get lucky enough to play some uncomplicated leading man or superhero. But if you learn how to act any role, he said, the options get better. That hit me hard about six months into the job. I had thought about quitting, feeling like an idiot for abandoning my plan to go to law school in order to stand on some moldy old set saying, "But, Greta—I love you!" over and over again. However, having spent hour after hour observing the people around me, younger and older, I realized that what was considered good acting was hard to do. I owe that to O'Brien. He told me to view the soap as a means to an end. "Don't ever think that this is all you are or could be," he said. During his breaks from the show, he would go off and perform plays like *Light Up the Sky* at the John Drew or *King John* at the Mc-Carter. Val Mahaffey was doing *Top Girls* downtown. John Pankow had understudied Peter Firth in *Amadeus*. Tuck, who became a good friend, performed all over the country in *Equus*, *The Crucifer of Blood*, *Big River*, and *The Kentucky Cycle*. At nearly every turn, it was drilled into me that the goal was to learn how to act and that such learning could best be achieved in the theater.

After work, which ended at around three or four o'clock, we would go downstairs to Hurley's, a Rockefeller Center restaurant, where O'Brien and other members of the cast taught me how to drink by following their example. We would order some small plates of food, just substantial enough to prepare the way for the booze that was to follow. Then it was post time. The sound track of this drinking scene, however, was different. I was no longer in some damp, suburban woods in Massapequa. No one was going to burst in here and order me to take out the garbage or shovel the snow or tell me that my parents' check had bounced. I didn't have to cut my neighbors' grass to pay my bar bill. I'd light another cigarette and think, "Who the fuck cares where I have to be at six thirty? This is where I want to be. This is what home feels like now." I'd get warmer, sillier, cozier. In this honey-colored state, if there was a woman between the ages of eighteen and fifty nearby, I feigned interest in whatever she was interested in, so long as she let me believe there was genuine hope for some kind of future for us. Sitting at a bar in New York City in 1980, I was falling in love, but not with a woman in a silk dress, her face turned away, her love poured out for someone else. As I learned to drink alongside some of the best actors I would ever meet, I was falling in love with show business and the people in it.

I also fell in love with alcohol, my most excellent friend. The clinking of the ice, the luminous colored bottles arranged behind the bar, the bartenders and waiters in starched white shirts, the tablecloths, the hors d'oeuvres and Rothman cigarettes (O'Brien's favorites) made everything seem right. I drank Canadian Club in the winter and Boodles Gin in the summer. All of it combined to relax me for the first time in my twenty-two years. Most important of all, I was with people I liked and whom I believe liked me. No matter how many stupid questions I asked or ill-informed opinions I expressed at the bar on 49th and 6th, I was home. Outside, snow was falling. They were lighting the tree, and skaters were twirling around the famous rink. Somewhere back in Massapequa, my siblings were finding their own forms of escape. At Hurley's, everything was tranquil and warm. When I went back to my apartment after those gatherings, I was uncomfortable and lonely. At times, I'd do anything not to feel that way. Once you have found some joy, you never want to be without it.

I lived on 58th between 1st and 2nd. The East 50s were filled with pretty brownstones, little neighborhood shops, and an unusual number of middle-aged gay men. So when O'Brien invited me to join him and some of his fifty-something friends for dinner and drinks, lots of drinks, I merrily rolled along. These were men who hailed from the era of *The Boys in the Band*, not Stonewall. They were bankers and bosses. They were management. These gents were quiet, pre-AIDS Executive Gays. In Rod Stewart's song "The Killing of Georgie," the eponymous male hustler dies on the corner of 53rd and 3rd, the precise coordinates of O'Brien's favorite stomping grounds: Ambrosia, Rounds, and the East Five Three. Perhaps David's friends thought I was fucking him. If he wanted them to think it, I never knew. Years later, a mutual friend guffawed and exhorted, "He was in love with you!" Maybe so. I was certainly in love with him. Although I was never interested in men sexually (God, how much better my life might have been if I was!), at that time I would only let relationships with women go so far emotionally. Therefore, while I often practiced my acting on them (and they on me, I'm sure), I only cared about moving my career ahead, whatever that meant at the time. And sitting at the East Five Three with David and a gaggle of flambéed, wickedly funny queens was more fun than anything else. It was more anywhere than anywhere else.

One Saturday afternoon, walking down 1st Avenue, I ran into Ken Harper, the theater producer who had scored on Broadway with *The Wiz*. Harper, who was friendly with one of our producers, George Barimo, occasionally lurked around the studio. Muscled up and predatory, he caught me en route to the laundromat. The opposite of O'Brien in the nuance department, Harper made small talk briefly before he said, "May I ask you a question?" I nervously grunted some reply. He seamlessly offered, "Is your ass as hairy as your chest? Because if it is, I'd like you to come up to my place and sit on my face for an hour." All the blood went down to my ankles. I laughed, but not the affectionate laugh I often had for O'Brien. I coughed up my version of Annie Hall's "La-di-da," something like "Ha . . . well . . . ha . . . ok . . . well . . . ha!" and whisked off. Reminding me that gay men are like any other men in their ardor, Harper's pitch had me wondering how much infidelity there was in the gay world. I resolved to chart my own course among the Sunday afternoon sitting-on-the-face circuit.

O'Brien eventually invited me to his house on Fire Island. I accepted but asked if I could bring the woman I was dating. Trained at the London Academy of Music and Dramatic Arts and ever the gentleman from Chicago, he seemed to stumble only slightly before replying, "I insist!" That weekend, Chloe or Siobhan or Francesca ferried over with me. She must have wondered herself what she was doing there, as I spent the whole time talking with David. It was as if he and I were on the date and my girlfriend was our queer dear pal. He raised the shades on a window looking out on the water. "I give you Patchogue by nightfall," he announced. I cackled loudly and thought to myself, "I really am in love with this man." My date smiled awkwardly.

The executive producer of *The Doctors* was a tough old broad named Doris Quinlan. Her associate, Susan Scudder, was the contact that my coffee-klatching guest at the health club had introduced me to. In a meeting that lasted maybe thirty minutes, the producers had signed me to a two-year deal. They asked me my name, as in stage name, and I told them I didn't have one. "People call me Alex. My family calls me Xander." They squinted and Barimo said, "Xander Baldwin . . . that doesn't work." Thirty minutes in the business and I was already primed to abandon my name of twenty-two years. I told them that my father was called Alec. They lit up, and one of them proclaimed, "That's it. That's your name. We'll put Alec Baldwin on the contract, and from now on that's your name." Barimo tensed slightly and leaned in. "So, you can sign this deal here and now, or go out and get an agent. But he'll only be able to bump it up the ten percent to cover his commission." I shrugged and said, "OK, sure. I'll sign right now." I signed "Alexander R. Baldwin III" and thought about how I was now the third Alec in that line as well, thanks to a trio of flinty TV producers working in off-off-television. "You will need an agent eventually, though," Susan Scudder said. "I want to send him over to Bloom." The others, looking at me like a used car they had just bought, murmured their assent. "Bloom," Doris said with a wry smile. "Sure. Why not?"

At first glance, J. Michael Bloom looked like Henry VIII as he is depicted in history textbooks. From certain angles, he also resembled a younger version of the actor Charles Laughton. He was slightly bug-eyed, and his face broadened below the nose, giving his mouth a splayed Donald Duck–like mask. With his trimmed and fluffed tufts of hair in blue and silver, his over-sized aviator-style prescription glasses and three-piece suits, he sipped a river of Pepsi-Cola poured over ice at his desk, chain-smoking Kent III cigarettes while speaking in a velvety FM radio voice. Bloom might have been a character in a Coen brothers movie, except he was real. Obviously, he'd been an actor at one time. He didn't ooze theatricality. He gushed it. Hailing from the Ken Harper school, Bloom had a reputation for cruising young male clients, to the point of harassment. Young up-and-coming actors working in film, TV, and commercials would ask me, "How do you put up with that guy?" He massaged this one's thigh or tried to corner and kiss this one in his office. None of that concerned me. I like people who are smart and funny, and Bloom was one of the smartest and funniest I would ever meet.

When I started in the business, there were certain arrangements between the actors' unions and talent agencies. In California, due to some Byzantine rules, a "franchised agency"—one that was vetted by the actors' unions—could not represent an actor in both commercials and "legit" work (stage, film, TV). So LA agents would send you off to another company, whose agents would rep you for advertising. In New York, that wall did not exist, and Bloom built a successful business exploiting that fact. While he repped great actors in theater, film, and TV, he also had a commercial and voice-over department that earned him a significant amount of money, and allowed him to develop up-and-coming theatrical clients. Bloom signed me after our initial meeting, knowing we had to wait out the soap contract before we could book anything under his watch. I kicked around New York during that period from August 1980 to October 1982 and periodically auditioned for films, plays, and voice-over jobs.

Bloom, while grandiose and self-promoting, was also patient and encouraging. He and his staff wanted their roster of actors, at least the ones they believed had any talent, to work in the theater. There were next to no real stars on their roster, so the flow of sarcasm could be irksome. At one point, Nevin Dolcefino, one of the agents in the theater department, said, "Pass me a roll of Alec's résumé, I have to go to the bathroom." It was around then that I think I got the message. I did a couple of showcases in tiny theaters, but serious work onstage in New York would not present itself for a while. Bloom, in an attempt to inspire me, took me to the theater regularly. In the summer of 1981, we drove to the Berkshires to visit Williamstown and the Berkshire Theatre Festival in Stockbridge. At Williamstown, we saw an adaptation of Euripides, Aeschylus, Homer, and Sophocles entitled *The Greeks*, directed by Nikos Psacharopoulos. The remarkable cast included Celeste Holm, Blythe Danner, Donald Moffat, Kate Burton, Edward Herrmann, Roxanne Hart, Jack Wetherall, Roberta Maxwell, Carrie Nye, Dwight Schultz, Josef Sommer, Emery Battis, George Morfogen, Pamela Payton-Wright, Jane Kaczmarek, a young Gwyneth Paltrow, and Christopher Reeve. It was as if Psacharopoulos attempted to put everyone who was great or would be great in the New York theater all in the same show. From there, we drove down to Stockbridge to see Hector Elizondo perform in Miller's *A View from the Bridge.*

It was forty-eight hours of Bloom exposing me to great acting and great actors. He encouraged me to believe that, with enough work and some degree of luck, I could climb my way into their ranks. He had thoroughly instilled in me the idea that if you didn't make your bones in the theater, your acting career was built on sand. Bloom's encouragement meant the world to me. At that point, I had worked on the soap for nearly a year. The cynicism I initially felt toward the soap was gradually replaced by a commitment to use this to my advantage and to move ahead to jobs that provided greater challenges. As we sat parked in his convertible sports car, I thanked Bloom for his belief in me. He put his hand on my shoulder and smiled. Then he jerked me toward him and shoved his tongue in my mouth. He was strong and pressed me against himself, seemingly bent on devouring me. Stunned, I pushed him away and took a deep breath. Bloom, who'd been here before innumerable times, barely contained a sheepish grin. I turned to him and said, "You're my friend, so I'm gonna let that go. But if you ever do that again, I'm gonna break every bone in your body." He nodded, as if to say, "Got it," and then we drove off back to New York. He never made a move on me again. And our real friendship was born.

I had gone to NYU with a guy named Gary Lazer. Right after we left school, we were roommates on 29th Street and 3rd Avenue in Manhattan, a nondescript block just around the corner from the Belmore Cafeteria, the twenty-four-hour restaurant and cabbies' hangout featured in *Taxi Driver*. Lazer was a young stand-up comic and lived the life of one; by that I mean I think his mother paid a portion of his rent. At night, I would stuff the next day's *Doctors* script in my pocket and follow Gary and a small cadre of his buddies around to the lesser clubs, where they would perform at open mike nights. They even got a booking here and there. Joints like Who's on First and the Good Times were where I got my first good look at the clever and incredibly neurotic people who seek approval through laughter for a living. Gary was funny, and effortlessly so. Through him I learned that true comedic timing is a gift. If I could actually make Gary laugh, I had accomplished something. We'd go to clubs, he'd do his act, and we'd get buzzed. I slept on the couch in our living room most nights, as I had to be up at six a.m. to go to work, while Lazer took the bedroom in the back of our dumbbell flat, where he'd smoke a half a pack of cigarettes from one a.m. to three a.m. while he read books.

The women in our lives were instructed that if they left our apartment in the early morning, they should avoid going west on 29th to Park Avenue, lest they came upon the supermarket of hookers who were finishing off their last pieces of business at sunrise. Men sat in their cars with Jersey plates, their heads tilted back, eyes closed, while some brassy orange wig bobbed up and down at steering wheel level. This was New York in the '80s, before the Internet and Grindr. Prior to the age of "broken windows" policing or the Central Park Conservancy, New York was pretty much a mess. There was graffiti on most of the subways and garbage strewn on the tracks. Most of the streetlamps in Central Park were busted, along with a lot of the benches. Living below Houston was a new idea. Every ad for real estate there underlined the "fixture fees" required to bring commercial, even light-industrial, spaces up to residential code. I dated a girl who was an artist and lived in Tribeca, which was a virtual outpost then. We'd wake up in her loft, and she would say, "Roll up the futon and help me put it in the closet." The place was her studio, and if she got caught sleeping there, she'd be evicted. Politicians talked about preserving some of Manhattan's last great manufacturing spaces and fought against the residential development of Soho. But no one was coming back to make thread or nuts, bolts, and washers. With remarkable speed, the pressure to convert the gorgeous cast-iron buildings along Prince and Spring, Grand and Broome, turned the market upside down. Suddenly everyone wanted to live in Soho, much like the Brooklyn influx of recent years.

In 1981, Gary and I moved to the apartment on 58th and 1st, around the corner from the 59th Street Bridge and the Roosevelt Island tram. I fell in love with Linda, a nineteen-year-old who lived across the street. She was the first woman I ever dated who was born and bred in Manhattan. I went with Linda to visit her cousin in Los Angeles, my first trip to California. Like a lot of my travel when I was younger, it was constrained by lack of money, ingenuity, and inspiration. We spent the whole week hanging out at her cousin's house in the Valley, with no car. We might as well have been limbless.

As I couldn't broaden my professional horizons much, due to the soap, I did small showcase productions, some for only ten performances. After work, I lounged around the city, drinking while watching Gary in clubs. And once in a while, I went home to Massapequa. Compared to the nightlife and the fruitless auditions I was going on with directors like James Ivory and John Sayles and for theater companies like Manhattan Theatre Club and Circle Rep, going home felt like a chore. Home began to change around that time, as my mother had gotten a job at the local shopping mall doing marketing research. The company that hired her was called Quick Test, and it was essentially a brigade of women, mostly housewives and college girls plus a few guys, who cornered people on the floor of the mall and asked them a series of survey questions. If the shopper was lucky, she would be invited to come to the office to sample anything from hosiery to fabric softener to hand lotion. My mother changed, markedly, once she started getting dressed up, getting her hair done, and going to work for the first time in decades. At times, she seemed transformed, grateful for the companionship that any professional life brings. My father began a descent in the opposite direction. With other kids heading to college, his expenses were higher than ever, and my parents' combined income still didn't make a dent.

Many years later, my wife Hilaria once said to me, as a means of underscoring some forgetfulness on my part, "When I'm not with you, I still exist." That comment reminded me of how wrapped up in my own concerns I was during this period. I saw my siblings infrequently, something I look back on with a lot of regret. By contrast, my sister Beth was a steady presence in the lives of our siblings even after she moved out to marry her boyfriend, Charlie, when she was nineteen. She had met him when she was sixteen, and although he was a tough, working-class young guy from a family of firefighters and cops, perhaps not her type, nonetheless he gave her a way out of our parents' drama, which was now steeped in resentments. Beth wanted to make her own home and quickly. It didn't matter if the guy she made that home with didn't go to Harvard or take her to Paris. Like me, she was conditioned to believe, "As long as the bills are paid." Remarkably, she would replicate our very household by having six children of her own.

Beth had moved out when I was almost seventeen. Soon after, when I went away to college, I could sense how difficult things were becoming for my siblings when I spoke with them now and then. When they were out of the house, they found companionship, joy, and identity. When they came home, they had to traverse a minefield. I would call my mother and she often sounded sad, as she must have perceived that she was getting close to some transition. My father was almost impossible to reach in the age before cell phones. I pictured him sitting in the driveway for a long moment before he sighed and finally went in. Calling the house was painful, and brought on feelings I wanted to run from.

I recalled that when I was around thirteen or fourteen years old, my brother Daniel and I found out that the local town park was offering tennis lessons during the summer for a very low enrollment fee. The instructor was an older student in our town named Jimmy Luchsinger, who, along with his brother Jack, was a sports legend in our school. As Daniel and I stood at the bottom of the stairs talking, my father overheard us and said, "I will get you the lessons." He then added, in his typical fashion, "But if you miss one lesson, it's over." A couple of days later, he came home with two of the old Wilson wood racquets with "Davis Cup" emblazoned on them. Our mouths fell open. As we offered our thanks, he went in to the den, turned on the TV news, and hid behind the *New York Times*, which was the wall he built around himself. When that paper was up at half-staff, you might try your luck. But full staff meant stay away.

As he lay on the daybed, he would fall asleep and often remain there overnight. One of my strongest images of my father is of him stretched out on the daybed, his shoes dangling over the edge, the soles worn and two large holes visible from wear. He smoked cigarettes for years, and once he quit, he smoked a pipe filled with

Amphora Brown tobacco. When the pipe sputtered, it sent tiny embers onto his shirt. One day, I opened my dad's closet to look for something, and in the sunlight, I saw the dozens of pinholes burned through each of his shirts. No moths were here, only Amphora Brown. He never did anything for himself. Nothing, that is, that mattered. When he wanted to binge on something, he sat down with a bucket of blue crabs and a jar of mayonnaise and ate the whole thing.

As we clutched the tennis racquets, beaming, he lowered himself onto the daybed, holes in his shoes, his shirt, and his psyche. The pressures and frustrations that swirled inside him barely concealed a pent-up rage that actually served to tamp down some greater sadness.

At one point, around the fall of 1981, my father moved out. As always, I learned about it from Beth. Everyone was stunned. He had no money to sign a lease somewhere else, so he went to Massapequa High School, his other home. He carried with him his mother's frugality, compassion, and conscience. He had that key ring that could choke a hippo, with the keys to everything, including the faculty lounge, where there was a couch no better or worse than the one at our house. He slept there, and he showered and dressed in the coaches' locker room. Surely some knew what he was doing, but they said nothing. Finally, after a couple of months, my father told me that Frank, the chief custodian, approached him and said he would lose his head janitor's job if the situation continued.

During his summer job at the rec center, my father had hired a young woman who was his former student. Bright and positive, Linda brought to my father's everyday life the wit and warmth he lacked at home. Linda was his O'Brien. Later, after Linda had finished her degree, she returned to Long Island to teach in a nearby town. With nowhere to go and no money to fund his escape from the crushing realities of his family life, my father moved into Linda's home. The animosity this triggered within my family was epic. Even I, living somewhat blithely in Manhattan, was pulled into the tumult. My mother played her usual victim card, telling me she had no money for her bills, including food, so I got my father on the phone and threatened him. I said I would give my mother the necessary funds to take him to court. I could feel his pain, anger, and sense of betrayal through the phone as I sided with my mother over him, an unfamiliar position for me. After that, we spoke even less often than before. But the handwriting appeared on the wall once he left that indicated that it had fallen to me to fill whatever gaps I could.

By the summer of 1982, Michael Bloom was telling me to seriously consider heading out to LA for the network television pilot season, and another excuse to distance myself from my family and their problems presented itself. And although my father was also running away from home, it was too late for him. Right at the time that Bloom was enlisting me to go west, my father was diagnosed with oat cell carcinoma, an aggressive form of cancer. The doctors at the area hospital told him they had found a tumor in his left lung. He chose, for a critical period, to ignore them. It was time to go without again. Like when he and my mom decided to have six children, it was time to rely on Providence again. And by the time he was back in a hospital for tests, the cancer had spread significantly. I asked him, point-blank, if he felt he was in real danger. He said no. And for a period that lasted for several months, he lied to me. My mother lied to me. My sister Beth lied to me. They all told me he had a very good chance of beating it.

I decided I would drive cross-country to LA, sublet a place there for four months, and give it a go. My contract on *The Doctors* was up in October of 1982. The three producers pressured me to extend for an additional four months. In September, I told the new executive producer, Gerry Straub, that I wasn't going to sign up again. In a hysterically funny moment, I walked down a studio hallway with Barimo behind me, and Straub shouted, "You're making a mistake! What? You think you're gonna go out to Hollywood and become a big star?"

"Well," I thought, "maybe a little star." The short span of the extension had seemed odd, and later I found out why. The show was canceled in December, for good.

While Beth was bringing her own children into the world, Daniel was at Ball State in Indiana, Billy was at the State University at Binghamton, Jane was finishing high school, and Stephen was polishing his legend on the streets of Massapequa, I got into a Volkswagen Karmann Ghia with Tuck Milligan and headed to Los Angeles on January 7, 1983. While I snorted and drank my way to Hollywood, my sister Beth ferried my dad to work on whatever days he wasn't at Sloan Kettering and, later, Mount Sinai. Every day, the man I looked up to for his bottomless reserves of power, his intense sense of duty and unswerving commitment, grew weaker and weaker, all out of my sight. When I left New York, I left behind Gary, my dad, and my TV dad, David. Only Bloom, whose California office was beginning to thrive, would be available to me for the next phase of my life. He would become among my dearest friends, as my life turned fortunate and gratifying on one hand, and abruptly and numbingly painful on the other.

5
Perpetual Light

Tuck and I had shared a small rental cottage in Amagansett the summer before and had become good friends. It was during that period that I fell in love with the East End, and Amagansett in particular. We lived the life of two bachelors, with a very small beach house and not much else. The days were spent cooking at home, punctuated by visits from the occasional kindhearted female visitor, drinking and sleeping on the beach—things I'd never want (drinking) or have time for (cooking) again. But the beach in Amagansett is a good place to get acquainted with God.

On our cross-country drive, I may have alarmed Tuck, my future roommate, with a preview of what was to come regarding my developing self-destruction. I suggested to Tuck that our route be guided not only by places where we had family and friends, but also by where I could deepen my relationship with cocaine. Drugs and alcohol, much to my own surprise, would become an increasingly powerful force in my life. At first slowly, then a sudden, rapid acceleration. All of the feelings behind it were the "self-centered fear" that AA's Big Book discusses. The self-centered fear that we would either not get something we wanted or lose something we already had. My life was changing in so many ways, most of them good, but others, painful. I was lonely and scared. I missed my family, the simplicity of being myself, of being accepted, even loved, simply for who I was. I often dreaded performing and, even more, the performing you had to do off camera. I was alternately tense, cocky, needy, inspired, or depressed. I felt that tremendous opportunities were in front of me and, therefore, there was no turning back. And as I wanted everyone to believe that I had it together, I was unwilling to ask people around me for help. I left my home with a case of OCD, a consuming desire to earn a respectable living, if not make a fortune, and a nagging need for attention that would fill the holes my parents were too enervated to address. But sometimes, dreams where I would go back to Massapequa and wait for my dad to come home and watch the late night movie show with him would flood me with feelings that I didn't know what to do with. So I drank. I took drugs and I drank. The chance at a career in Hollywood represented ever greater change for which I was poorly prepared. So, LA would prove to be the Kitty Hawk where my addiction really took off.

Our first stop was the Virginia suburbs, where the woman I'd first seen lying on the floor of my freshman dorm at GW, none other than Avis Renshaw, now lived with her husband and kids. We had stayed in touch. Her husband, Steven Cox, resembled Montgomery Clift as photographed by Dorothea Lange. My nickname for him was Male Model Farmer. They owned a farm and grew things. Avis had purchased a pizza oven, installed it in her garage, busted a hole in the wall to allow access to the oven from inside the house, and, thus, birthed Mom's Apple Pie Company. They had a lot of kids, one of whom, Biansa, later became my assistant. Avis was happy. She had a home and a family, things it would take me another thirty years to find. After a day of envying Avis and Male Model Farmer, we drove on.

Tuck was living the life of a real actor and, therefore, was not obsessed with box office numbers or red carpets, the adoration of fans and critics, or special treatment in restaurants, hotels, and other public places. He had, and still has, the career that nearly all actors should expect after their apprenticeship, one that is about the work. In this situation, performing roles in the theater is your life. If some degree of security comes your way, like a soap opera or any paying gig, some means to take the pressure off and earn a couple of bucks, that is welcomed. During our friendship, I've seen him act in several productions, from La Jolla to New York to Palm Beach. A skilled and dedicated stage performer, he's traveled the country and, as a result, developed a skill that truly great thespians possess: sizing up one's overnight accommodations.

En route to Tuck's hometown of Kansas City, we stopped in Indianapolis and pulled into a nondescript motor inn. It was late and we were beat. The desk attendant checked us in and handed over the keys. Once inside, I moaned about hitting the sack, but Tuck said, "Not so fast." The boy from the Show Me State wanted to do a bit of inspecting. With a flick of the wrist, he turned down the bed to reveal gray sheets covered in spots of some indeterminate source. "We're outta here," he snapped. "What's the problem?" I asked. "These sheets haven't been changed in weeks!" he said. He called the desk. A night-shift security guy showed up with supposedly cleaner sheets. In the doorway, Tuck said, "What's this?" "Your fresh sheets," the guard muttered. "Keep 'em," Tuck snorted. We went to the desk, said no thanks, and got our thirty bucks back. Thirty bucks. Years later, I'd end up staying in hotels where a hamburger was thirty bucks. And the movie I was shooting while staying in that hotel hardly measured up to the artistic standard that Tuck has spent his life pursuing. That's one rule in Hollywood: the shittier the project, the more they pay you.

In Kansas City, Tuck's dad, a "Missourah" gentleman of the old school, took us for the obligatory stop at Romanelli's for a roast beef sandwich. Next, we visited Dallas and Tuck's brother, Bill, a former military pilot who went on to work for Delta Air Lines. Tuck, the youngest child, was the lone "artist" in his family. I related, as my own home had lacked any cultural trappings. Though acting had never been my goal and I had grave doubts about my future while heading to LA, living with a comedian like Gary and then an actor like Tuck was rubbing off on me. Gradually, people outside the business seemed dull, guarded, and predictable. Part of falling in love with acting is falling in love with actors. And before money began to contaminate the whole enterprise, there were so many to fall in love with.

We then drove through the Texas panhandle and headed toward Santa Fe to see Amy Irving, whom Tuck had performed with in Seattle. In Chillicothe,

Texas, we got caught in a speed trap, where the speed limit seemed to drop from 150 miles per hour to 25 inside of a block. We were pulled over and taken into the police station, which appeared to double as the local DMV, courthouse, and feed store. Late in the frozen evening, standing in front of a schoolroom-style retractable chart bearing the schedule of fines, we could overhear the arresting officer saying to the judge, "But they got traveler's checks from the Chase Manhattan Bank IN NEW YORK CITY!!!" It was the Pace picante sauce commercial brought to life. We then drove to Flagstaff to rest, drink, and blow a kiss to one of the wonders of the world. "I give you the Grand Fucking Canyon," Tuck said as we walked onto the viewing platform at the edge of the South Rim. We took it in for about twenty minutes, the last pure thing I'd do for some time to come. Then we jumped in the car and headed to LA.

One week after we had left New York, we arrived in West Hollywood to find that the apartment we were subletting wasn't ready. The great stage actress Roberta Maxwell, whom I had seen at Williamstown, and her husband, Phil Dunne, an audio engineer for the likes of Elton John, needed a couple more days to move out. Our first night in LA, we slept on the floor of Toby and Bob, a couple whom Tuck had worked with in New

York. It was there that I met and fell in love with Ken Page. I was falling in love every half hour back then, enamored as I was by this newly discovered crowd. Ken, a great musical theater actor who had come to LA to branch out, having played roles in *Cats* and *Ain't Misbehavin'*, is one of the most talented Broadway performers I would come to know. Through Tuck I met a few other New York actors, directors, and writers who had relocated to LA: David Marshall Grant, Victor Garber, and a writer named Ron Dobson, who would eventually become the best friend I would ever have.

After a few days, we finally moved into Roberta and Phil's. Roberta, a dark and stormy Canadian, and Phil, a lanky and chirpy Brit, lived on Larrabee Street, above Sunset. When they were finally vacating the place, Phil paused to lay out his dos and don'ts. In a scene reminiscent of a *National Lampoon* movie, Phil finished his checklist saying, "Now, in this closet"—Phil indicated his closet—"in this box"—Phil indicated a box inside the closet—"are my mah-stah pressings of Elton's reck-hords." Along a wall, heading up the stairs, were framed gold records from some of the Elton John recordings Phil had engineered. "Please do not touch them. They are vinyl pressings from the original mah-stah tapes, and I tell you, you must never handle them. Please. I must insist. Don't even take them out of their sleeves. I implore you." Well, I think we had them out and on the turntable before his car hit the bottom of the hill. We pulled the trophies off the wall, too, as the prospect of snorting cocaine off framed Elton John gold records while listening to "mah-stah pressings" of "The Bitch Is Back" was just too tempting.

I met some smart and wicked characters in LA in 1983. Through the actress Hillary Bailey, our other roommate, I was introduced to a small group of writers who worked in network sitcoms. They typed away at an early form of computer in their apartments in the Hollywood Hills, pumping out episodes of some of the most successful comedies on the air. An afternoon of writing, and boom, they were done. Then we played tennis and drank while I listened to them bullshit about a business that I was barely in. But because they were in it, I could listen all night long. Driving is everything in LA, so drugs suddenly seemed more practical than booze. People drank, but that was often how they balanced the high of cocaine. As these guys were civilized sorts, we'd go to dinner at Lew Mitchell's Orient Express, the old "gourmet" Chinese joint on Wilshire near the Miracle Mile, before we blasted off for the evening. It was the LA equivalent of Hurley's. I watched them eat squab in lettuce cups. Imagine this New Yorker in LA, where pigeons were on the menu.

Tuck and I had a phone answering machine, and as neither of us had a job, we reveled in recording long, self-indulgent outgoing messages, usually employing ridiculous dialects. The result was bad Monty Python. One day, we got a message from an old friend of Tuck's, Dick Clayton, a bygone actor who had appeared in films like *The Hunchback of Notre Dame* with Charles Laughton before going on to a big career as an agent, representing James Dean and Burt Reynolds at the Famous Artists Agency. Clayton, polite but firm, said, "I don't know what that is, Tuck, but you ought to knock that off. No one wants to sit and listen to that over the phone. It's not very professional, and I think it makes you look bad, if I may say so." A lesson about Hollywood as a serious business, courtesy of James Dean's agent. We changed the outgoing message.

Los Angeles quickly became a blur of Thomas Guide maps, gas stations, burger joints, studio parking lots, and bars like Barney's Beanery and the Formosa Café, which were the Polo Lounge and Dan Tana's for out-of-work actors. I went to lots of auditions for films, TV shows, and some TV commercials. TV commercial calls in LA highlighted how the business differed from New York. In New York, guys showed up for auditions with a game face on. Commercials were viewed as a trite yet necessary evil, so you'd chat about what else you were working on, typically in the theater or film. In LA, the guys who sat around the holding area talked about hang gliding, biking, horseback riding, surfing, hiking, or anything else one might do under the perfect Southern California sun. Each was a perfect specimen in terms of height, fitness, hair, and skin, and nearly everyone was named Chad, Rick, or Steve, with maybe one or two Coles. They were male models auditioning to play cowboys, cops, or the guy half of some perfect-looking straight couple. In New York, actors talked about the latest play at the Public Theater. In LA, they talked about the newest cars, diet shakes, or workouts.

In the majority of my early auditions, I was either dreadful or totally unmemorable. But it didn't matter. I was perfect for TV in the '80s. I met Jean Guest, the mother of director Christopher Guest and the head of casting at CBS. Jean was a kind, intelligent woman who seemed to be in my corner in those early days. After a series I shot for CBS was canceled, the network signed me to a holding deal, paying me a relatively small stipend in exchange for simply not working for anyone else. In one meeting, an opaque colleague of Jean's said, "We like you and want to try to find a good fit. We'll keep throwing something against the wall until it sticks. We want you to be the next Bill Bixby." In New York, the carrot might be a career like Pacino's.

In LA, it was the chance to be the heir to the star of *My Favorite Martian*.

The series I shot was called *Cutter to Houston*, a drama where Shelley Hack, a wonderful actor named Jim Metzler, and I played doctors bringing our talents to some Texas backwater, each for our own complicated reasons (I was a physician/drug thief who was sentenced to work there as community service, if you can imagine such a thing).

The pilot was written and directed by Sandor Stern, who had a heart attack in the final days of shooting it and was replaced by another director. The show was eventually taken over by the producer Gerry Abrams, father of the prolific J. J. Abrams. We wrapped the pilot at the end of March 1983.

By then, the California sun had seduced me a bit, as I drove up the Pacific Coast Highway and hung out at Zuma, La Piedra, Pescador, Matador, and Nicholas Canyon Beaches in Malibu. I thought that if I found a lot of work in LA, I might live in Malibu, which possessed a wonderful sense of community. Beyond the lifestyle, LA represented the chance for me to learn more about the business than I could in New York. I thought about staying a bit longer, driving around California, seeing the place in a way I never had time for when I was working all day. But right about that time, my sister called to tell me to come back home as soon as I could. Everyone there had underplayed my father's condition, and now his health had declined precipitously.

In my first few days back in New York, I learned that my father had only weeks to live. The lymphoma, detected in August of 1982, had raged through his body and was now in his lungs. Initially, he went to Mount Sinai on the recommendation of his brother Charles's second wife, Vera, for whom promising treatments involving macrobiotic dieting bought more than a year of comfort and some hope. But after this period of remission, her cancer recurred and she died. At Sloan Kettering, they had essentially told him to go home and die as comfortably as he could. My sister told me that he dragged himself to work until some of his students' parents complained to the administration that his appearance "upset" them. He called my sister Beth and, throwing in the towel, asked her to take him back home to Linda's house, where he'd been living.

My uncle Charles found a hospital in Philadelphia that agreed to see him, so when I got back to New York, I traveled by train to the Mercy Catholic Medical Center's Misericordia Hospital. Charles, battle-hardened as he was by Vera's illness, was at my father's side much of the time. When I arrived, the halls seemed so ominous: dark, long, and wide. The walk to my dad's room seemed to take forever. When I entered the room and finally saw him, I was speechless, and not only because of his sallow skin or the tubes coming out at different angles. It was the look in his eye, a look I had never seen before, that crushed me. I saw fear in this brave and self-abnegating man. This was not my father. He spoke only once that first afternoon, to tell me that he wanted neither a wake nor a funeral. He wanted to be cremated and his ashes scattered in Lake Coeur D'Alene in northern Idaho, the place he had dreamed he might retire.

My brother Billy and I spent the night at a weird motel where the lounge, called the Frank Sinatra Room, featured a trio of middle-aged guys playing and crooning the hits of the Chairman of the Board on Friday and Saturday nights. One wall had a mural, perhaps fifteen feet wide by eight feet high, a knock-off of the cover from Sinatra's *Main Event* album from 1974. Maybe this was God offering us something truly bizarre to take our mind off of the situation. Just across a narrow alley, my father was suffering unimaginably, while we drank and listened to "The Shadow of Your Smile," performed by the Frank Sinatra of South 54th Street, Philly.

The next morning, my dad opened his eyes, and as a tear rolled down his cheek, he said, "I'll never see my grandchildren." Then, overwhelmed by morphine, he went back to sleep. An oncology resident from India asked, "Did your father ever work in heavy industry?" No, I said. "Near a steel mill or factories?" No, I said. "Your father has a very high lead content in his blood," he informed me. I told the doctor that my father had coached riflery in a high school for twenty-eight years, and he ventured that an unventilated shooting range may have been a cause. There, for over a quarter century, lead dust was inhaled not just by my dad, but by his team members and my brothers and me as well. Other area schools had installed ventilation in their shooting ranges long before. Some months later, my sister asked school officials to provide us with sample material from walls, flooring, and ceiling tiles to assess the level of toxicity. These men, my father's colleagues for decades and some his longtime friends, denied our requests and gutted the rifle range, incinerating all of the material in order to shield the district, and themselves, from the litigation we were exploring.

On April 15, I was back in New York to meet for a general audition with the casting director John Lyons, and read "Let us sit upon the ground . . ." from *Richard II.* It was probably bad, but John only smiled and said, "Well, I've never seen that done that way before." Though some casting agents were assholes, others genuinely cared, like Lyons and the late Howard Feuer. In 1986, I auditioned for Peter Shaffer's *Yonadab*, and at one point, the director, Peter Hall, expressed concern about the paucity of my theater credits. Feuer, who was short, corpulent, and spoke with a wheeze, blurted out, "Well, he's very stage-worthy!" Dear, dear Howard. I owe so much to people like him.

After the audition, I took a long trip by subway, then bus, to Yonkers to meet a bail bondsman. It seemed that my brother Daniel had either borrowed or stolen a car and had been arrested while visiting my brother Billy at college in Binghamton. I had to post the bail so that Daniel could get down to Philadelphia to see our father. I got to the bail bondsman's office and, matter-of-factly, he said, "I am authorized to use deadly force, if need be, to bring him in. You realize that, don't you?" After a pause, he repeated, "Deadly force . . . if necessary," his tone suggesting that he was rather fond of deadly force. I signed the bail papers to spring my brother and made my way home to the apartment on 58th between 1st and 2nd. I walked up the three flights of stairs, opened my door, and got a glass of water. It was five p.m., and I hadn't been in the door five minutes when the phone rang. It was my sister Beth, convulsing. I could barely understand her until she got out the words "Dad died." I don't remember anything after that. I don't remember the cab ride to Penn Station, the train ride to Massapequa, or the taxi to our house. When I got there, my mother, Beth, and I seemed to unconsciously move into the den, where we stood near the daybed that my father had slept on for many years. I felt as if I had fainted and come to in that room. My journey to LA had been not only encouraged by my father but also underwritten, in some sense, by the lies about his health, lies that had brought us to this awful place. I started to sob uncontrollably, and I blacked out again, awake but unable to hear or recall anything.

My father was the first person for whom I was charged with arranging a burial. His wake was held at the Massapequa Funeral Home. Prior to the services that evening, the owner, a man not much older than me, quietly asked me if I was ready to bid farewell to the body. I hesitated, not quite sure I wanted to see my father's body, and that must have showed. The man leaned in and said, "One day, I assure you, you may see your dad walking down the street or sitting in a park. You'll swear it's him. So I urge all of the family members to view the body and say a proper good-bye. That way, you have no doubts." The thought had never occurred to me. The next thing I knew, I was in the room, standing over my father. With makeup, he looked a good deal better than when I'd last seen him. He was beloved in my hometown, and that night many, many in our town came to his wake. My mother sat in a widow's chair and received the condolences of half the town, with no acknowledgment of the state of their marriage.

After my father's death, my relationship with my mother would hit an all-time low. As I look back, I attribute this to her fear and economic insecurity as a widow. However, we now entered a period where I was more of an ex-husband than a son. My mother had often relied on Beth and me to function as lieutenants in her army. However, as I spent more time in Los Angeles working, my mother's needs and her inimitable way of expressing them drove us to a frosty, unpleasant place.

The funeral was held at our church, St. Martin of Tours Catholic Church in Amityville. Another Catholic church, St. Rose, had opened nearer to us in Massapequa, but by then we were dedicated St. Martin's parishioners. It looked like every seat was taken. I came in and out of my battered state, picking up on snippets of the Mass text. I stared at the floor. Then, I heard the priest recite, "Eternal rest grant unto him and may perpetual light shine upon him." I cracked again, but it was different this time. The word, as I learned, is "keening." I thought I might pass out. My sister reached over and squeezed my thigh and whispered, "You've got to stop." But I couldn't stop, because this was incomprehensible. My father couldn't be dead. That wasn't possible. The only person in the world I trusted was now gone and everything would be different. Throughout that day and beyond, I worried about the lost opportunities to thank him for his generosity and selflessness. I fantasized about the clothes I would have bought him, the trips I'd have sent him on. Many in my family needed help, and I tried to provide that help, but I always imagined that, in his case, I would have done anything to thank this man. Anything. He had sacrificed so much to carry me on his back up this hill of life.

Two years later, while shooting a TV show, *Dress Gray*, at Warner Bros., I noticed a man sitting at a picnic table at an outdoor commissary. It was my father. I froze. Then I walked a few steps toward him. The funeral director had been right. It was not my dad. After that began the unconscious and ultimately unhealthy search for someone to substitute for him.

6

The Love Taxi

The weeks following my father's death, I spent more time back home with family, which made me realize how much I had missed them. Perhaps unconsciously, I had created this bogus myth that I had crossed some ocean to make my fortune by going to Los Angeles. The truth is that I was simply uninterested in going home, back to a place that required me to explain who I had become. I wanted different experiences now. The one person who had a genuine interest in my life, as well as an insightful perspective, was gone. Meanwhile, my mother floated in a haze of grieving widowhood. My sister Beth was off beginning her own family. My sister Jane was just a kid who fell between the cracks of my reality, which was sad because she was and is such a bright person and is engaged by learning in the same way that I was.

While I was home for this grieving period, I relied on my brothers, by then ages twenty-three, twenty, and seventeen, to cope and on a wholly different level. I had money in my pocket, so we partied. During the summer of 1983, it was a weird mix of sweet and unsettling to go out "on the town" with them when the town was Massapequa. The white-flight suburbs were now the easiest of places to buy drugs, to get fake IDs, and to walk into bar after bar. By six a.m., we'd hit the Sandbar in Seaford, and I would see some of my friends' dads. As dawn broke outside, there was Mr. Smith here, Mr. Jones there, my dad's peers stewed at the hour when my father would have been in the kitchen making breakfast. I thought about how good we'd had it with him as our father, and how alcohol drowns our dreams, silences our beliefs, and relieves us of our responsibilities. Although my brothers and I had some laughs that summer, none of it felt right. I didn't want any of us to grow up to become the guy sitting on the next bar stool at the Sandbar.

Tuck had gone down to West Palm Beach to appear at the Burt Reynolds Dinner Theatre in a production of *The Apple Tree*, so I flew down there to join him. He and his female costar were put up in a couple of condos in a swell building by the beach. We spent the days sleeping by the pool, waterskiing, and drinking while attempting to win over some girls who worked at the theater. If mourning your dead father and presenting yourself in a state of overall numbness were an aphrodisiac, then I might have made a better impression upon these women. Some women go for needy men. However, I do not recall any of them taking me up on my offer. I went home to Long Island a week later, still feeling lost.

When I got back to New York, I got a call from a very young and very beautiful woman named Janine Turner, whom I'd met in LA when she'd auditioned for the *Cutter to Houston* pilot. She told me that she came to New York regularly and promised to call me when she did. When we met at the old Café La Fortuna for coffee, I told her about my dad's death, and she was genuinely moved. After she went back to California, she sent me a beautiful and thoughtful letter. I selfishly felt that there weren't enough people checking in on me during this difficult time, so Janine's letter made a real impact on me. Janine was only twenty-one and completely without cynicism. Thus, I found myself smitten by what is often the greatest aphrodisiac of all: sincerity. So that's how Janine Turner became my first show business love. Within a matter of months, we were living together in LA, getting engaged, and then just as quickly heading for a breakup while I was in the throes of my self-destructive behavior.

Once, while Janine was performing the musical *Grease* at a dinner theater in Denver, I had, of course, made the necessary connections to procure my illicit pharmaceutical needs. I went to brunch with Janine, her mother, and her mother's parents, who were out of a Norman Rockwell painting. Everyone sipped coffee or wine while I retreated to the bathroom every fifteen minutes. At one point, Janine's grandfather leveled me with a look that said, "There's somethin' not right about you, boy." If only he knew the extent of it. Janine and I broke up a few months later. She was an extraordinarily kind woman, but we were too young to be making those plans.

At the same time, the pilot for *Cutter* was picked up, and I raced back to LA, excited to be working as a lead in my first prime-time show. We shot eight episodes, but the result was tepid reviews and unspectacular ratings. Even as inexperienced as I was, I knew the show wasn't working and that something had to give. I learned then that producers never give the prognosis of a show in fear that everyone will start to phone it in. One day a director named Bernie McEveety walked on the set, and a crew member muttered, "It's the Hangman." I asked what he meant, and he said, "They bring him on to wrap up the last few episodes under budget." McEveety, a polite and quiet man, would snap, "Cut, print, fine!" after one or two takes. Within a couple of days of McEveety's arrival, word came down that we'd been canceled. The excitement of scoring any job as an actor comes with that dichotomy. The movie bombs, the play closes, or the TV show is canceled, and your joy is quickly replaced by disappointment. But you try to remember that it's not your fault. At least, not entirely. Finding an audience is a difficult task and failure is the norm.

CBS signed me to a holding deal, whereby one is paid a fee to work exclusively for one company for a period of time. The results of that deal were shows like *Sweet Revenge*, a TV movie with Kelly McGillis, and *The Sheriff and the Astronaut*, a very bad pilot from a very good writer named Gerry Di Pego. Di Pego had written *Sharky's Machine*, which starred Burt Reynolds, and was a movie I liked a lot. I couldn't imagine how the writer of that ballsy, gritty script had also come up with this soft, precious TV show.

It became clear what a small town LA was. While I was shooting these odd little TV projects, I was actually six degrees from some seriously talented people. Di Pego wrote a screenplay that Reynolds had decided to direct himself. Goldie Hawn's first husband, Gus Trikonis, directed me in a TV movie with Stephanie Zimbalist (whom I adored). Gus had acted in the movie *West Side Story*, and his wisdom about the business made an impression on me. He told me, "Work is work. Just try to be the best thing in whatever you're doing." I tried to take his advice to heart, even though what I was doing seemed weak and wasn't drawing a significant audience. I gathered, therefore, that it must have been agents, producers, and casting people talking about me and my potential, regardless of my recent work, that brought me the first audition for a project I thought was truly special.

In the pre–O. J. era, the Jeffrey MacDonald murder case was a big media event, on par with the crimes and trials of Jean Harris, Charles Manson, and the Menendez brothers. In 1970, MacDonald, a US Army surgeon assigned to the Green Berets at Fort Bragg, was accused of killing his pregnant wife and two daughters in their home. The author Joe McGinniss responded to an invitation from MacDonald to tell his story, and ended up writing the bestseller *Fatal Vision*, in which he submits that his subject is, in fact, guilty and labels him a "narcissistic sociopath." NBC was producing a TV movie based on the book, and I got a call to audition for director David Greene to play MacDonald. Greene had directed the forgettable TV movie I did with Kelly McGillis and the more well-received *Rich Man, Poor Man*, among others.

On an overcast New York day in 1983 as I headed to my audition, the thought of being considered for this job made my head spin. The prospect of working with Karl Malden, Eva Marie Saint, and Andy Griffith, who had already been cast, was overwhelming. Before the meeting, I headed into a bar down the block. I quickly belted down two Canadian Club and sodas, steeled myself, went to the appointment, and nailed it. When Bloom called me to tell me I'd landed the job, I was deliriously happy. Dramatic acting roles were always the goal, and now a great opportunity to play this cunning murderer was in front of me. But then Bloom informed me that we had an interesting dilemma. The producers of the CBS prime-time soap opera *Knots Landing* had also called and wanted to meet with me about joining the cast. *Knots* was perched in the top ten every week and therefore I would simply go along for the ride. Bloom was deliberate and clear. "No question, you should do *Knots*," he said. "It's already a big hit and you will be seen by many millions every week. The TV movie will get aired once with a rerun and be gone. The MacDonald role is great, but *Knots* comes with an added bonus. The role is Julie Harris's son."

Working with talented people is one of the great gifts of show business and an area in which I've been lucky over the years. A few of these people, however, have stood out above the rest. Some are famous; others are not. Some are bright, compassionate, and unpretentious; others are not. But no one I've worked with during my career has come close to Julie Harris, in terms of the reservoir of humanity, talent, and professionalism that she embodied. It was Julie, and all the feelings that she provoked in me, who made my decision to sign up for *Knots* an easy one. (And a good one. Later, when I ignored those instincts to work with the right people, bad things happened.)

Julie appeared on the show for eight seasons as a series regular. She approached the job like she did all of the stage roles that had garnered her five Tony Awards on Broadway between 1952 (*I Am a Camera*) and 1977 (*The Belle of Amherst*). She took the work seriously. She was professional every minute of every day. The crew moved around her as if she were the queen. She elevated the work of the other cast members. When I read the upcoming scripts and saw that I had scenes with Julie, I was excited to go to work.

My character, Joshua Rush, was Julie's character's estranged son, who became the love interest of Lisa Hartman, the show's young ingénue. Joshua was a mess. He had mommy issues and daddy issues. He was a minister's son who was a preacher himself and eventually jumped off a building. My scenes were a bit overcooked, and I was still trying to figure out how to work around the cast of actors who had built this show into a hit without any help from me. I learned that any screen time on an ensemble show is time taken from someone else. Some of the other actors aren't so happy about that.

When the camera rolled, I simply focused on Julie, and she took you where the scene needed to go. When encountering her warm eyes and her soothing voice, I sometimes wondered what it would be like to have a mother that present, that soulful. But comparing my own mother to Julie was, obviously, unfair. Julie was an actress being paid to express those feelings. Nonetheless, confusing acting with reality can be an occupational hazard. I would make small talk with her in her dressing room, and we became friends. She would occasionally invite me to the Brentwood home where she stayed while she shot the series. After the show wrapped, she'd return to her home in Chatham, Massachusetts, or go off to do a play. *Knots* was a job. It was a good job. But the theater was her life.

Manipulating their public relations was a large order of business. One day, sitting in the driveway of a home where we regularly shot, Julie sat quietly, knitting. As I was discussing with Lisa and some others the question of which publicist I should sign with, Julie looked up and said, "Oh, Alec. Don't get a publicist. Let the work speak for itself." How I've wished, over the years, that I had taken her advice. Publicists, and the courting of the media that goes hand in hand with them, have created as many problems as they have solved in my life. If only I had followed Julie's lead in all things. While Julie taught me that there was nothing to be ashamed of in doing jobs simply to make a living, so long as those jobs fueled other creative efforts, the other actors on *Knots* were all big TV stars who saw things somewhat differently.

Working with someone as iconic as Julie, I wondered what impressed her. Julie's career cut a swath through the heart of twentieth-century theater, film, and TV, and I wanted to learn what memories stood out to her. In her dressing room one day, I asked her what the most special moment of her career had been. What was she proudest of? She paused for a long moment and said, "I'm one of only two actresses to kiss Jimmy Dean in a movie." Julie had done so in *East of Eden*, the other actress being Natalie Wood in *Rebel Without a Cause*. Over time, I asked Julie about Raymond Massey, Claire Bloom, Elizabeth Taylor, and Brando.

Of all that galaxy of names and experiences, kissing Dean was what lingered.

One night in Gleneden Beach, Oregon, where *Knots* had gone on location to shoot a couple of weeks' worth of picturesque exteriors, Julie shared her most priceless sentiment with me. I drove Julie back to the hotel after having dinner in Lincoln City. Sitting in front of the Salishan Lodge, I asked her, "Are you anxious to go home?" "No," she said. Surprised, I asked, "Aren't you ready for this trip to be over?" Julie said, "I don't wish anything to be over. To wish something to be over is to wish your life to be over."

I wondered if the closeness I had with some people in the business would last, or if it was all just of the moment. Was my home now the set of a show, where a kind of instant familiarity was bred, and was it always meant to melt away? Somewhere in the loneliness and insecurity of being among people I didn't know while seeking some bond with them, I searched for ways to kill those feelings. I subsequently bonded with others in a more self-destructive way. One night, in my room at Salishan, I lost myself to those feelings. It's a story I don't like to tell. I don't want to tell it. But it's so real and unreal at the same time. That night changed my life forever. It had its own staccato rhythm, distorted sound, and spasmodic imagery. It went something like this:

SALISHAN LODGE, 1984

There's that knock at the door that I've been waiting on for over an hour and they told me it would be only thirty minutes and they always say it will be thirty minutes, these FUCKING PEOPLE! Why won't they just do what they say they're going to do? Motherfuckers. SNAP!!!

When I called room service, I fumbled for the words, saying something like, "Hello? Room service? This is Mr. Baldwin in Room 224. I have some guests arriving for lunch and I know how busy you can be and I was wondering if you might send over a bottle of champagne NOW!"—punching certain words, as I am slightly deaf when high. "I won't have to bother you later and I would appreciate that. One bottle of champagne. NOW! Baldwin. Room 224."

My hair is a bird's nest, my black T-shirt sweaty and covered with white chalky crescents. The *Today* show is on, signaling officially that I've stayed up all night getting high and smoking cigarettes, calling people back in New York and LA to keep me company and nurse me through this run. All the while that I'm on the phone, I'm wondering, do they know? Can they tell? It's getting a little hard to breathe. But Jane Pauley is my center. Jane is my center. Breathe, baby, breathe.

I lie down and focus on Jane and she will talk me down. She's like Naloxone coming out of the TV. If I just sit and focus on Jane, this will pass. Her goodness will counteract all of this shit. Another knock.

A merciless and unstoppable death squad has been marauding up and down my nerves throughout the predawn hours. By sunrise, it's clear that they're going to torch the whole village. I put up no resistance. I am their hostage, simply feeding the troops more drugs and filing for the spiritual bankruptcy that cocaine always demands. Cue "Midnight Rambler," as the Rolling Stones are always the soundtrack when I'm driving this road. I'm looking at Jane, but hearing Mick. KNOCK, KNOCK!! I'm on my feet and moving across the room like I'm hopping over hot stones. Not bothering to pull myself together, I look through the peephole before I open the door. The sun, with its effortless power to shame, jumps at me. The man's back is to me and I can't get a look at him. Could he possibly know something? Fuck. When he turns, he looks like a Rick or a Steve, a bit whiter and older than I anticipated, and that throws me. Is he a fucking cop?! I open the door, the sun crashes in, my heart rate spikes up. CRACKLE!!

Oh, no. I feel an unfamiliar tingle move over my chest. Forty-year-old Nancy Reagan Country room service Rick assesses me. My eyes are looking everywhere but at him. Then he hands me the champagne bottle, in a bucket, and the glasses. The booze is all I see now and I tip him and he goes and I'm closing the door with my ass so I can open the bottle as fast as I can, because I'm gonna do WHATEVER IT TAKES to solve this. Jane, I'm coming! Don't finish without me!

POP!! . . . goes the champagne bottle. Shhhhhh, Jane is speaking. She's like chicken soup. Breathe. Up it goes and down it goes and I drink the bottle in four gulps. It's eight a.m. I've been snorting cocaine since around four the previous afternoon. By midnight, one of the two girls I've been hanging out with at the crew hotel, about thirty miles away, said something crazy and wonderful. "Our husbands are going on a fishing trip tomorrow morning. They leave real early. You get some more coke and come to my house and we will do whatever . . . you . . . want." She lays out the offer like we're discussing subletting an apartment. They leave, presumably to stage their bedtime at home. At around one a.m., I knock on the nearby hotel room door of a guy in the crew who I knew had what I wanted. He was a casual user, not twitchy. He was friendly and together. For him, cocaine was an amuse-bouche among other available relaxations during an evening out. He opens the door and I've broken his heart, it seems. "You?" he sighs, in the way that someone signals that they now know a sad truth about you that you both wish they didn't. "I got these two girls," I stammer, as if that explains everything. He sighs and leaves to grab the stuff. He shoves it at me, saying, "Don't come back."

I drive from the crew hotel up the coast to Salishan, where the cast is staying. In the car, a rare moment of clarity descends on me and, as is often the case, it's a movie that screens in my head. A car slows on a dark, leafy road. Inside, a man, a big guy wearing outdoorsy clothes, says, "Bob, did you bring the propane for the stove?" Bob, also big, says, "Shit, I thought you did." "Jesus, Bob. We gotta go back." What Bob will go back to, obviously, is his house, which I am settled into for a night of partying with their wives. As they walk into the living room, they'll find me naked on the floor, drink in one hand and Trivial Pursuit cards in the other, playing a friendly game of Strip Trivia with their spouses. The requisite cocaine lines, paraphernalia, alcohol, and cigarettes are on display.

I pull over to the side of the winding road. My eyes are wide and I am hyperventilating. Thank you, God, for intervening with this insight, this gift. Fuck. If they'd shot me, I would have deserved it. Or maybe stabbed me. Then they'd chop me up! My eyes are really wide now. I'm breathing harder. Fuck. Thank you, God. Maybe twenty minutes later, I return to my hotel, holding on to not only the couple of grams of blow, but also some sick, lingering remorse that I'm not deep into the Strip Trivia tourney by now. In the hotel, I am alone with my least favorite company, the guy who complains to me about his life and criticizes me about mine, more than anyone I know.

I sit and pack cocaine, musket-style, into cigarettes. I gently roll out some tobacco, then mix the drug with it and pack it in. I adopted this method some years before, in order to walk along Columbus Avenue and get high while cruising the Upper West Side. I turn to it now to calm myself with something familiar. That's right. Calming myself by smoking cocaine at three a.m. Or perhaps I'm doing this because addiction forces you to a place of inevitability that must include overwhelming risk, shame, or death.

Jane is speaking, but it is not having the desired effect. Shortly after Room Service Rick is gone, I realize I have hit that place where none of it is working. I cannot get high and I cannot come down. I've walked out on a ledge, only to find that I lack the true resolve. But I've also closed the window and there's no way to get back in. I think for a moment and decide to give it one more try. Now I'm slightly panicked. My heart is like a speed bag, thumping very fast in my chest now. As I dial the phone, I think how I've never been this aware of my heart beating before. RING RING!! Not ever. RING RING!! "Room service? This is Mr. Baldwin again in 224. Yes, I did get that delivery, however my friends have informed me that they will be a somewhat larger group and I'm thinking that perhaps we'll need ANOTHER bottle of champagne, NOW, in order to accommodate everyone, so, yes . . . er . . . ah . . . Baldwin, room 224."

Knock, knock. It's Rick, staring straight ahead with a jaundiced look as he hands me the bill to sign. As I turn and put the paper on the counter, I follow his gaze over to the now empty bottle of champagne, upside down in its bucket. I turn back and he says, glancing over my shoulder, "Shall I take away the empty bottle?" His expression seems sad. Seeing myself reflected in this guy's eyes, I glimpse a chance, in that moment: a last, unrecoverable chance. I actually sober up for four seconds. He's Angel Rick now. He's here to save me, not to deliver room service. But Mick keeps singing:

He don't go in the light of the morning
He split the time the cock'rel crows

So I resume, muttering "Sure, sure" and gesturing him out. As I close the door, I feel as if I'm on a surfboard and an enormous wave is gathering. I'm now left to ride this colossal beast to the shore all alone. I take a few more gulps and I lie down and light a cigarette.

My heart starts fluttering. I sit up, gasping a bit for air. Jane is smiling. I lie down again and begin to breathe deeply and sharply, trying to calm myself down from an emerging megapanic. I inhale, attempting to push the air up toward my clavicle and down toward my lower back. I'm scared. My speed bag heart drums away inside me while my skin begins to feel wet and cold. As I reach my right arm across my body to get another drink of champagne, I begin to go completely deaf. Did Jane just look at me through the TV and mouth, "Oh, Alec"? Now the speed bag is replaced by a hummingbird, trapped inside my chest, trying to get out. It's too fast. My eyes start to tear up. I start to whimper. Am I overdosing? I press my right palm over my heart and my left one over the right. I am trying to massage my heart and contain the hummingbird while gulping in air. I am fucked. I am so fucked. I actually know it now. The wave is gathering me. It's going to fling me like a fucking paper airplane onto the floor. The bird gets faster. The wave is curled over me. Then there is this bizarre pause as the beat stops. Now my heart feels like a bubble gum bubble is blowing up inside of it. Puff, the bubble gets bigger. Puff, bigger still. Puff, and I have no idea what is happening and then the bubble pops. There's a pop inside my chest. POP! Then I black out.

When I open my eyes, I have no idea how long I was lying there, knocked out by a hummingbird. When I raise my head, I find I can't move without some corresponding tachycardia. Each motion awakens the bird. When I stop moving, the bird is quiet. I crawl across the carpet to the phone on the other side of the bed, a twenty-foot journey that takes me thirty minutes. I call a woman in the cast who will understand, I'm hoping. When she picks up, she sounds appalled. It's nine a.m. on her day off. I try to tell her I think I need the kind of help someone needs when he's just overdosed on cocaine, but I don't use the word "overdose." More than his own health, more than his life, the addict clings to the lie.

We drive to the emergency room, where the doctor asks if I'm on drugs. I think, "Fuck you, asshole. You're gonna take my blood and find out." In this business, even taking a standing eight, let alone getting knocked out by drugs and booze, is frowned upon. And a diagnosis of addiction can follow you forever. So I lie and tell him, "We've been working hard, Doc. Long hours. I took some speed." He stares down at me on the gurney. He must be good at poker, because his expression doesn't say, "You lying little shit," which

I assume he's thinking. Maybe he's seen lots of lying little shits like me come through there: black, white, rich, poor, promising, or hopeless. Or maybe he's an angel, too? He seems kind when he says, "I'm going to give you something to sleep." Although I can't move my body, a tear rolls down the side of my face. "What's the matter?" he asks. I say, "I'm afraid I'm not going to wake up."

I slept the next thirty-six hours. I woke up Monday morning and had the day off. I was still rooming with this guy, however, who was trying to kill me. Tuesday morning, I went to work and never spoke with anyone about what happened. The girl who drove me to the hospital simply asked, "Are you OK?" as if I had poison ivy.

I returned to Los Angeles, alternately scared out of my mind and grateful beyond words, and went to a meeting of Cocaine Anonymous, an association of people who measured their lengths of sobriety more in months, weeks, and days than years. Due to the overwhelming grip cocaine had on its largely younger membership, relapses were more frequent. But as I had been warned in my first AA meetings, abstinence from drugs requires abstinence from alcohol as well, because otherwise the addict substitutes drinking for drugs.

And that's just what I did. Rather than pull over to my dealer's house at four p.m., I'd hit a bar. I'd never been much of a drinker compared to others I'd known. But I now found myself spending the fall of 1984 keeping my feelings and my drug addiction at bay by drinking liquor in LA bars.

By that point, Tuck and I were living just off of the Ocean Front Walk in Venice in an apartment that looked out onto the water and the surge of beachgoers who flocked there on weekends. Venice was a Bleecker Street–type carnival of humanity, vendors, and food. The walkway was a filthy and garbage-strewn mess by Sunday evening. On Monday mornings, the beach cleaning crew arrived, a small brigade of sand-sifting trucks and workers who spent the day soaping and rinsing the benches along the promenade. By Tuesday morning, it was as clean as the entrance to Buckingham Palace. The smells and sounds of those Tuesday mornings became my *Bright Lights, Big City* moments. A sparkling, clean Venice made me think that maybe I could be cleansed, too.

In the winter of 1985, Larry, an old friend from New York, came to visit me at the beach, and for the first time in six months, I got high. He drove away after just an hour or so, claiming he was off to procure more coke. He never returned, leaving me to pace the floor in a desperate, metronomic march, waiting for him. That was it. That was the last day: Saturday, February 23,

1985. I spent most of Sunday sleeping, thinking, pray-
ing, and accepting. On Monday morning, I went to an
AA meeting in West Hollywood. To tell you what was
said there would be a violation of the principles of anonymity that I respect. I'm comfortable telling you I am
a member, but I'll leave it at that. I haven't had a drink
or recreational drug since that day over thirty years
ago. I surely have not had the courage to face all of my
issues in the way AA gently recommends. However,
I am profoundly grateful for discovering the program
that saved my life. As frequently as I have gotten in my
own way throughout my sobriety, I shudder to think of
how much more painful and destructive my behavior
might have been had I not been sober. Most important,
through AA, I have a renewed relationship with God,
a relationship I call upon every day. A couple of short
years later, Larry died of AIDS from IV drug use.

AA teaches you to make no serious decisions in your
first year of sobriety, including moving, changing jobs,
and getting into serious relationships. I obviously ignored the last part as soon as I met Holly Gagnier, who
visited the *Knots Landing* set one day to see her father,
Hugh, the cinematographer. Beautiful and funny,
Holly would be my girlfriend, off and on, for the next
five years.

Knots Landing was a good opportunity, but it wasn't my show. The cast was a lovely bunch that had formed a family, and Joan Van Ark, who played my sister, made me feel like a real sibling. But I didn't want a career like that of my castmate Ted Shackelford, whereby you come in week after week and do the same thing every day. The women in the *Knots* cast ruled the roost, and the show's creator, David Jacobs, expressed his beliefs, curiosities, and passions through the three female leads, who were given more interesting things to do on-screen than the men. The producers of *Knots Landing* had my character commit suicide, and although I had mixed feelings about leaving, I was off the show in the spring of 1985.

In the beginning, I had thought I might try acting for a while and see if it fit. As the work I was offered became more interesting, it became my life. The challenge of doing it well at an ever-higher level appealed to me more than anything else. It also took its toll on the rest of my life. I dated a bunch of women from 1980 through 1985. The cycle was always the same. I fed them crumbs and water and insisted they pretend it was a five-course meal. The moment work presented itself, and another chance to get ahead, I rushed into the arms of The Business. I discovered that in my private life, I was a chauffeur. People got in. I drove them around. Everyone seemed to arrive somewhere except me. I was a taxi that brought women to their next relationship and, hopefully, a better one. They got out of the cab and got married, had kids. I just kept reading scripts, going to meetings, trying to hustle my way into the movie business.

By the end of 1985, I had been in Los Angeles for a few years and California had begun to seem like a bit of a political loony bin, with Reagan having won reelection the year before. The lens of sobriety forced me to see everything more clearly. I wanted to go home. When I flew to New York on a red-eye for an audition, the city's stark reality overwhelmed me. Jet-lagged and hungry, I walked to the old 79th Street Coffee Shop on Broadway. That morning I thought, as some elderly folks shuffled by, "New York's got so many old people." A moment later, "New York's got so many fat people." And then, "I never realized how black New York is," as I noticed at least a third of those on the street were African-American. "New York is so old and fat and black," I thought. Coming home from LA, the land of the trim, youth-obsessed, and racially polarized, made me realize that I had been away too long. I ate breakfast, went home, and slept. Once I was in my right mind, New York seemed just right. Perfect, in fact. I sublet my half of the Venice apartment, bought a little place on West 80th Street in Manhattan in December of '85, and in the spring of 1986, I moved back to New York. Within a month, it would prove to be one of the best decisions I had ever made.

7

Prelude

The first Broadway show I saw was *Shenandoah*, starring John Cullum. Our high school bused us into New York for a field trip to the stock exchange, police headquarters, the United Nations, the botanical gardens, or Broadway. New York in the 1970s was filthy and unlovable, but while watching a good Broadway show, you could forget that. And inside the grimy Alvin Theatre, Cullum showed me, for the first time, what acting talent truly is. Leading men on Broadway like Cullum, Philip Bosco, and Len Cariou may have lacked the symmetrical features, perfect bodies, and ability to hold a close-up solely with a style like Cary Grant or Bogart. But they more than made up for it with wit, technique, and timing. Cullum had that theater eating out of his hand.

When I returned to New York in 1986, the Manhattan Theatre Club produced Joe Orton's black comedy *Loot* with a cast that included Kevin Bacon. The show garnered good reviews, and though subscribers may have yawned or slept through Orton's signature language and madness, true Ortonphiles showed up in the final days of the run to laugh convulsively at the late English playwright's dark and twisted take on family, sex, and politics. I was told that the legendary producer David Merrick attended one of the last performances and decided to move the show to Broadway. Bacon, on his way to starring in many films, could not make the move with the rest of the cast, so I got a call to audition for the role.

The producer, Charles Kopelman, gave me a copy of *Prick Up Your Ears*, John Lahr's definitive biography of Orton, where I read about the playwright's role in the cultural life of "Swinging London" in the '60s and his tragic end, bludgeoned to death by his lover Kenneth Halliwell. (Gary Oldman played Orton in a film version of the book, which was released the following year.) John Tillinger, the director, warned me from the moment I was cast that we would only do a "put in" rehearsal, due to the brief window of time before the opening. Thus, it was eight days of "Kevin did this" and "Kevin did that." There was a smattering of apologies from people assuming they were offending me with a rehearsal that bordered on puppetry, but I couldn't have cared less. I loved every minute of it. The role of Dennis, the undertaker's apprentice, was a small one, so the obstacle wasn't about memorization, but about my nerves. We previewed briefly, as all the other cast members were ready to go. It all seems a blur now, but the opening night was indelible. I made my first entrance feeling like I'd been fired out of a cannon. On that stage I tasted, for the first time, the joy of doing a well-oiled show. Knowing what I was going to say, how the other actors would respond, and the ultimate effect it would have on the audience became an addiction.

Charles Keating played the patriarch (a pejorative in Orton's worldview), Zoë Wanamaker was the nurse, and the talented Zeljko Ivanek played Hal, my character's lover. All three of them were such a pleasure to watch. But the otherworldly and brilliant Joe Maher was the Meadowlark Lemon of this team. Maher could bend a line, a phrase, or even a syllable to suit his desires. You couldn't take your eyes off of him. I'd first gotten a glimpse of Maher when I'd auditioned for Tillinger four years prior to replace Max Caulfield in Orton's *Entertaining Mr. Sloane*. Awed by his playfulness, pomp, sinister sexuality, and thunderous eruptions of conceit and indignation, I thought, "Imagine having gone to school with this guy!"

Throughout the run of *Loot*, which lasted only three months, I stood each night by the desk of the stage manager, Peggy Peterson, while she called the show. I was nearly hypnotized by Maher as, again and again, he tickled the crowd and his fellow actors with his signature zany effusions. In one scene, Maher brandished a book, intoning, "You have before you a man who is quite a personage in his way. Truscott of the Yard!" He then snapped open the book to indicate his picture. Beforehand, Joe would go to a newsstand and buy male porn magazines like *Honcho* and *Mandate*, cut out a shot of a guy with an appendage the size of a wrench, and paste it into the book. Zeljko's next line, "It's you," was meant to be thrown away, as if his character was unimpressed. But Zeljko and I could barely contain ourselves. Zeljko would spit the line out, stifling a laugh. That alone indicates how funny Joe was, but he was also kind and instructive offstage. Working with him was the most fun I've ever had. Wicked, funny Joe, I miss you.

As soon as the show closed, I was back on a plane to LA to audition for a film. In the beginning of my movie career, I met with casting directors frequently, and that year I was lucky enough to meet Jane Jenkins and Janet Hirshenson. Jane and Janet are two of the biggest names in casting in all of Hollywood, but when you talked with them, they were kind and generous, unpretentious and professional. Meetings with them were like going to the school nurse. If they brought you in and they liked you, they wanted you to get the job. In those days, when I had to audition for a role, I never knew if I was going to be offered the job until the end of the casting process. Eventually, I got to a place where I rarely have a discussion about a role without an offer, but the old days were more fun. The expectations were low. The excitement was real. For every job you were cast in, no matter how small, you had immeasurable gratitude.

I went through the casting process with Jane, Janet, and the director John Hughes, and got the role of Davis McDonald, the leading man's best friend, in the film *She's Having a Baby*. It was set to star Kevin Bacon, coincidentally enough, and Elizabeth McGovern. Hughes, slightly awkward yet smart and funny, reminded me of a resident assistant at a college dorm, having focused his films on the woes and triumphs of the young. I loved shooting with him, as he was very thoughtful toward me on my first real movie. Liz was that rare kind of actress with both beauty and talent but devoid of ego and insecurities. She reminded me of Katharine Hepburn. She knew who she was. Kevin was quiet, and his shyness suggested that the nature of movie stardom itself was a bit of a rash for him. We shot the film in Chicago and LA, and when it was over, I wanted more. I was attracted to the slower, more thoughtful pace of the movies, the professionalism on the set, and the belief that film is an art form.

The Hughes film was also my first time seeing a truly top cinematographer at work. Don Peterman, who had shot *Flashdance*, *Splash*, and *Cocoon*, among others, was a reserved guy who began my education about the camera. The first lesson he taught me is that the camera is the real star of every movie, and your first priority as a film actor is to get your relationship right with it. How you have prepared, how you look, how truthful you and the choices you make for your character are only matter if they are revealed to the camera. Otherwise, it's like painstakingly crafting a painting only to hang it on the wall backwards.

In the summer of 1987, I made a trip to the Williamstown Theatre Festival to do an odd little adaptation of a Sherlock Holmes novel. Believe it or not, I played Holmes. My Watson was an actor named Brian McCue, whose honesty and subtlety I can never forget, even though we worked together for a mere two weeks on what was otherwise a trifle of a production. It seemed that every time I did a play, I worked with someone who taught me something.

After that, movie parts started to come in a flurry. I went to read for David Geffen and Tim Burton for *Beetlejuice.* Once we started shooting, I sat in my trailer wondering what the hell I had gotten myself into. Jeffrey Jones, Glenn Shadix, Catherine O'Hara, and Michael Keaton chewed up the scenery, day in and day out. Comparatively, I just stood there doing almost nothing. I asked Tim if he was getting what he wanted from me. He murmured something about the living characters being scarier than the dead ones. I thought of my character as a milquetoast antique collector and told him I thought I'd channel Robert Cummings. Tim just stared at me and said, "No. Don't do that."

Soon after, I met with Jonathan Demme for *Married to the Mob.* The male characters in Demme's films are divided between violent or corrupt degenerates (*The Silence of the Lambs, Something Wild*) and soft-spoken, thoughtful, or just plain odd men (*Stop Making Sense, Melvin and Howard*). He cast me in the role of Michelle Pfeiffer's vulgar gangster husband, who fell squarely into the first category. I learned a couple of lessons on this film. One was the idea that directors might mistake your performance for your own persona, and in a way you may not like. And though your job is to deliver, to be that person as best you can, underneath is a quiet little plea that says, "Please don't think this is who I am." Also, I loved working with Michelle, who, like Julie Harris, tempted you to confuse acting with reality. Poor Michelle, having to deal with everyone falling in love with her. I would imagine that for some of the actresses I have worked with, like Diane Lane, Julia Roberts, Michelle, and, yes, Kim, it must be exhausting.

Next, I played a small role in *Working Girl* for Mike Nichols, which was a treat. I also got to work with the legendary cinematographer Michael Ballhaus, who had shot the remarkable *Death of a Salesman* with Dustin Hoffman and Malkovich and directed by Volker Schlöndorff. Nichols, witty and imperious one moment, warm and paternal the next, educated me about the invaluable contributions of his set and costume designers, among others. In this case: Patrizia von Brandenstein and Ann Roth, respectively. Years later, Ann and I worked together on *Streetcar* on Broadway. On set, Nichols knows where he is going, leaving you to come to work every day and say, "Yes, sir." There are few of these men left, almost none, actually. I have missed the chance to work with Coppola, De Palma, Jarmusch, and Lumet. But I was fortunate enough to shoot, however briefly, with Nichols, Frankenheimer, Scorsese, Cameron Crowe, and Woody Allen.

Oliver Stone, by contrast, introduced me to the director as hostage taker, a man who knew that either you needed to work, or you didn't want to get sued for leaving the set, or both. I shot the film *Talk Radio*, Eric Bogosian's hit stage play adapted for the screen, with Stone. We shot down in Dallas, and after only a couple of days, I wanted to go home. Working with him felt like being trapped with the Barton MacLane character from *Treasure of the Sierra Madre*. Stone's "technique" was to generate as much tension on the set as he believed the film required. With sarcastic asides and a passive-aggressive tone throughout, Stone drove the cast and crew to drink a lot each night to blow off steam, which was not an option for me. Stone is a brilliant screenwriter and has directed some very good films. And he is certainly not the most unpleasant person I've worked with. But Stone opened my eyes to the Machiavellian filmmaker who would throw his own mother down a flight of stairs if it would help him get his project financed, get the shot he wanted, or simply get his way.

I showed up in Memphis to shoot *Great Balls of Fire!*, which starred Dennis Quaid. The director, Jim

McBride, should have just cut all of my scenes and sent me home. The film is fantastic and alive when Dennis is on-screen and completely forgettable when he is off. I met Jerry Lee Lewis on set one day. As I greeted him he roared, "What kind of a handshake is that? That's a sissy handshake," and shoved my hand away. He tormented the producers about payments to secure his services to work with Dennis at scheduled rehearsals. "Jerry's sick," his handler told a producer. "What's it gonna take to make him feel better?" the producer asked. Ten thousand in cash was the reply. What choice did the producer have but to pay? Lewis was incredibly gifted. And he was an asshole.

Miami Blues reunited me with Jonathan Demme, but this time as a producer, as his friend George Armitage, a talented writer, was directing. Tak Fujimoto, the director of photography on the film, was another of the greats I had the good luck to shoot with, but the true prize here was the chance to film with probably the best actress I've ever worked with: Jennifer Jason Leigh. Jennifer is brave and honest and eschews vanity in her performances like no woman I've ever seen. On that set, she reminded me, oddly enough, of the actor Paul Muni in terms of her unguarded intensity and her brave choices.

Boarding a plane from New York to LA, sometime in early 1989, I paused before I sat to take note of the fact that, in the two dozen seats making up the first class and business cabins alone, at least eight or ten men were reading a novel written by Tom Clancy. *The Hunt for Red October* had been published in 1984, followed by *Red Storm Rising*, *Patriot Games*, and *The Cardinal of the Kremlin*. People were turning the pages of Tom's books by the millions, all over the world. Paramount Pictures was just getting around to making a movie of *The Hunt for Red October*, and I was on my way to meet the director, John McTiernan, to audition for the part of Jack Ryan, the protagonist of all those books. The meaning of that incredible opportunity really hit me on that airplane.

My agent, Michael Bloom, had made it clear that Kevin Costner was the first choice for the role, but that Paramount didn't want to pay his fee. They may have gone to twelve other guys in the meantime, but in the end, it was I who wound up in a makeup chair with McTiernan, the producer Mace Neufeld, and some makeup people as they scrutinized the color of my hair. The hair conversation lasted longer than any I would have on that set about either the script or the character. Rehearsing scenes on the set before we had begun shooting, McTiernan would look at me and say, "It's too much about props and staging with you. Can't you just stand there?"

McTiernan is from the "shooter" class of moviemakers. He has little, if anything, to offer actors. But in terms of the kind of films he makes, John has the essential skills of the black belt camera geek. His movies are costly, so he is hired by studios to steer a massive tanker into a harbor successfully, spending many millions of dollars in the process. Like nearly all directors, he hires actors who come ready. He points the camera and you do the preapproved thing you've been hired to do.

The joys of making the film, beyond its potential for box office success, were many. The movie checked several boxes on my "I want to work with that guy" list. Jan de Bont was the cinematographer, before he went off to direct his own films such as *Speed* and *Twister*. While shooting the submarine interior sequences, de Bont had to find a way to shoot in a contained space and still keep it interesting. I think those scenes look fabulous.

One day, the great Peter Firth showed up to play a small but pivotal role: the Russian officer on board the *Red October* who has his neck broken by the defecting Captain Ramius. Firth, now older and no longer the lovable enfant terrible who seduced audiences in his seminal stage roles in *Equus* and *Amadeus*, effortlessly slalomed through a long monologue in perfect Russian, proving why he is one of the best actors of the last many years. Tim Curry, Courtney B. Vance, Scott Glenn, and Sam Neill were also in the cast. The ever-gracious James Earl Jones was the dramatic equivalent of Joe Maher, patient, kind, and helpful. When I met Sean Connery, however, it all got a bit surreal for the boy from Massapequa.

Mace Neufeld threw a party at his home a few days before we began shooting. Nonetheless, Connery, the legendary movie star visiting the world's movie capital, wasn't allowed a drink or a bite of food. His wife, Micheline, was his trainer. As a tray of champagne glasses hovered in his direction, Connery reached for one, only to have his hand lightly slapped by Micheline. "No, no, no, Sean," she chided. "You cannot 'ave zee champan-ya!" Hors d'oeuvres followed. Again, Connery attempted. Again, Micheline blocked him with a slap and "No, no, no, Sean. You cannot 'ave zee paste-ah-reez!" Looking like a high school wrestler struggling to make weight, Connery looked at me and frowned. "It's not going to be much of a party," he murmured.

I came to watch Connery shoot on his first day, even though I wasn't on the schedule. He almost didn't make the film, because an illness had forced him to withdraw from the project. The producers had hired Klaus Maria Brandauer to play Sean's role. But before Brandauer showed up, word came down that Sean was recovered and ready to work. McTiernan told me that Paramount figured out a way to make Brandauer "go away." When Connery walked on the set to begin shooting, appearing trim and fit, he stunned me. From his steel-gray hairpiece to the cuffs of his shirts, from the trim of his beard to the fit of his wardrobe, Connery was a movie god. "A great day, comrades. We sail into history!" he said. No matter that the revered Soviet tactician had a Scottish accent. My first lead role in a big movie was with Double-O Seven. It didn't get any better than this.

Tom Clancy showed up on set one day, and McTiernan, Neufeld, and a rather tense producer named Larry De Waay escorted him around. Tom knew that no one on that set would be there if it were not for his books. He told me that while he was running an insurance company in Maryland, his approach to writing his first novel was to research as much as possible in the public domain. He'd then add material based on interviews with military types who agreed to speak to him, at times even offering classified information, as long as it wasn't attributed to them. "I filled in the rest with my imagination," he told me. He was clearly on to something with this formula: the book sold three million copies.

Unfortunately, the producers seemed to barely tolerate Tom. This isn't surprising, however, as Hollywood executives always insist on putting in their creative two cents. And Clancy didn't hesitate, between cigarettes, to mutter little comments under his breath. He was on the record with me with his opinion of the script. I'm certain that he realized how much was at stake for him at Paramount. If things went well, he would be in Stephen King territory. If not, he would simply be a very rich novelist instead of a ridiculously rich one with both feet firmly planted in cinematic history.

We started shooting on my thirty-first birthday. I had rented a house close to the lot in Beachwood Canyon, and my brother Billy was living with me while he shot the movie *Internal Affairs*, also at Paramount. We drove out to Malibu every weekend with a group of friends, and fell in love with the northern head of the peninsula near County Line. We would lie out at Zuma Beach and do as little as possible. The beach in Venice was too crowded with vendors, revelers, and palm readers, but Malibu reminded me of the beaches back home. One Sunday afternoon, driving the long route back to Beachwood, a friend and I stopped to watch *Batman*, whose ubiquitous billboards actually suggested an interesting movie. At a late-afternoon screening, my friend and I were perhaps the only two adults not accompanying a child. Having worked with Tim Burton on *Beetlejuice*, I was even more curious. On-screen, I saw Kim Basinger, whom I had seen in films like *The Natural* and *Fool for Love*. The kids in the theater perked up over the Batsuit and the Batmobile. When Kim came on-screen, they frowned and wanted to get back to the action. I, on the other hand, turned to my friend and said, "She's a very beautiful woman."

Back on the set, I dined one afternoon in the commissary with two Paramount executives, Don Granger and Gary Lucchesi, while we discussed their idea of casting me in John Milius's film *Flight of the Intruder*. I didn't know what I wanted to do next, but an effects-heavy military-hardware picture wasn't it. Lucchesi turned to Granger and said, "I know what he wants. He wants the good stuff." I stared at them for a moment and said dryly, "Yes, I suppose." Once we wrapped *Hunt*, as we referred to it, I went home to New York. Soon after, an offer to audition for *The Godfather, Part III* came. As I read the screenplay while sitting in Central Park, I would literally hum the theme from the original *Godfather* as I turned the pages. The role eventually went to Andy Garcia, but on that one afternoon in New York, what a fantasy I had!

I wanted to stay home in New York for a while. I felt confident that movie work was mine to be had. I wasn't looking for a play to read, but my agent sent me one called *Prelude to a Kiss*. On a quiet autumn day, I read it straight through. With its mythical premise, odd characters, and beautiful writing, the script put a spell on me. If you know the show, you know there's no pun intended.

Prelude taught me something profound about the true nature of love. Like Craig Lucas's other work, it shows us unusual people thrust into extraordinary circumstances. The story of Rita and her soul-swapping journey with an elderly man was a big hit when we played at Circle Rep. The theater was small, so the show sold out easily every night, particularly after Frank Rich's rave review ran in the *Times*. Norman René directed, as he had Craig's other plays, and the cast of *Prelude* was phenomenal; Larry Bryggman, John Dossett, the incomparable Debra Monk, and Barnard Hughes all shone. Barney, though, came to us seriously injured, fresh from falling off the stage during a performance. He fell again, this time down the stairs at the 96th Street subway stop, just two weeks into our rehearsals. In the dressing room we all shared, our names were taped along a wall to mark our space. I wrote "Keith Richards" in Barney's spot.

The star of *Prelude* was Mary-Louise Parker, who was like no other woman I'd worked with before.

Mary-Louise, already on her way to becoming one of the princesses of the New York theater, was the darling of not only Norman and Craig but also, apparently, all who came in contact with her. She was quirky and, like Joe Maher, also bent a line here and a pause there to reshape her performance again and again. She was unpredictable. With her big eyes and lanky frame, you weren't sure if she was a ballet dancer or a murderer. However, my prevailing memory of the show is of walking out onstage every night and, without fail, actually falling in love with her over and over again. The play, both in its writing and direction, made those feelings inevitable. The music made an enormous contribution as well. I can never hear Toni Childs's song "Walk and Talk Like Angels" without starting to cry.

The show was successful enough that Fox Studios, which was headed at the time by Joe Roth and Roger Birnbaum, bought the film rights. But before that, the show went to Broadway and the producers approached me about doing the role again. After ten years in the business, work seemed abundant and economic security wasn't an issue. Yet I chose not to go to Broadway, seduced by the prospect of my first million-dollar payday to act in Neil Simon's *The Marrying Man*. It was a devastating mistake, and without a shred of doubt, the single decision I made that changed my career and my life forever. I had followed my instincts from the beginning and they had served me well. Now, I walked away from a play that was considered for the Pulitzer Prize to go shoot a very forgettable film for the money. I allowed myself to be sold on the idea of ignoring my own beliefs to spin the wheel in the game of movie stardom.

Once you abandon your instincts and begin polling people about your choices, once you attempt to reshape yourself into someone you are not, it affects nearly every decision you make. You begin to see your entire life through a distorted prism. After I chose *The Marrying Man,* I completely lost my sense of who I was, and so many things went wrong. Within eighteen months, my self-loathing about this decision played a big part in my one grand attempt to set things right again.

8

Back to One

Moviemaking is a profoundly collaborative process. The goal, therefore, is to work on a movie set with a great group of people, top people who are recognized as among the best in the business. Props, sets, accounting, publicity, locations, wardrobe, music, production design, stunts, writing, camera, continuity, direction, acting—they all blend together to make a form of magic. Watch *The Godfather*, a movie in which all of those things come together magnificently. Nearly every frame is a work of art.

The actors and actresses who are invited to join those productions are talented, but luck plays a big part, too. There are men and women throughout movie history whose performances are but one component of a vast undertaking. The force of their personality doesn't drive the film. Their acting choices are simple and clear. They're not Gary Oldman playing Lee Harvey Oswald in Oliver Stone's *JFK* or Daniel Day-Lewis as Lincoln or Anthony Hopkins in *The Silence of the Lambs*. Movie stars are, more often than not, simple men and women who project strength and integrity on film. You can call it heroism or character. The list of actors who are invited to front big studio films is short. And once you get on it, you will do almost anything to stay there.

In the spring of 1990, I headed to LA to shoot *The Marrying Man*. Neil Simon is, of course, a legend. His plays and films have sold more tickets than you can count. When you begin to study acting, Simon's writing is a station of the cross, right up there with that of Shaw, Williams, Miller, Mamet, and Shepard. In 1990, Neil was only sixty-three, five years older than I am as I write this, but he seemed older. During *The Marrying Man*, Simon looked tired at the table reading of the script he attended, while collecting the expected laughs, tributes, and signs of approval. When the reading ended, the leading lady on the picture, Kim Basinger, asked Simon a couple of questions that hinted at how sexist and dated she felt some of Neil's writing was. She was right. *The Marrying Man*, set in the 1950s, was based on a real-life story about Harry

Karl, who was later Debbie Reynolds's husband. Karl married a lounge singer he met in Vegas. There was a lot that was funny in the script, but some of it felt stale. The director, Jerry Rees, was a sweet young guy out of Disney animation who didn't have the nerve to opine about the script.

Kim, on the other hand, had plenty of nerve. We had just met, and I was already struck by how candid she was. Visibly flustered by Kim's questions, Simon gave her a tense smile. Later on, one of the producers, surprised by Kim's boldness, told me to keep in mind "what Simon was used to." He went on, "Always try to remember what people are used to in this business. Simon is used to everyone laughing, then he gets a big check." As we filed out of the table reading, Neil approached me and thanked me for doing the film. He was, in every respect, the perfect pro. I asked if the "notes" he had received troubled him. He smiled and said, "We've got lightning in a bottle with her. It'll all be fine." He had probably faced far worse in Hollywood and on Broadway. Putting a picture together is a lot of work. You don't take it apart without a good reason. Eventually, Neil incorporated a few of Kim's comments.

Shooting *The Marrying Man* was difficult. At times, it was awful. There were some good scenes, the cast was great, and I thought the story of Harry Karl made for a good movie. But the production was overshadowed by the ongoing battle between Kim and Disney, as Kim attempted to exert yet more control over the movie than Disney was prepared to allow. One day, Jeffrey Katzenberg, who was in charge of the studio at the time, asked me to come to his office. Once I was there, he wasted no time informing me that it was their studio, their money, and their movie. Actors were employees and expected to do their jobs and create as little trouble as possible. "I can get the guard at the gate to play your role. It makes no difference to me. The film itself is the star," he exhorted.

At the time, I was offended. Years later, I found his honesty refreshing. Less than a year after *The Marrying Man* (and *Dick Tracy*, as well), Katzenberg published his infamous memo shellacking pretty much the entire industry for their profligate spending and overall bad decision-making. That memo meant, among other things, that a lot of people in the town were overpaid and some of them unrealistically so. The reaction to that was, at best, somewhat mixed. Within a few years, however, Katzenberg's memo was viewed as prescient. Eventually, Katzenberg offered me work voicing animated characters in films like *Madagascar: Escape 2*

Africa and *Boss Baby*, and I've enjoyed working with him again.

During *The Marrying Man*, however, an article appeared in the movie magazine *Premiere*. The story, which painted Kim as an out-of-control brat, was largely fiction. It read as if Disney's PR people had faxed it to Susan Lyne, the chilly editor of the magazine. I knew that the article's oft-quoted anecdote about Kim insisting on only Evian water for washing her hair was false, but that lie would follow her for years. By this time, we were dating. Naturally, I tried to take up for Kim. My publicist at the time told me, "Who do you think *Premiere* is beholden to, a couple of actors who make a movie or two a year? Or to a major studio that releases twenty or twenty-five pictures every year?" The piece made us look like two spoiled, ridiculous children. I can only begin to imagine what was being said off the record to the media. An important die was cast during that film, as I began to think that defending Kim from any and all trouble was becoming my job.

When the film ended and I was scheduled to pack up my rented house and go home to New York, Kim invited me to move in with her. As the *Premiere* magazine piece broke, Mace Neufeld, the producer of *Red October*, called me. Every inch the old guard Hollywood type, he offered little small talk before he got down to cases. "Get rid of her," he said. I was standing in the living room of Kim's house. Instinctively, I lowered my voice, for fear that she would hear me. I replied with something stupid like, "What do you mean, get rid of her?" Neufeld shared his views on my choice of girlfriends. "There are a lot of women out there for you," Mace said. "When the timing is right, then of course you'll want that. But this is a very important period of your life. You've got to get rid of her because she's just gonna pull you down." But like it would for any man who believed he was in love, that suggestion went in one ear and out the other. I thanked Mace and hung up.

Years later, I realized that Mace had been telling me the cardinal rule of Hollywood stardom: that you must make it the most important part of your life, above all else. Take the example of Tom Cruise. I don't know exactly what Scientology offers, but I have speculated from time to time about what its followers derive from their commitment. In Cruise's case, I've asked myself, "What could Tom possibly want or need that he doesn't already have?" He is talented, handsome, and rich. He is admired by everyone he works with. He is a cornerstone of latter-twentieth-century movie history. And to top it off, he seems genuinely happy. Does Scientology function as some kind of coach that not only gives permission to its flock to unabashedly pursue their dreams, but demands that you go for it, without apology, keeping your focus on yourself and your goals?

I didn't quite see my career that way. My obligations to my family and to a woman I had invested so much in prevented me from placing my work above everything. Also, Kim presented herself as a pure, uncompromising iconoclast. There were many things she might have done to advance her own career. Instead, she dismissed the many sexed-up roles, and a lot of money, that were thrust at her while she hoped for something better. She lived in a modest house in a modest neighborhood, abjuring a self-conscious lifestyle. As attractive as those qualities seemed, however, there were other things about her that I wish I had given more weight to when we first started dating, such as her reflexive reliance upon "advisers" who often wrongly urged her either toward or away from conflict in her life and work. (This would become abundantly clear down the line when divorce lawyers were involved, but at the time it rang only faint alarm bells.) However, as I was developing my own sense of cynicism about the industry, Kim's lack of pretentiousness was like oxygen. She didn't always go about her business in the smartest way, but Kim knew that Hollywood was full of shit and that, unless you were going to go all in, the less seriously you took it, the happier you'd be.

In 1991, my mother developed breast cancer, a diagnosis that would eventually bring her as much joy and triumph as an advocate for victims of the disease as it initially brought her illness and fear. A lifelong believer in Western medicine, my mother never met a pill she didn't like in her quest to combat her many aches and pains. She was falling apart and she was frightened and overwhelmed. Although my relationship with my mom had never been that deep, I had begun to take more of an interest in her health and well-being. On Saturday nights (I worked most Friday nights), as I was heading out for the evening in whatever city I was in, I felt a pang of sadness for her and would call and chat with her, knowing that her house was empty and that she was alone. A lifelong *Jeopardy!* watcher who wanted me to invite Alex Trebek over for dinner, she could always be found in bed in the evening, the TV blaring away. She'd watch *Magnum, P.I.* or *Law & Order.* Later, when *NCIS* was added to the rotation, she would ask why I wasn't on that show. "I just love that Mark Harmon!" she would sigh. I imagined Alex Trebek, Mariska Hargitay, and Mark Harmon all at my mom's dinner table. She'd be in heaven.

In the summer of 1991, just returned from shooting the film version of *Prelude*, I came to Bob Rehme's office on the Paramount lot to meet with him, Mace, and the director Phillip Noyce. *Red October* had been a success, so it was time to discuss the next installment of the Jack Ryan series. Rehme, an arid, patrician Southern Californian by way of Cincinnati, was Mace Neufeld's partner and a man I'd had little to do with during the making of *Hunt*. I had sensed that something less than wonderful was brewing earlier when I learned that McTiernan would not be returning to direct the sequel. Mace had offered some explanation, but people at movie studios lie or obfuscate at least five times before breakfast, so I ignored him. McTiernan himself suggested to me something about his schedule or something in his deal. But now, in the room with the current "team," Rehme glared at me like I was a communist at a HUAC hearing he was conducting.

As I talked, measuredly, about what I thought of the current script, I felt as if no one in the room was really listening. When I suggested adding a scene in a pub where I thought we could see Ryan's face on the front page of every newspaper on the heels of his heroic stunt, prompting a small, nondescript gaggle of British pubgoers to sing "God Save the Queen" in his honor and top off their tribute by handing him a pint, they all just stared at me. Unbeknownst to me, their nonresponsive looks, I would soon find out, were the first signal of my exit from the film series. They had trouble concealing the fact that they really didn't want any notes from an actor who wasn't going to be playing the part. But nothing was mentioned in that meeting. It was just odd and frosty.

After the meeting, I flew through Chicago to Syracuse, which took all day. My mother and sister Beth had moved there a couple of years earlier. The next morning, I accompanied my mother to her consultation, during which she was told she needed to have a double mastectomy. I developed a deeper level of concern for her right there in that room. While I stood in a conference room at the hospital making calls, my office patched me through to Mace. The call brought to mind the classic film *Sorry, Wrong Number*, when an apoplectic Burt Lancaster must convince his invalid wife to go to the window and cry out for help or she's going to be murdered. (Great movie, by the way.) My call with Mace wasn't quite that high-stakes. Nonetheless, he asked where my deal was at and why it wasn't closed. I told him that I was trying to schedule both the film and a chance to star in *A Streetcar Named Desire* on Broadway the following spring. "You've got to close this deal and get this done," Neufeld said, his voice a tad strained. "The play, the dates, it will all take care of itself. But sign that deal."

I spent the next day or two with my mother while she recovered, then flew to Long Island for the weekend. When I got to my friend's house in the evening, it was still early in LA, and I called the office of David Kirkpatrick, the very successful and very self-absorbed executive in charge of the sequel. On that call, Kirkpatrick told me he wanted me to sign a deal with neither a start date nor a stop date. The movie would start when it was ready and end whenever it ended. That meant the film had no schedule, which was untenable and absurd. I asked when that information would become available and he didn't have an answer, suggesting that it wasn't my concern. The premise that he had no real idea when the film would begin was ludicrous, since all studios have schedules linked to release dates. I had gone from costarring in the first film, which had done well at the box office, to the place where all of my suggestions, inquiries, and requests were now intrusions. Kirkpatrick said I had until Monday to make up my mind.

The final piece of the puzzle came in a call from none other than the normally phlegmatic John McTiernan, who asked how my deal was progressing. After

I filled him in, he took a long pause, sighed, and told me that Paramount was illegally negotiating with another actor, a big star, to take my place. He told me he was scheduled to shoot a film with this big star. The producer of that film called him to say that the big star was out because he was moving on to another project and "You're not gonna believe which one." McTiernan told me that Harrison Ford was going to replace me in the sequel.

John told me he spoke with Ford and asked if he was aware that Paramount was in an active negotiation with me. Ford's reply, according to John, was "Fuck him." Ford wasn't merely employing a different strategy from me in the same game. He was playing a different game entirely. In need of the next franchise to keep the flame of his stardom burning bright while earning him tens of millions more, what choice did he have? The carpenter who walked onto a set and then into movie history knew that these roles were his legacy.

Ford is one of the most successful stars in movie history. He has abundant fame, wealth, and the adulation of an adoring public and everyone in the town. One thing he does not have is an Oscar, which must frustrate, if not burden him, after his long career. Ford's lack of any serious accolades for his acting is somewhat odd. In a review in the *LA Weekly* of his performance in the Scott Turow drama *Presumed Innocent*, the critic wrote "watch Ford's acting go from beige to taupe." He certainly has had every advantage. He has worked with the best directors. One would assume that his projects have budgets for the best writers, designers, craftspeople, shooting schedules, and casting. They have lots of money for marketing and ad campaigns during awards season. Every single asset that Hollywood can bring to bear is rolled out on behalf of his films. And yet Ford is, Oscar-wise, empty-handed.

Years later, when I met him in LA at a benefit reading of a play that his girlfriend was in, he smiled politely and muttered some greeting. I realized then that the movies really do enhance certain actors, making them seem like something they really aren't at all. Ford, in person, is a little man, short, scrawny, and wiry, whose soft voice sounds as if it's coming from behind a door.

Earlier that year, while shooting *Prelude* in Jamaica, I had met with Phillip Noyce, who seemed to want to have a constructive conversation about the next Jack Ryan film. But Noyce is a studio director to the marrow. Given his marginal talent and the attendant insecurities, he wouldn't dare tip me off as to what was going on, assuming that by then he knew the details. In fact, he probably wet himself at the thought of the eventual outcome.

I considered whether I wanted to have the kind of career where you are, by and large, asked to do the same thing, over and over, like Ford or Bruce Willis or, eventually, Russell Crowe. Certainly there are ever-larger paychecks, but never any surprises. I suppose I could have said yes to Paramount's unconscionable demands and held on to the role. But if that choice meant more time with David Kirkpatrick, Bob Rehme, Phillip Noyce, Don Granger, and all the other "gentlemen" I had washed up alongside in LA over the past five years, I wasn't so sure. Then I thought of the decision-making that had led me to scuttle the Broadway production of *Prelude* in order to do *The Marrying Man*, and things became clearer in my life than they had been for some time. I told them I wanted to do both *Streetcar* and the film. They said, essentially, "Fuck you and good riddance."

The fact that Paramount was negotiating with two people at the same time was infuriating enough. I often wonder why people in those circumstances don't simply call you into their office and tell you they don't want to work with you anymore. I'm sure some settlement could have been reached. But as studios, networks, and talent agencies increasingly hire self-serving, rapacious types such as Kirkpatrick, it's less likely. I could just see the Paramount group high-fiving each other for having engaged Ford while not having to pay me a dime. The most unpleasant part, though, was that Barry London, another cookie-cutter exec at the studio, took it upon himself to announce my departure to the press and blame it all on me. I had "overplayed my hand at the negotiating table" was how one report put it. I learned that when you're not Harrison Ford, simply asking for the schedule may be "overplaying your hand."

Eventually, *Patriot Games* was made with Ford in the role of Jack Ryan, and it made less money than *Hunt* when adjusted for inflation.

On a movie set, the cry is "Back to one!" to alert the cast and extras to reset to their original positions before the camera is rolled for the next take. Whenever I arrived at a place where the film business felt uncomfortable or downright unsafe for me, the place I often returned to was the theater. Onstage, we trust that the material works, we assume all of the actors are genuinely talented, and the work itself is the focus, unencumbered by the bullshit that often interferes with moviemaking. Back to one, indeed. It was time to go home. It was time to do a play. As far as I was concerned, it is *the* play.

9

What She Was Used To

Standing on a footbridge in Chicago on an April evening in 1991, the freezing temperature at a degree only Chicagoans could comprehend, I spoke with Michael Gruskoff, the producer of the film version of *Prelude to a Kiss*. "When is this thing scheduled to come out?" I asked. "Hopefully, by December," he replied. "Good," I said. "Because we're going to win everything. Best picture, actor, actress, direction, screenplay." The more seasoned Gruskoff managed a slight smile and said, "That would be nice."

Adapting *Prelude* to the screen had proved to be difficult. Finding a cast that satisfied Norman and Craig as well as the Fox executives who had bought the rights was the first challenge. During that process, however, my next opportunity to meet a truly great actor materialized when Norman called me to say that Sir Alec Guinness was interested in the film and, pending the meeting, inclined to do it. I thought I might faint. Before long, I found myself seated across from Guinness at the old Wyndham Hotel in New York.

As had happened when I had met or worked with Pacino, De Niro, Tony Hopkins, Julie Andrews, George C. Scott, Meryl, Ava Gardner, McCartney, Gregory Peck, Tony Bennett, Brando, and the other artists whom I had admired, even worshipped, the sight and sound of Alec Guinness unleashed a torrent of his most famous cinematic accomplishments in my mind. Legendary movie moments began unspooling: The young Guinness in *Great Expectations*, admonishing John Mills not to "fill one's mouth to its utmost capacity." As Fagin in *Oliver Twist* ("What right have you to butcher me?"). His Academy Award–winning performance in *The Bridge on the River Kwai. The Horse's Mouth, Our Man in Havana, Lawrence of Arabia, Doctor Zhivago, Star Wars,* and too many others to name. Alec Guinness, a totem in film acting, was now right before my eyes, making one simple request. "I'm afraid I must shoot the film in New York," he stated quietly. "I must be able to Concorde back and forth to London to see my wife." Norman had told me that Guinness's wife was ill and that he needed to visit her periodically while shooting.

Quite quickly, however, my dream of costarring with Guinness disappeared as the Fox execs rode roughshod over Norman and Craig's casting desires. Ultimately, to shoot the film in New York was too expensive, so Guinness had to withdraw. Naturally, Norman had wanted Mary-Louise to claim the role that was rightly hers, but Joe Roth, the head of Fox, and Roger Birnbaum, his second, protested. They insisted that Mary-Louise and I would need to be bolstered by a big name in the role of the old man, and strongly suggested Jack Lemmon or Art Carney. Norman told me he would rather not make the film if it meant hiring someone he did not see in the role. And then, in what reminded me of the Julie Andrews/*My Fair Lady* casting tale, Mary-Louise was gone and Meg Ryan was playing the lead. As a concession to Norman and Craig, the remarkable theater veteran Sydney Walker was cast as the old man.

Roth, a successful executive who'd also directed with little or no success, had overseen countless films from his office, but seemed to have learned next to nothing about how to create one. He and Birnbaum had me in to see them on a couple of occasions, hoping to enlist me in their cause of placating Norman about specific

creative decisions they had made. In one meeting, after
the film was finished and had been screened for test
audiences, Birnbaum announced, "We have to cut the
kiss." Roth sat by, nodding pensively. By that, Birnbaum meant the eponymous kiss, the kiss between the
old man (now embodying my wife) and me, THE kiss,
which is the incontrovertible emotional climax of the
film. "What?" I asked. "We have to cut it," Birnbaum
said. "At the screening, there was audible groaning."
Roth repeated, "Audible groaning." This would be
Prelude to a Hug. Their idea was like suggesting that
The Longest Yard be moved to a basketball court to
reduce the number of cast members, but still titled *The
Longest Yard*. Birnbaum, whose round, boyish face,
expressive eyes, and silly intonation reminded me of a
borscht belt comic out of *Broadway Danny Rose*, just
stared at me. "It's gotta go."

Norman and Craig told me they would sue. The
idiocy of the Fox note was plain, so the kiss stayed.
But the whole thing began to slowly swirl downward.
Meg is a wonderful actress and was at the peak of her
career then, but she was not Mary-Louise. We finished
the film, and when it came out, Fox put minimal effort
into supporting it. Some of the blame has to go to all of
us for the final product because, during the shooting,
we all began to wonder what it might have been like if

Mary-Louise had been there. That winter, I was invited to Craig's Christmas party. In a throng of people, music blaring, Mary-Louise appeared. She saw me, burst into tears, and bolted away. I realized that there really are rare occasions when there is one person who is meant to play a role. That was true of Mary-Louise. The movie tanked.

Normally I try to avoid working in the summer. Being from Long Island means that an extended celebration of the beach, boats, and sunsets feels like a birthright. However, when my agent, Michael Bloom, was contacted on the heels of *Prelude* about the film version of David Mamet's Pulitzer Prize–winning play *Glengarry Glen Ross*, I broke my usual routine. Like *Prelude*, this would be another adaptation of stage material, but the two films were night and day. Pacino was set as the lead, Ricky Roma. But Bloom had an instinct about the project due to Pacino's reputation for being in and out of certain projects, including *Glengarry*. So Bloom made a suggestion to the producers: if Pacino faltered again, let me play Roma. They agreed. Pacino flip-flopped again, Bloom called them on it, and count to three, I was set to play Roma. But Pacino is the person they wanted in that role, so when he reconsidered, the producers asked Bloom "if I would mind stepping aside." It was just a few months after the

Red October situation. I was now dealing with a group of people who politely asked if I could accommodate them, unlike the assholes at Paramount who violated agreements and stabbed people in the back as a matter of course, so I chose to accommodate them.

Al played Ricky, and I took the role of Blake, a part not in Mamet's original play. Mamet's work, in my mind, is often about predation among human beings. I was told that Blake is there to incite the other men, men who are not criminal by nature, to commit a crime. Blake is the screw that turns and pressures them to do something desperate. Blake, with his turgid language and metronomic delivery, is sent to hammer home the message: if you don't make money, and make it right now, you're out.

The rest of the cast was like an acting school, an assembly of men so varied in style, I knew that whatever happened here, it was going to be special. The cast included Kevin Spacey, Ed Harris, Alan Arkin, and Jonathan Pryce. While I came to rehearsal with a fondness and high regard for everyone, I outright worshipped Jack Lemmon. The great actor and film star was a role model to me, especially for the signature key he often played in, a combination of weakness and valor, doubt and resolve, anxiety and clarity. Few actors have appeared as vividly human as Lemmon did on-screen. He had starred in so many great films, including *Mister Roberts*; *Bell, Book and Candle*; *The Apartment*; *Days of Wine and Roses*; *The Odd Couple*; and *The China Syndrome*. Lemmon, despite the corrosive tone of Mamet's material, was an unerring gentleman of the old school throughout. Here, perhaps, was the great opportunity I had missed with Alec Guinness. Lemmon is breathtaking in the role of Shelley "The Machine" Levene and the fact that he wasn't even nominated for an Oscar is a crime. He should have won it.

The director, James Foley, is a smart guy. He had a great script. He brought in the talented Juan Ruiz Anchia as cinematographer. With a cast like that, a good director chimes in specifically and as needed. Foley stood back and let everyone do their thing. He did offer me a truly fabulous piece of direction. I was anxious about shooting a scene in which I so relentlessly harangue some of the greatest actors in the business. Foley said, in so many words, "It's like that scene in *Patton*, where George C. Scott slaps the soldier in the medical tent. He's doing it for the coward's own good and for the benefit of the other men. Patton asks, 'You call yourself a soldier?' Well, this is, 'You call yourself a salesman?' You're doing it for their own good."

That was all I needed, something to authorize me to lean into these guys without fear or doubt. People are always commenting to me about that scene in *Glen-garry*, commending me for those blistering moments, but I've still never really understood audiences' appetites for that kind of double-barreled acting. Mamet's pieces are tough. You have to give the horse the stick out of the chute and all the way to the finish line. It's mean and it's relentless, and if you're not exhausted by the end, you haven't done the job. But as I get older, I'd rather do a more thoughtful role, like Henry Drummond in *Inherit the Wind* or Willy Loman in *Death of a Salesman*. Or I even fantasized about doing a comedy, a television sitcom written by some truly funny and crazy people! That sounded like fun.

As the *Red October* fiasco came and went, the fall of 1991 found me sitting on a couch in Kim's house in LA believing that our relationship was coming to an end. In the past, I had a timer set, an unconscious alarm that went off at a certain point and told me to move on. My outer limit was around eighteen months. I'd met Kim in April of 1990. Now it was November of the next year, and the pressures of *The Marrying Man*, Kim's failed real estate development deal in Braselton, Georgia (a very good opportunity that was just poorly executed), and her overall anxiety as a private person living a public life were mounting. My commitment to doing *Streetcar* had enabled Kirkpatrick to torpedo my

Paramount deal, although I'm sure they would have figured out how to get rid of me even without it. Now it was time to go do that play. Kim said she felt Broadway was where actors go who can't make it in the movies. I bit my tongue instead of saying that the opposite was more often the case. For some, the movies are where you go when you don't have the talent for the stage.

My entertainment lawyer at that time was the colorful, reedy Jake Bloom (no relation to Michael), a guy who reminded me of a thinner Jerry Garcia. Bloom was one of the most connected and adroit players in Hollywood. So when he called to tell me that, in the wake of the Paramount implosion, he wanted me to meet another agent, I sensed how much trouble I was in. One Bloom in my life was poised to push the other Bloom over the side of the ship. Michael had been the only agent I'd ever had.

I was in a rut, and as Jake Bloom suggested, I needed a tow truck to pull me out. Ron Meyer, one of the founders of Creative Artists Agency (CAA), arranged for me to come to his Malibu home to talk about leaving Michael Bloom and coming to CAA. Meyer, an ex-marine, is a compact, bespectacled man with the look of a wrestling coach who favors cardigan sweaters. His lack of pretension is legendary. But in Hollywood, a town overwhelmed by its obsession with personal power, Ron Meyer is the OG. Together with Mike Ovitz, he transformed the business. The formation of CAA heralded a period of unusual power for agents who packaged their writer, director, and actor clients into deals that created a sellers' market that spelled huge fees for them.

I asked Meyer which agent would do my day-to-day, meaning the person with whom I would communicate about offers, etc. He said he would be that person. I laughed out loud. How would someone like Meyer, who headed a company that handled the biggest stars in Hollywood, find the time, let alone the interest, to cover my career? Meyer promised to handle everything personally, and he wasn't kidding. Over the course of the next few years, right up until he sold the agency and went on to his lengthy run at NBC Universal, Meyer took my calls like I was his brother. People joke that Ron would take calls as he was being put under for surgery. But the truth is, he was generous and forthright with me in a way I was unprepared for. "We'll just keep throwing it against the wall till something sticks," he would say. Eventually, the offers for starring roles in big films would become fewer and further between, but Ron gave it everything he had. I remain indebted to and fond of him to this very day.

The painful task of parting with Michael Bloom occurred in a small café near the Miracle Mile in LA. Bloom had been in this boat before, having watched several of his stars-in-training move on to other, usually more powerful agents and agencies. Also, by 1988, his business was on the ropes. That year, the Writers Guild of America had taken its members on strike from March 7 to August 7. At 155 days, it was the longest strike in their history. The town shut down, and the ripple effects were staggering. Restaurants, dry cleaners, private schools, travel agents, florists, clothing stores, limo companies, you name it, everyone was affected. Some B-level agencies in Bloom's league folded. Others were smart enough to merge, and though their power was diluted, they survived. Bloom, with his outsized faith in himself, refused such merger offers. He couldn't imagine working for someone else. His name was on the door and it had to stay that way.

At a café that day, Bloom cried. I think I cried, I don't remember. (I am a pretty good crier.) He asked if Kim was in some way an influence here, as she was already with CAA. Kim had in fact voiced the opinion that I needed a change. (When Kim spoke about Bloom, I reminded myself of the changes that Mace Neufeld had recommended.) But the reality was that when I was in trouble and I needed answers, the heads of studios didn't even know Bloom's name, let alone return his calls. Underlings would get back to him, offering little in the way of hard information. When I was struggling with the Jack Ryan deal, Bloom called Stanley Jaffe at Paramount many times. Jaffe never called him back.

Ron Meyer could never be Bloom, and I would miss our trips to the West End of London and our long dinners in New York after a show, critiquing everyone and everything we'd seen. But I knew I had to climb out of this well I had been thrown into. I told Bloom we were done, and I headed to New York to start rehearsals for *Streetcar*. In the coming years, mutual friends told me that Bloom took my decision hardest of all his clients' defections.

As I prepared to begin *Streetcar*, a decision that forced me to rethink my career, I was questioning other things as well. Life with Kim was largely centered around the narcissistic passions of two childless actors. We worked most of the time, and when we weren't working we were thinking about work. But troubles on the set of *The Marrying Man*, along with Kim's age (she turned thirty-eight in December of that year), had seemed to let some of the air out of her tires. I, on the other hand, needed a break from the sweepstakes mentality of Hollywood, and I went to New York knowing that I needed a break from her and her self-absorption as well. Kim could be funny. She could be a mess. But, most of all, Kim was about Kim. I needed to heal and she wasn't built to comfort her significant other. Kim lived to be understood, not to understand. To heal, I needed a meaningful experience, a mountain to climb. So Tennessee Williams would help me by providing me with one of the greatest challenges of all.

I had seen a production of *Streetcar*, directed by Nikos Psacharopoulos, at Lincoln Center in 1988. It had starred Frances McDormand as Stella, the wonderful Frank Converse as Mitch, Aidan Quinn as Stanley, and Blythe Danner as one of the best Blanche DuBois I've ever seen. I've always admired Aidan and thought he was good in the part of Stanley, in a production I'd actually auditioned for myself, but he seemed to hold back, like he was asking permission for this or that. At one point in the play, Stanley slugs his wife, and in less than five minutes, she comes back to him and they go to bed. Unless the director makes cuts or you're doing some revisionist production, it's World War II New Orleans and you play these roles without comment or apology.

When I'd studied acting at the Lee Strasberg Institute on East 15th Street, I'd met Elaine Aiken, who became my friend and private coach. When I worked on scenes from *Streetcar* with her, she would say, "Honey, you're either sexy or you're not. No acting lessons can help you there. This guy is an animal. You can't be polite about it. You've got to be clear. It's more than 'You want something, you take it.' When this guy wants something, he'll destroy anyone who gets in his way."

Gregory Mosher, who, along with Bernard Gersten, had reshaped Lincoln Center Theater, was directing this production. The cast included Jessica Lange as Blanche, Tim Carhart as Mitch, and Amy Madigan as Stella, as well as Jimmy Gandolfini and Aida Turturro in supporting roles. At the first rehearsal, an actor read a line from the New Directions edition of the play, and Maria St. Just, the coexecutor of the Williams estate, snapped, "That's not the line!" Mosher arrived the following day, plopped down three other somewhat varied editions of *Streetcar*, and said, "What line do you want?" The Williams estate had yet to codify the playwright's papers, and the extant texts of his classic dramas contained certain inconsistencies. Many had blamed the disarray of Williams's official papers on Maria, who, through some unusual arrangement with the playwright toward the end of his life, wound up having approval of everything, including the casting of his shows. Mosher is smart and funny, and just the type of person I needed for this situation. He warned me that Lady St. Just (she was the widow of some guy with a title) would have notes about everything, and he was right. During rehearsals, Maria would ask if she could get a lift home in my car. On a couple of occasions, early on, I acquiesced. During the ride, she tore everyone in the cast to pieces and then sought my opinion on them, too. She was a shrill ferret of a woman with a British title and the power to at least try to tell us all what to do. Fortunately, Greg got her to fade into the background.

Jessica Lange had never performed on Broadway at that point, and making her debut playing Blanche DuBois in *Streetcar* was a very daring move. She was a celebrated film actress who had been nominated for an Oscar several times and would eventually win twice. It was assumed she was awash in theater culture and history, but her stage credits were slim when we started rehearsal. What many observed about the production was that if you were in the first ten rows, she was wonderful. If you were onstage with her, she shone in the role. To the majority of ticket holders, however, she failed to project in the way to which they were accustomed.

Greg Mosher was assumed, at one time, to be the heir to the Mike Nichols Chair in Film and Theater before a corporatized show business eliminated that position. Capable in ways that translated into great success directing early productions of Mamet's work in

Chicago, and later in his great run with Gersten at Lincoln Center, Mosher is the smartest guy in the room and doesn't have to work to remind you of that. He just shows you and usually in an elegant way. He was enormously helpful to me in the role, both in terms of the text and in the psychology of taking on a role overshadowed by so iconic an actor.

I had never once hesitated to take the part, never once doubted I could play Stanley. And, up to a point, I never thought about Marlon Brando and the threat posed by comparisons to him. Brando, however, was twenty-four when he appeared on Broadway. I was thirty-four in 1992. I always contended that Stanley's self-absorption, bullying, and passions were best served by a younger man. Therefore, in order to straddle the need to serve the script and my own hesitancy to lay into the brutality too hard, I tried to make it funny where I could. Other male actors my age would constantly say to me, "It must be great to get all of that anger out of your system every night." My response was, "I don't have that much anger in me." Indeed, some nights I wanted to ad-lib a scene with Blanche in which we sat down, had a beer, and talked out our differences, ending up as good friends.

On opening night, though, it hit me. Brando owned the role to the exclusion of all pretenders. Now, I was the latest pretender, sitting in my dressing room, suffocating under the weight of a Broadway opening. What the hell had I done? Mosher came to see me, and I told him how I felt. Mosher, as kind as he is bright and talented, told me, "Marlon Brando is sitting up on Mulholland Drive right now. He's three hundred pounds, he's sixty-eight years old, and he's not coming down here to do the show. So, if they want to see it live, you're it. You're Stanley now." He wished me luck and headed out. Onstage, Williams's writing has the effect that all great writing has on an actor. It steadies you. It emboldens you. You ride an elevator to the top floor of a building, you jump off the penthouse balcony, and you fly. Just put one foot in front of the other, one line after the other, one moment after the other, and you are walking on air. It was the creative experience of a lifetime.

I worked out pretty hard for the role. My trainer was a boxing pro named Michael Olajide, whose son, Michael Jr., fought professionally under the name "Silk" Olajide. Olajide, a Nigerian émigré, was a gregarious and patient man who called all of his charges "Champ": "How are you today, Champ?" Or, "OK, Champ, let's hit the heavy bag." Fred Ward had gotten me into boxing while we were shooting *Miami Blues* about four years earlier. Fred and I walked into the 5th

Street Gym in Miami and right into the legendary Beau Jack, a world-class fighter who ran the place where Ali trained when he was photographed "knocking out" the Beatles in 1964. Over the years I fell in love with that form of training, which eliminates any downtime. The bell rings, you move. The bell rings, you stop. Repeat. Repeat. Ninety minutes of that, and you start to feel pretty good.

Olajide had me lift weights for thirty minutes after the bag, rope, and sparring work. I put on twenty pounds of muscle. I felt like if I hit a building, the building would wince. If someone leaned on me on the subway, I was ready with the look you flash only when you can back it up. I felt invincible. I was becoming Stanley. But the physicality of the role, the animal lack of self-consciousness, is counterweighted by the character's obsession with and love for Stella. Each night, it was like *Prelude* again. Amy Madigan was more Annie Oakley than the languid beauties normally cast in the role of Stella, but she is a woman who beams talent, heart, decency, passion, and technique. She is right there at the top with Mary-Louise and Jennifer Jason Leigh as one of the greatest actresses I've worked with. With the deepest respect to Ed Harris, I fell in love with his wife on a regular basis, too, and loved her with all my heart and soul. In the iconic moment where

Stanley wails for the loss of his one good reason to live, I imagined having and losing a woman as wonderful as Amy/Stella, something I would not know in my own life for some time to come, and the pain just poured out of me.

Performing the role of Stanley took a real toll on me physically. I broke my knuckles while pounding the Kowalskis' kitchen table ("Every man is a king. And I am the king around here!"), which I swear was made of hickory. After I injured my hand, I kept at it until the knuckles turned a blackish blue. I switched over to pounding the left side of my chest with my right fist, in a basic ape-like manner. Eventually, I crushed a nerve in my chest. One night, as I dropped down to do some push-ups offstage, my left arm just collapsed—my pectoral muscle was simply dead. To add to my problems, the stage of the show was pitched, or raked in Broadway terminology. If you turned toward another actor while opening slightly to the audience, you stood on a slight incline, one leg lower than the other. After six months of that, my back went out. I never had a back problem in my life until *Streetcar*, where I developed back pain that would eventually drive me nearly mad. I enjoyed saying those lines and being that guy, but I literally hobbled to the finish line. Having also added twenty pounds of weight, I finished the play injured, exhausted, and bulky. Rather than do what I could to take the weight off, I kept lifting as I turned thirty-five and then headed toward forty. One day, a guy in the gym said, "You work out like the Cowboys are gonna call you to carry the ball this season. I got news for you. They're not gonna call." Within a few years, age and a diagnosis of prediabetes made weight gain an issue in my life. The vanity that propelled me through *Streetcar* had its price.

On the opening night of the play, we all gathered at Sardi's for the party. Many of us were tense in anticipation of Frank Rich's review. Rich, the powerful and unsparing critic from the *Times*, occupied a place beyond the one Ben Brantley does today, as Rich actually knew what he was writing about. Brantley seems to serve a function for the *Times* similar to Page Six in the *Post*, insofar as his writing is random, uninformed snark. There was no digital edition of the *Times* then. The paper would hit newsstands in New York just past midnight. Kim and I headed home from the party and arrived near my apartment as the paper literally hit the shelves. "Don't read that," she said. "I mean, you don't really believe that, do you? You don't believe anything those people say?"

Rich had been kind to me just a couple of years earlier when *Prelude to a Kiss* was at Circle Rep. The commercial success of our production hinged on his review. But I caught Kim's intention, which was to make sure I didn't enjoy the evening too much. She had once told me, as a kind of self-penned letter of recommendation regarding her on-the-job performance in romantic relationships, "I am so 'for' the other person. You couldn't be any more in the other person's corner than I am." Now, Kim had grown tired of bad publicity about Evian hair rinses and failed real estate investments. She seemed to demand that everyone be as miserable as she was. In 1992, I had the old Record-a-Call answering machine in my apartment. The morning after the opening, the tape was filled with the scores of congratulations from friends who quoted the *Times* review, as Rich was positive toward my performance. Elaine Aiken, who had helped to coax a bit of Stanley out of me, framed the review and hung it in her acting studio.

Jessica Lange is a tough woman, but the challenges of *Streetcar* tested her. When all the reviews came out (mixed for all of us, actually), Jessica must have been perplexed and certainly hurt. She was rather remote to begin with, and the response to her performance simply made her retreat while at the theater even more. But she was used to winning, so after our show, she picked herself up, dusted herself off, and went on to build a whole wing of her career dedicated to the theater. She did *The Glass Menagerie* in New York, *Streetcar* in London, and in 2016 won the Tony Award for best actress in O'Neill's *Long Day's Journey.* For me, *Streetcar* was also pivotal. McTiernan, not a dramaturge by any stretch, said that the Jack Ryan character's story was essentially "a boy goes down to the sea and comes home a man." He was right. I showed up at Paramount a boy and left *Streetcar* a man. It was in losing *Hunt* and gambling on *Streetcar* that I realized who I was, what I could do, and how little I cared about most of the moviemaking in the era I was working in.

In the fall of 1992, I went off to shoot *Malice*, a tepid thriller written by a young Aaron Sorkin and directed by Harold Becker, whom I enjoyed working with. Bill Pullman is a talented actor and a great guy, but the best opportunity the movie offered was the chance to be photographed by the great Gordon Willis, who shot a slate of Woody Allen's richest films, not to mention *The Godfather.* Gordon's signature chiaroscuro meant we were lit low. Very low. In one scene, I turned to Bill and said, "Do you think if we left here right now, anyone would even notice?" Gordon was tough, but what an honor it was to shoot with him.

At the end of 1992, Kim was informed that the producers of a film she had pulled out of intended to sue her. By the spring of the following year, her career and her finances would be sunk like the *Titanic*. In 1993, Kim would enter a courtroom and be mauled by opposing attorneys, the jury, and the judge. Years later, when we divorced, it was the lessons from this trial that she would apply in a concerted effort to have the last word, to control the outcome, and to effectively represent herself as the victim in any and all disputes, which is what Kim was used to most of all.

10

The Pink and the Gray

I had first met Kim in 1989 on the set of *My Step-mother Is an Alien*, a comedy she was shooting with Dan Aykroyd, while I was on the Fox lot to meet with Jim Cameron about a role in *The Abyss*. Her personal costumer, Linda Henrikson, thought that Kim, after a divorce from her first husband and relatively brief relationships with Prince and the producer Peter Guber, among others, was ready to meet someone. When I called Linda, whom I had worked with on *Beetlejuice*, and said I would be around for a visit, she arranged things, and the next thing I knew, I was in front of Kim as she was asking me, "You're the guy in the boat movie, right?" referring to *Hunt*. I didn't see her again for a few months, when we started the Neil Simon film. There was a playful side to Kim that prevailed in the early days. Wry one minute and awkward the next, with her angular features framed by her signature corona of blonde hair, Kim is a creature, an object like a leopard or an orchid or a magnificent mountain lake. At times, her attempts to dress down and disguise herself in public were laughable. Kim is Kim, from five feet away or five hundred, on the red carpet or in the grocery line.

If you've never been sued in a civil court in this country, particularly in California, you're really missing something. Civil trials, like the ones I have observed in Los Angeles, provide you with insight into the darkest corners of human malice, greed, corruption, and cowardice. They're like a hockey brawl, Bush v. Gore, and *One Flew Over the Cuckoo's Nest* all rolled into one. You see judges posing with a mock certainty and air of control when, in reality, they are pawns in a game controlled by big law firms seeking profits.

Well before I set foot in a family law court, I had attended much of Kim's trial in 1993, when she was sued for breach of contract by the producers of a film. In the fall of 1992, while I was shooting *Malice* in LA and western Massachusetts, Kim had signed with a new agent, an old guard character named Guy McElwaine. As agents often do, he wanted to sweep aside as many of her pending commitments as possible, as he would not get a commission on those deals. *Boxing Helena* was such a project, and Guy told Kim that he would extricate her from it. Additionally, the script explicitly called for nudity and sexual contact that required Kim's approval, none of which had been spelled out to her satisfactorily by the director. Other actresses had been approached about the role before Kim, and Madonna had actually been hired for a time before walking away with little fuss. However, when Kim decided to leave, the producers, feeling powerless and thwarted, were determined to make an example of her. They sued her, and the case went to trial in early 1993.

During pretrial preparation, Kim rehearsed mock cross-examinations with her lawyer Howard Weitzman. Sometimes, she would come home in tears for fear of what lay ahead. Jake Bloom, who in addition to being an agent also one of Kim's lawyers, told her to settle the case. Hollywood is a place where the pay scales are so out of proportion that Bloom's suggestion made perfect sense to everyone involved. "Give them a million to walk away," Bloom spouted. "That's definitely better than getting in front of a jury." He was, in hindsight, wise on that front. But Kim would hear none of it. The idea of handing over a large sum of money to these producers while she was certain that she was right was out of the question.

When the producers appeared in court, it was plain to see that they would likely earn more money in that courtroom than they ever would in their careers. The director, Jennifer Lynch, the daughter of David Lynch, had apparently inherited his unruly hairstyle but none of his talent. Lynch parlayed her unkempt appearance and inarticulate demeanor into an image of herself as the victim of "Big Hollywood" and its bullying tactics. Her producer, Carl Mazzocone, a soft-spoken, obese man, also dialed up the victimhood in order to lobby a jury that ultimately was more than inclined to side with the have-nots.

The plaintiffs' attorney was Patricia Glaser. I have written about Glaser before, but perhaps that characterization could use a finer point: in the courtroom, she was like a creature out of *Jurassic Park*, in appearance, body language, and demeanor. Glaser is one of the most contemptible people I have ever encountered, a cartoon rendering of the rapacious litigator, representing everything that I believe is exploitative and unfair about our civil system. Her opening salvo was, "Now, we all know what it feels like for the pretty girl in school to get everything she wants." Glaser, not the pretty girl, wanted to take Kim down in some schoolyard-style Betty-vs.-Veronica dynamic straight out of *Archie* comics. Naturally, she won.

Kim had dressed herself with great care every day before heading to court, in order to avoid appearing too extravagant. Some mornings, sitting on the edge of the bed, wondering what to wear or not wear in order to project the "right" image to a jury of strangers, she would quietly start sobbing. It was heartbreaking.

The case proceeded for several days without any clear cause for alarm until it was announced that Kim's agents, who were co-litigants in the complaint, would be dismissed from the case. Thus, the entire burden of any potential verdict and subsequent award would fall on her alone. The judge further ruled that the jury would not be informed that the deep-pocketed code-fendant was now out. The jury should level its judgment for damages blindly, without regard for Kim's financial position.

Everyone in the courtroom twisted the truth or out-right lied. On one telephone call during the pretrial period, one of Kim's lawyers spit at her, "They're going to lie! So you have to lie if you want to win!" But she didn't lie. Not once. In the end, they handed her a bill for $8.9 million. She filed for bankruptcy in the hope that the verdict would be reversed on appeal. As was widely reported at the time, the judge, a disgrace to the bench named Judith Chirlin, strode across the court-room and hugged the two plaintiffs in full view of the jury. In September of the following year, the verdict was thrown out due to Chirlin's improper instructions to the jury. However, the damage to Kim's reputation was done.

During the trial, I didn't work and stayed in LA to attend the proceedings. During that time, Walter Hill, the great screenwriter and director, approached me about a remake of Peckinpah's *The Getaway*, which he wanted to direct using his original script. The producer, Larry Gordon, wanted Sharon Stone to play the female lead, if only for the financing she would bring. I asked him if Kim, who desperately needed to go back to work to take her mind off of her troubles, could play the part. Gordon agreed, but only after slashing the budget considerably. With less money on hand to shoot, Walter walked away and Roger Donaldson stepped in.

Quite often, when evaluating actors and their creative choices, the public fails to see them as husbands, wives, mothers, and fathers. Entertainment writers and critics in particular, who are assumed to actually know something about the business, never seem to understand that performers want to alternately stay home or get away from home, to do something heavy and dramatic or something light and fun, to dig into a performance and give everything they've got or just pick up a paycheck. With *The Getaway*, I just wanted to be with Kim. I wanted her to get back on her feet and shake off the effects of the trial. We went off to Arizona and shot all over the state. Beginning in Phoenix, living at the great old Biltmore Hotel, we made our way to Prescott, Jerome, Sedona, and then finished down in Yuma, where on one shooting day the temperature hit 126 degrees.

We brought with us our movie family: hair and makeup, wardrobe and stunts, stand-ins and assistants who formed the personal crew we had assembled over several years of moviemaking. On the first day of shooting, Kim was compelled to sign papers declaring bankruptcy in response to the verdict. However, my overall idea worked, as in the ensuing weeks, she genuinely seemed to relax and enjoy working.

The first thing critics do when you remake a film like Peckinpah's is to make a negative comparison to the original. Just like with Brando and *Streetcar* a year earlier, not once did I ever consider I could top Steve McQueen in the movie-star department. McQueen became an icon by perhaps doing less than any film star in history. His acting was so casual that at times it barely registered on-screen. His voice, his line readings, his whole demeanor seemed like he was a few moments away from a siesta. And yet it worked. Stage acting is about doing half a dozen things, all at the same time, and doing them well. Movie stardom is about doing two, maybe three things on camera, but doing them to perfection. Stars like McQueen taught me that sometimes the trick is to do nothing at all.

On the last day of production, at the very hotel where the cast and crew were staying, Kim and I ambled around the pool, shooting a scene where Doc McCoy and his wife, Carol, are reunited after his prison term in a Mexican hellhole. When they called "Cut!" on the last take, Kim pushed me in the pool. Everyone laughed and then much of the crew jumped in after me. That night, we held a party at the hotel bar. Everyone showed up and got drunk, and Kim and I could finally share a smile about how the two spoiled monsters in Susan Lyne's *Premiere* magazine article managed to shoot a picture where everyone had a good time. All the more reason it was so hard to go back to LA to face Kim's ongoing problems.

Going home meant facing a mountain of appellate and bankruptcy court filings. I wanted to continue the feeling of hope and positivity that the Arizona trip had fostered, even slightly. So I went to Tiffany's in Beverly Hills and bought Kim a ring. One afternoon, I sat in our backyard with Kim's sister Ashley and her husband, Joe. Joe was a quiet, shy Southerner and one of the most decent and easygoing guys I've ever met. I had told Joe and Ashley of my plan. Neither of them endorsed it and for different reasons. Ashley knew Kim was cursed in her romantic relationships. Joe joked that it was the men who married into the family who were cursed. I brought up the subject of marriage to Kim infrequently. When I did, I sensed alternately that she was enthusiastic or that I was putting a saddle on a wild horse. I thought my idea of getting married was a chance to start over, albeit through that most traditional of commitments. Ashley just looked at me sweetly and sympathetically, as if to say, "One can never tell with Kim."

Undaunted, I drove Kim to Taft High School at the foot of the hills along Ventura Boulevard, where we would often run on the track. As we walked along the track, there were kids playing soccer while others jogged past us. Did she see the proposal coming? I couldn't tell. When I asked her to marry me, believing at that moment that, united, we could face her mounting difficulties, she seemed genuinely confused. She didn't say yes. She didn't say no. She was, to say the least, overwhelmed by all the turns her life had taken.

Choosing to propose directly on the heels of the court case was, in hindsight, bad timing. My tendency to want to fix everything, and my belief that I can, got the better of me. Was this poor kid from Massapequa now prepared to make someone else's troubles disappear by supplying the necessary funding? Was I confusing pity with love? Nonetheless, we were married in August of that year. About a hundred friends and family members came. The wedding was held at the home of a friend in East Hampton, on the beach. Naturally, I made all of the arrangements.

The term "fugue state" best describes the remainder of 1993 and all of 1994. Kim almost never worked. When I went on location, she was less inclined than ever to visit me. It seemed like the only laughs we had, the only closeness I actually detected, was during the big Northridge earthquake in January of 1994. The earthquake was the quintessential California rite of passage for me. There were long lines everywhere as San Fernando Valley homeowners struggled to stock up on everything from groceries to gasoline. I'll never forget these seemingly insignificant, flimsy metal straps that held a hot water heater in place and how I scoured the Valley to buy one. One afternoon, when all the gas lines had been turned off in our neighborhood, ruling out the possibility of cooking at home, I found us a hot meal from a local Italian restaurant that had a generator. When I walked in with the food, it was a scene out of one of those movies where the survivors of a plane crash are rescued in the snowy mountains.

I was the hero just by showing up with pasta and a salad.

I went to New Orleans in 1994 to shoot *Heaven's Prisoners* with the wonderful Mary Stuart Masterson, who, as Kim seemed to recede more and more, I probably fell in love with while we were shooting. Teri Hatcher, by no means anyone's first choice for the role of Eric Roberts's wife, turned out to be tough and brave. (I always enjoy when an actor comes to set and ends up changing your mind about them.) Kim came down once, for a weekend, then flew back to LA to figure out how to get out of the hole she was in. When I was home, appellate lawyers and bankruptcy lawyers called the house regularly, pleading for direction regarding Kim's case. Kim wouldn't take their calls, so the responsibility fell to me. Two or three times a week, lawyers asked me for certain direction or approvals, most of which meant more money in fees. Although, eventually, Kim's verdict was reversed on appeal, the path to that ruling was agonizing.

On New Year's Day 1995, on the front page of the Sunday business section, the *New York Times* ran an article entitled "The Basinger Bankruptcy Bomb" about powerful people who had sidestepped significant debt through strategic bankruptcy filings. In it, Kim was portrayed as a capricious, irresponsible woman who flagrantly exploited bankruptcy law, living extravagantly in spite of a pile of bills she refused to pay. (Remember, the verdict was ultimately overturned, providing a textbook example of the kind of case that bankruptcy protection was designed for.) The writer of the article, private investigators later uncovered, lived in Texas, had never come to New York, and had never seen my home in New York or Kim's home in LA, both of which she described as either "lavish" or a "mansion." She was wrong on both counts.

After reading the article, Kim vibrated with anger. She spent the day on the phone with her lawyers, wondering what she had to do to catch a break from all of the misrepresentations of both the case and her in the press. That very evening, we were scheduled to fly to Lima and then on to the Peruvian rain forest to shoot a documentary for Turner Broadcasting, but Kim declared that the trip was off. Just the slightest criticism in the press could set her off, and this piece was unfair and inaccurate in several ways, so much so that her attorneys wrote a rebuttal that the *Times* printed a week later. As we headed to the airport, Kim was brimming over with embarrassment and indignation.

I spent the morning screaming at Kim's lawyers about how I wanted to kill the *Times* reporter, perhaps also sensing that all of this wasn't very good for me either. Kim only sat and glared at me. Yet, somehow, we managed to get in the car and head to the airport to shoot the film, which was about the illegal exportation of exotic birds. The trip up the Tambopata River to the Tambopata Research Center, slightly west of the Bolivian border, was an awkward, uncomfortable experience. The week we spent in mosquito-netted lean-tos with the legendary documentarian Robert Drew, his wife, Anne, and our crew was not what I had envisioned. Our time away from the noise and vulgarity of the US media, however, turned out to be the thing we needed to begin to breathe again.

Once we were back in LA, I decided that we needed to get out of town again, if only for a weekend, to rest and try to reconnect. Marriage is a fragile and, presumably, valuable object. Even as we deliberately smash it on the ground, we are compelled to sweep up all of the pieces and attempt to put it back together. Also, I feared divorce, as I equated it with a deep, personal failure. We drove up to the San Ysidro Ranch for a weekend. Soon after we got back, Kim discovered she was pregnant.

During the first three years Kim and I were together, I had completely cut myself off from thoughts of having a family. With Kim, she led and you followed regarding any important, life-changing decisions. After we were married and throughout her legal battles, any limited talk about children was weighed against how it would stall her career revival. For me, the idea of forgoing a family was difficult. I recall one moment when, watching a man carry his sleeping child through an airport, I said to myself, "I'll never have children." I sighed, shoved down those feelings, and boarded a plane to go to work.

Then our daughter, Ireland, was born. The moment that your first child arrives is a transcendent one. And, regardless of the state of our marriage, Ireland's birth inspired Kim and me to set aside whatever doubts or fears we had and allow the day to be the remarkable event it truly was. Ireland was a healthy, beautiful baby. Like any husband, I spent that day dedicated to providing whatever assistance I could to my wife. But for most of it, I was simply overwhelmed by the arrival of my daughter. At one point, I tried to recall how I imagined this day would play out. This child, this person, is finally arriving; what would she be like? I would stare at Ireland, mesmerized, and say to her tiny being, "My God, it's you! I wondered who would show up and it's you!" After sleeping in the chair next to Kim's hospital bed that first night, I went home to shower. In our bedroom, I lit a candle and thanked God for Ireland and prayed for the health of mother and child. I have lighted a candle or, for lack of one, a match, every night since. Twenty-one years. If I was on a red-eye, heading home to New York, I lit the candle when I arrived home in the early morning. If I've missed a night, I am unaware of it, as there's surely the chance I passed out here and there. But, I don't think so. Every night, for twenty-one years, I go to sleep and say, "I love you, Ireland."

When Ireland was an infant, Kim designed a thank-you card for the many thoughtful people who had sent along gifts. The card was perhaps one of the more powerful insights into Kim I had ever come across. On the cover was a naïve illustration that showed a bare tree colored in a muted matte gray. Stuck in one of the high branches was a bright pink ribbon blowing in the wind. There it was, I thought. There was the meaning of Ireland's arrival in Kim's life: our child as the only sign of hope, of light, to come into Kim's world.

My friend Ronnie once said that I had loved Kim the iconoclast who didn't care what anyone thought. "Little did you know that included you, too," he quipped. I had felt that I was losing at this game for some time. Everyone wants to believe that they are capable of making someone they love happy, be they a spouse, lover, sibling, or child. I believed that kind of union, that happiness, was my destiny. When you finally face the bitter reality that they will never be happy in the relationship because they are incapable of being happy anywhere, with anyone, you implode. You are powerless.

Love is an object that we hold in our hands. It is visible and it is ours to share. Sometimes, the person you love withholds theirs from you. But it is still there, hidden behind their back, kept from your view. Until one day, the one you love stands in front of you with both of their hands at their sides and their hands are empty. There is nothing there anymore. Nothing. After Ireland was born, all of the love Kim had went to her child. And every moment we were together after that, the emptiness that resulted moved us toward the inevitable.

With my sister Beth and our Easter baskets.

On the couch in Brooklyn,
waiting for Ed Sullivan
and the Beatles.

My fifth grade class reenacts the Apollo moon landing.

Richard Nixon offers his support after I lost the election at GW.

RICHARD NIXON

LA CASA PACIFICA
SAN CLEMENTE, CALIFORNIA

April 10, 1979

Dear Alex,

From our mutual friend, Mark Weinberg,
I have learned of the disappointing
results, as far as you are concerned,
of the recent George Washington
University student body elections.

The important thing is that you cared
enough to enter the arena, and I urge
you to look upon the contest as a
learning experience which will serve
you well in the future.

May the years ahead for you be filled
with success in your chosen field of
endeavor,

Sincerely,

Mr. Alexander R. Baldwin, III
2000 South Eads Street   (Suite 827)
Arlington, Virginia 22202

With Michael Bloom at Athens Pump Room in Chicago.

With Mike Nussbaum in Mamet's *A Life in the Theatre* at the Hartman Theater in Stamford, CT (1987). © *T. Charles Erickson.*

Another scene from *A Life in the Theatre.*
© *T. Charles Erickson.*

Perfecting my roar in Caryl Churchill's *Serious Money* at the Royale Theatre (1988). *Photograph by Martha Swope © The New York Public Library.*

Meeting one of my heroes, Gregory Peck, at a People for the American Way benefit in 1990.

With Barnard Hughes and Mary-Louise Parker in *Prelude to a Kiss* (1990).

With Larry Bryggman and Debra Monk in *Prelude to a Kiss*.

Bored out of my mind on the set of *The Hunt for Red October*. © *Bruce McBroom/ mptvimages.com.*

In uniform as Jack Ryan in *The Hunt for Red October*.

Boxing training at the old Times Square Gym in New York. *Photograph by Michael Tighe.*

Taking direction from Martin Scorsese on the set of *The Aviator* (2004).

With my firstborn child, Ireland.

With my wife, Hilaria, and our children, Leo, Carmen, and Rafael.
Mary Ellen Matthews.

11

Of Course, Of Course

The list of men I admire in the movies is quite long. It goes from Lon Chaney Sr. to Gable to Tracy to Fredric March. It includes Mitchum, Clift, Kirk Douglas, Lon Chaney Jr., Michael Douglas, Tyrone Power, James Garner, Burt Lancaster, Yves Montand, Colin Firth, Albert Finney, Robert De Niro, Robert Preston, Paul Newman, Peter O'Toole, Gregory Peck, Maximilian Schell, and Gary Oldman.

My favorite movie actor is William Holden. Onscreen, Holden is handsome, graceful, charming, and funny. He is tough and resourceful enough to handle himself in any type of predicament. In a range of films from *Golden Boy* to *Bridge on the River Kwai* and *Sabrina*, from *Sunset Boulevard* to *Stalag 17* and *The Wild Bunch*, Holden could do it all. I knew that developing a style like his was not practical. He was an original and tough to imitate. Plus, the scripts in those days were tailored for him. Writers today, in most cases, don't necessarily write for a particular actor. But what I wouldn't give to have been born in 1925 or so, to have survived the war and gone on to a career in films in that Golden Age of the 1940s and '50s.

In small and not so small ways, many young actors seek to latch on to the persona of a particular star and channel that star in their early work. Some newcomers try to bring their Brando, Dean, Mitchum, Pacino, De Niro, or Nicholson to the roles. Women may try, especially when they're young, to pull in everything from Monroe to Katharine Hepburn. They may try to emulate, not only in terms of style but also career choices, someone who is a contemporary like Meryl Streep, Cherry Jones, or Cate Blanchett. Young actors have to come up with something and haven't had much experience. So why not steal from the best?

I don't remember stealing from anyone, at least not in any overt sense. (Maybe a bit from Joe Maher!) But an actor who says they don't borrow from others in their early years is a liar. I'd see an actor like Edward G. Robinson snarl a line ("Yeah, see?"), and at some point, I'd think, "I'm gonna snarl like Edward G." Cagney was so cocky—let's sprinkle a little of that in there. Bogart was so subtle, so silky, yet so playful—let's layer a little of Bogey into this line. Let your face relax while holding a faint smile, like you just woke up from a nap, like Mitchum. Make the zingers zing, like Nicholson. Say the line with a smoldering, quiet tone, then thunder on the last phrase, like Pacino.

I suppose the contemporary actor who I most wanted to emulate was Pacino. Al's passion, intensity, and sexuality, all of his now legendary signatures, took my breath away. The scene in *Serpico* when John Randolph presents Serpico with his gold shield, a bullet hole bored into Al's face, his indignity, disgust, and rage are barely containable. As Randolph presses the badge onto Al's chest, Pacino collapses in tears that, to this day, go straight through me. I didn't want to imitate Al. But I wanted to learn from him. The task was to maintain a reservoir of emotional truth, pain, and love.

Even though Marlon Brando's film career seems far in the past now, for some he remains a sort of gold standard. No doubt, Brando is a monolithic talent. He reached an undiscovered place in terms of emotional truth and complexity in film acting. And he developed this gift at such a young age. But Brando's difficult relationship with the business, and with himself, left me wondering when Brando was acting and when he was mocking. His contempt for what he viewed as false or pretentious in Hollywood resonated with me. When he gave his all, the results were incomparable. But it became clear later in his career that he had no intention of giving his all in many films. A battered, fatigued Brando thought that simply showing up was enough. Perhaps actors with Brando's unmatched talent, and the attendant worship that comes with that, run the risk of such cynicism, even self-destruction.

Movie stardom amplified Brando's family issues, industry battles, and neuroses, ultimately overwhelming him. Pacino always struck me as different. Pacino seemed focused on balancing his two roles as actor and star, not easy given that his own accomplishments in the movies are legendary. He returned to the theater with some regularity, certainly, more than most at his level. Like Nicholson, when it was called for, he left his vanity at home and just played the role, and beautifully, as in *Angels in America*. In films like *The Godfather* and *Scarface*, he put the character's ugly nature on display. However, in films like *Dog Day Afternoon*, *Carlito's Way*, and *Donnie Brasco*, his ability to break your heart is like no other. I don't know about you, but I go to the movies to have my heart broken every now and then, and I've always relied on Al to bring that emotional wallop to his films.

Although I studied their work, I could never have

Holden's career, or Brando's, or Al's. Those careers are of their time. What I did have was Gus Trikonis's advice that I simply focus on trying to do my best in whatever film role I landed.

Once the Tom Clancy franchise was out of the equation, I didn't have to worry about protecting some squeaky-clean image. I learned that if you are willing and have an aptitude for playing an intelligent villain, your options change. Many actors, to this day, shy away from playing the bad guy. Even though those roles can offer great acting opportunities, some stars won't take the chance that such work might tarnish their image. In the case of stars like Cruise and Hanks, this is understandable. They have towering careers in the movies built upon a combination of integrity and heroics. When I watched Cruise in Paul Thomas Anderson's *Magnolia*, I thought he had won another Oscar. He was riveting. But perhaps someone told him to never do that again and, for Cruise, villainous roles disappeared.

In movies like *Malice* and *The Juror*, playing the "negative value" in the script (a phrase I borrowed from the great director Harold Becker) was both fun and not without a cost. Hollywood studio executives, so limited in their creativity, make things easy on themselves by ruling that you can't be the hero of a film if, in your last one, you stepped onto a school bus with a flamethrower. (Especially in one of their own pictures!) In the '90s, most of the films I had made after *Hunt* had underperformed, or were outright turkeys. *The Shadow, The Getaway, Heaven's Prisoners,* and *The Juror* offered me some wonderful experiences, but little luck at the box office.

When Rob Reiner asked me to do *Ghosts of Mississippi,* I thought that it was a real chance to gain back some ground in terms of my film career. The picture had been developed for Tom Hanks, and when he was unavailable, I got the call. But from the moment Reiner said "Action!," it was clear to me that he wished it were still Hanks in front of the camera. Back then, Reiner left little to chance and made films only with the biggest stars available. In spite of a very soft script ("Another civil rights story told through the eyes of a white protagonist," Coretta King complained to Myrlie Evers at the premiere. "Where is Medgar?"), making the film was very gratifying, although it did not succeed. However, in the summer of 1996, a script arrived that I had a hunch was my last real chance to save my movie career.

The first play by David Mamet that I performed in was *A Life in the Theatre* in 1987 at the old Hartman Theatre in Stamford, Connecticut, directed by A. J. Antoon. In 1972, Antoon held the distinction of being nominated for two Tonys in the same season, winning best director for *That Championship Season*. Antoon, a remarkably agile director, emphasized the importance of lighting, sets, and how the actor must move on the stage within his design for maximum effect. Antoon died of an AIDS-related illness in 1992, just five years after we worked together.

The piece is a two-hander and one of my favorites by Mamet. The other actor was the great Mike Nussbaum, a veteran of numerous early Chicago productions of Mamet's work, including this play. Every day I traveled from Grand Central to Stamford during a snowy winter. It was the theater, which means that along with compelling material, there were no frills. In late December, we began rehearsals using a banquet room on the second floor of a VFW hall near the theater as a rehearsal space.

Like nearly every actor trained in the past few decades, I am a great admirer of David's writing. Whether by way of scenes from *Sexual Perversity in Chicago* attempted in acting classes, our production at the Hartman, or filming *Glengarry Glen Ross*, I respected his ear for great dialogue. His roles for contemporary men are like no other. The lines that close act one in *Oleanna* make up some of my favorite writing in the theater. Carol struggles to communicate with her professor, John, saying, "All my life . . ." and stops. John replies, "Go on." Carol says, "I've never told anyone this . . ." And suddenly, John's phone rings. His wife is calling, and John's life punctures their halting foreplay. When John hangs up, a humiliated Carol snaps out of her unaccustomed vulnerability. The moment is priceless. Whenever I've seen it performed, I gasp slightly and I love teaching it in any class I've taught.

In July of 1996, a script arrived from my agent entitled *Bookworm*, written by Mamet. As was the case on maybe five occasions in my life, I sequestered myself from everyone around me and read the screenplay the moment I opened the envelope. When I was finished, I called my agent to say that I loved it, and in a couple of weeks I was in a conference room in a Beverly Hills hotel with the presumptive director, Lee Tamahori, the producers, and other actors reading the smaller roles. Playing the other lead role was Robert De Niro. I was, obviously, beside myself with the prospect of working with Bob. However, the character was named Charles Morse, and as tycoons go, De Niro is more Stavros Niarchos. De Niro did the reading and decided he didn't want to play the part.

I was offered the other lead role and waited for them to tell me who they would cast in De Niro's place. That month, I went with Kim, Ireland, and Kim's siblings and father to Figure Eight Island, just off the coast of Wilmington, North Carolina. We'd vacationed there for several years as it was a reasonable drive from Athens, Georgia, where Kim grew up and her family lived. I remember sitting on a bed in our rented beach house when my agent called to tell me that Anthony Hopkins had just been cast in the role of Morse. I literally welled up with tears of joy.

Just two years prior, the producer of the Oscars, Gil Cates, asked me to present a clip from a nominated film. I told Gil I would if that film could be *The Remains of the Day*, which was one of my favorites that year. I worshipped Emma Thompson and admired the director, James Ivory. The movie I shot with Hopkins would be one of the few of my films that I can watch. Its mournful treatment of the main character's struggle to connect with people in any meaningful way requires an actor of Tony's ability. Who plays existential angst better than Hopkins?

We began shooting that August on location all over Alberta, Canada. The cast and crew were in hotels and rental houses in Canmore, thirty-odd minutes from the gates of Banff National Park. It was decided to jettison the title *Bookworm*, which I preferred. The new title, *The Edge*, should have provided a clue as to how Tamahori, the producer Art Linson, and the studio execs

at Fox wanted to shape the film into more of a conventional action-adventure-drama than the baroque
thriller I thought I had signed on for. The script told
the story of Morse, an awkward, introverted billion-
aire, who accompanies his supermodel wife, Mickey
(Elle Macpherson), on a photo shoot in the Alaskan
semiwilderness. Unbeknownst to Morse (or maybe
not), his wife has been having an on-again, off-again
affair with the attending photographer, Bob Green,
played by yours truly. I loved the script because it was
simple and stark, throwing two men into desperate
circumstances, simultaneously mistrusting and needing each other. In several scenes, such as when a third
companion, played by Harold Perrineau, is killed, the
film mimics *The Treasure of the Sierra Madre* in its
moments of unbridled humanity.

In one rehearsal, Tamahori said, "This scene on
page fourteen. I think we should just cut the first four
speeches. David does tend to go on a bit." I felt that the
way David tends to "go on" was the very reason I was
there. At one point, I telephoned Mamet, who listened
politely to my concerns about the changes in the tone
of the film. Then he said, "Alec, these scripts are like
orphan children to me. I write them, they pay me, and
they belong to someone else." In terms of Hollywood
protocol, he was right. As he was not the director, he

wouldn't waste his time worrying about how the film was being made. During the actual shooting, Tamahori revealed that he had little, if any, affinity for dramatizing the tensions between Morse and Green. Instead, he relied on Bart the Bear, our Alaskan Kodiak castmate, to execute the kind of storytelling he could comprehend.

Ultimately, the stars of the film are two incomparable icons, the Canadian Rockies and Anthony Hopkins. Hopkins treated me to my favorite acting collaboration and the best view of a truly great actor I'd had since shooting *Knots Landing* with Julie Harris. With his classical training, subtly expressive face and limpid eyes, and an essential sturdiness and strength, he is my favorite living actor. No matter the role, there is always both the gentleman and the thug, the man and the beast present in so much of his work. I had studied Hopkins (and I do mean studied) going back to 1974, when he starred in the television adaptation of Leon Uris's *QB VII*. I'd then watched him in films like *Magic, The Elephant Man, The Remains of the Day, Nixon*, and, of course, *The Silence of the Lambs*. After we worked together, Tony, ever the pugnacious iconoclast, still delighted me in *The World's Fastest Indian*.

Hopkins has numerous gifts, and it is, of course, his voice that casts his spell. Like the French horn solo from Tchaikovsky's Fifth, he simply opens his mouth to speak and his work is halfway done. While many British actors imbue their work with something a bit more polished than Americans do, with Hopkins there is an added layer. Whether it's something sensuous or dangerous, it's palpable. While we were on location in Banff National Park, my sister Beth came to visit me. My sister Beth flew from Syracuse to Toronto to Calgary, then drove ninety minutes to the set, arriving rather tired. I found Hopkins lying on an air mattress, recommended for a neck and back injury that he joked he picked up while channeling Nixon. I approached him and said, "Tony, I'd like you to meet my sister Beth." Hopkins put down the newspaper, stood, and slowly looked up at my sister, his blue eyes like sapphires that he had often utilized to similar effect, no doubt. "Elizabeth," he purred, taking her hand, "what a pleasure to meet you." When he kissed the back of it, I thought that Beth, a married mother of six, was about to faint.

Another career lesson occurred while shooting *The Edge*. A year earlier, in 1995, I had become quite committed to the work of one of the entertainment industry's leading arts advocacy organizations, The Creative Coalition, founded in 1989 by actor Ron Silver in cooperation with then HBO CEO Michael Fuchs and a roster of actors including Susan Sarandon, Stephen Collins, Blair Brown, and Christopher Reeve. Silver had wanted to harness the energies of politically engaged members of the industry who were willing to work on behalf of specific causes. His basic idea was to invite his more activist show business friends to study the issues on a level they had not been exposed to before. Programs were produced wherein experts and scholars lectured the TCC members—including not only famous actors but also writers, producers, musicians, and agents—as well as the public. TCC raised awareness on a range of core issues that included arts advocacy and the responsibility of the federal government in arts funding, gun control, First Amendment rights and issues related to freedom of expression, the reproductive rights of women, federal and state enforcement of environmental regulation, and campaign finance reform.

At the 1995 retreat, which was held in New York, I vividly recall standing next to Chris Reeve and knowing that he would run for political office, probably the Senate, and soon. He had cultivated a more moderate and politically adroit stance while serving as TCC's president. He spoke more carefully and was less confrontational with our "opponents," and he admonished me to follow suit. The very premise of TCC, that movie stars could effectively draw the attention of legislators and impact public policy if they had been sufficiently briefed, was embodied by Chris. It was entertaining to walk the halls of Congress with Chris to lobby for the issues TCC had adopted. The congressional staffs and elected officials themselves reacted to Chris in a charged way. Members of Congress would beam when meeting Chris and shout, "Come on in here, Superman!" Two weeks later, he broke his neck and was paralyzed. Soon after that, I was elected TCC's president.

While shooting *The Edge* in Canada the following year, I informed the producers of a TCC commitment I needed to keep in New York. I went so far as to have them book my plane ticket to avoid any confusion about my trip. However, the late-evening flight from New York was delayed, and the connection, an odd Las Vegas junket to Calgary, took off without me on it. I wrote down the names and contact info of the flight crew in charge and called the first assistant director, a guy named Phil Patterson. Phil, who played a role similar to a sergeant in the army, seemed worried by my news, but took a deep breath and said, "We'll try to shoot around it. Get here as quick as you can." The next morning, I flew from New York to Calgary, stopping in Toronto. The trip took up most of the day. I arrived at work that Monday, in the late afternoon. We did a couple of uncomplicated shots, and I went back to my rented house in Canmore. The next day, I walked into my trailer to find a FedEx envelope from a Fox attorney named Bill Petrasich waiting for me. Fox was suing me for the lost production time.

After some inquiries, I was told that the head of the studio at the time, Tom Rothman, had envisioned someone else in my role, an actor who was either unavailable, unaffordable, or unwilling. Therefore, when the time came to make my deal for the film, Fox negotiators were taciturn, as they were negotiating with someone who was certainly not their first choice. Perhaps I had them over a barrel, to some extent, because the movie was in the pipeline and they believed they had to move forward. But when you are unwanted, your demands are always viewed as excessive.

When shooting films on location, I brought seven men with me: Carl Fullerton, makeup; Rick Provenzano, hair; Myron Baker, personal wardrobe; Fred Liberman, driver; Ted Haggerty, stand-in; Gary Tacon, stunt double; and Greg Pace, personal assistant. These guys had shot several films with me. They were my movie family. They also cost the studio some money, which may have pissed them off. However, the idea that a major studio would threaten to sue a lead actor on one of their films for missing work as the result of someone else's error or negligence, even though I had offered them all the proof they needed that it had been far beyond my control, was more than ridiculous. It was abusive. I went to Art Linson, the producer, and asked him to intervene.

A producer, I've been told, is a person who brings an "essential element" to the table to get a film made. That can be money, material, or movie stars. Linson, who had made films like *Melvin and Howard*, *The Untouchables*, and *Casualties of War*, was the type of producer who was "friends" with certain actors, which I assume gave him a leg up when submitting scripts for them to consider. Robert De Niro and Sean Penn fell into that category, and rather quickly, it became clear I did not. Linson did nothing to help me. I was now stuck in the middle of Alberta, my wife and young child at home in LA, with a director who had no business making the film and a producer who was content to watch the studio fuck with me as some kind of payback for my desire to bring the same crew I'd taken on the road with me for years. Years later, Linson, believing that his own career was the stuff of Hollywood legend, made his memoir *What Just Happened* into a 2008 film with De Niro playing him. De Niro called me and asked me to play a character based on myself in the film. It was a testament to the loyalty of Linson's friends that De Niro would even ask me such a stupid question.

With little hope that a good film would emerge from this scenario, I was left with Tony, the breathtaking scenery, the wonderful music of Jerry Goldsmith, and the cinematography of Don McAlpine. We helicoptered to the top of Mount Assiniboine, which, at 11,850 feet, is the highest peak of the southern Canadian Rockies. When we alighted from a helicopter at the top of Assiniboine, I felt as if I had died and gone to heaven. Prior to that trip, I thought Big Sur was the most beautiful place I had ever been. I may even have voted for the beaches in East Hampton, right in my own backyard, or Kruger National Park in South Africa. But in Alberta, everywhere you look is unforgettable. The people are lovely, too. Away from the ceaseless noise, hucksterism, and smugness of America, Canada itself is a balm to the soul.

During the shoot, I learned more about Tony. He was raised in the same town in Wales as Richard Burton, who encouraged him at a young age to attend the Royal Welsh College of Music and Drama. As he spoke, I envisioned this shy boy who liked to paint going on to become an Oscar-winning film star and receiving a knighthood from the queen. Tony spoke casually about his training at RADA and his early stage career at the National Theatre under the direction of Laurence Olivier, and stunned me with his assertion that Hollywood had always been his goal. But if I pressed him further, eager to hear more and showing him my own apprentice's heart, a smile would come across his face and wonderful stories about Olivier's vanity, playfulness, and, above all, talent would spill out.

In *The Edge*, my character, Bob, is one of the more vacuous characters I've ever played, and it was interesting, sometimes fun, recalling people I had known, even worked with, who lent me some idea for the character. Bob is intimidated by Charles's intellectual and psychological powers. It was not hard to play that while acting opposite Tony. At the end, Bob chooses to exonerate Charles's wife, Mickey, out of respect for Charles. It was easy to love and respect Tony in the extreme as well.

Years later, when I performed in Peter Shaffer's *Equus* on Long Island in 2010, I asked Shaffer if he thought it was worthwhile for me to see the original production, with Hopkins and Peter Firth, that is on tape at the Lincoln Center library. Shaffer said, "I don't think so, only because the cast did not wish to be taped. So Roberta Maxwell did not perform that show. Firth put on a North Country accent, completely out of character. And Tony impersonated Larry Olivier the entire performance." After a bit of a pause, he said, "Very naughty boys." This actually came as no surprise to me. Hopkins is funny and a wonderful mimic. On the set of *The Edge*, Hopkins and I had played a game of dueling Richard Burtons. The goal was to not only impersonate Burton but to distill the self-destructive genius down to his essence. Eventually, Tony won the game for all time with his almost haiku-like incantation: "Elizabeth! Baubles and stones. White wine. Marbella." Then he feigned passing out.

One of my favorite images from making films comes from shooting a scene with Tony, running through a glacier-fed stream, pursued by Bart the Bear. When we began the picture, the temperature was in the low seventies and we wore bug repellent. Weeks later, we wore thermal linings in our costumes as we spent the day in frigid water. Along the bank of the stream, the crew had situated a hot tub that we could jump into to stay warm between takes, as our costumes were already soaked through. I sat in that hot tub, smoking a great Cuban cigar and muttering, "Baubles and stones. White wine. Marbella." Here I was that little boy again, repeating the famous actor's lines. Only now, the famous actor was my costar and the lines were spoken to me over lunch. I'll never have it that good again. Not ever.

The final ten minutes of *The Edge* are the only piece of my own film work that I can ever watch and enjoy. The movie got decent reviews and made a nickel or two at the box office. I returned to Alberta for many years after the film wrapped to ski at Lake Louise, Kicking Horse, and Banff. I loved it so much, I thought I'd move there.

There was a period during the '90s when, if I asked a question, made a request, or sought a piece of information, before my sentence was even finished, the response would be, "Of course, Mr. Baldwin, of course." After *The Edge*, things would change, irrevocably, in my film career. In some ways that was a good thing, insofar as the less power you believe you have, the simpler life can get. And simple is good in acting. It just took me a bit more time to learn that.

12

So Long as You Know

After *The Edge*, I grew tired of the limitations of studio moviemaking. And just in time, as that system had grown tired of me as well. You have to sell tickets. There are actors who are drug-addled, fornicating madmen. They are bullies who not only lack talent but also create some degree of difficulty wherever they work. There are actresses whose vanity and lack of self-awareness are so dense, you could split the atoms of their egos and fuel a reactor. Their behavior makes little difference, so long as their movies make money. On the other hand, you can be professional, committed, appropriately curious, hardworking, and collegial. But if the movies tank, you're out.

The Edge was not successful in dollar terms. I asked my then agent, John Burnham at William Morris, if producers and execs would shun me because of the difficulties I'd had on films like *The Marrying Man*, *The Juror* (another incompatible director situation), and *The Edge*, as well as walking away from the Clancy series. Burnham's reply was a memorable one: "It's not that when they think of you, they hate you. They just don't think of you at all." Someone's got to kiss the girl, blow up the bridge, punch the villain, deliver the stirring speech, fire some type of weapon, and then kiss the girl again. I was thirty-eight years old, with mixed success at best, and the studio movie business was moving on with other people.

When you are an apple that falls from the studio movie star tree and you're ready to be made into the applesauce of the independent film world, the transition is frustrating and humbling, the greatest frustration being not the smaller budgets but the more limited time allowed to make a movie. Indie filmmaking means less time. A lot less. But it also presents a greater opportunity to produce your own films. Up to that point, I had exhibited only a slight interest in developing my own film projects. I had a company. I had creative partners. For a while, my partner was Walter Hill's wife, Hildy Gottlieb, herself a successful agent at ICM, and a great colleague. But convincing studios and production companies, large and small, to gamble their resources on your belief about what an audience will want to see is the most difficult job in the business.

When you are Hanks or Will Smith, you are the powerful engine in an expensive machine. Everyone around you wants to keep you tuned, ready, and on the track, because you usually win. There is no shortage of people poised to buy what you and your team create. Everyone else, however, is just another merchant in an unimaginably competitive market. In the beginning of my film career, my desire to make the most of whatever role I was given was my sole focus. The business side of the movies was unfamiliar to me, and I never had a serious thought about writing, directing, or producing, where many actors eventually focus their energies. I felt the job was to act, to improve at that and to grow. Anything else seemed like a distraction.

For those who find that acting simply isn't enough, the technical components of filmmaking are limitless and alluring. And the camera is king. On sets, over the years, some of the most brilliant cinematographers in history would nod at me and wave me over to the camera to look through the lens at their composition. Like when you're invited into the cockpit by the pilot, you rarely, if ever, say no. But none of this proximity to the "film school" side of the business sparked any interest in me. Talk of lenses and cutting points and which side of the room the camera must be on went in one ear and out the other. Often, the camera team informed me of some technical adjustment or realignment they wanted to make, and I'd joke that I was in the "Acting Division," while they were the "Science Division." On the set of *It's Complicated*, the great John Toll might turn to me and say, "The shot works better from over here." Or, "We need to change lenses because I think it looks better on a forty." I'd wink at him and say, "So long as *you* know." By this, I meant to indicate that the technical side had little or no effect on what I was about to do. My awareness of the camera and my relationship to it were my own obligation. Like nearly all good film actors I have worked with, over time I developed an innate, acute sense of how to adjust for the camera. The job was to act with others in a scene, but also, to the best of my ability, factor in the camera and, thus, the audience itself. The camera is the proscenium, and I always feel compelled to triangulate my performance with it and the other actors. Wherever the camera is, I'll unconsciously adjust to it.

There are not many directors who shoot films allowing for actors to simply "behave" in front of a camera in a realistic way, like Cassavetes or many of the great Europeans, and even Spielberg in films like *Saving Private Ryan*. Certainly those directors frame their shots deliberately, but inside of those frames, there is a latitude that is rare to find in conventional moviemaking. The normal order of business is for the actor and director to create the scene inside of an "invisible cage" imposed by the limitations of the camera, lighting, sets, and the script itself. Before you roll the camera, an Arthur Murray–esque pattern of preapproved moves is designed to lead you from one prearranged mark to the next. Once that staging is agreed upon, you are usually asked to re-create it, over and over again, varying only your intent, intonation, pace, and physicality.

As I became more experienced, the expectation was that I would bring more variety to the individual takes. If I asked the director if I could try something, the answer was usually yes, giving me more freedom to contribute ideas about scripts and character. A scene can be shot in a week or a day or an hour. Therefore, due to the normal limitations of time, my mind was often on simply manipulating the lines. I'd think, "How smart is the character? Is he a good talker, like Bill Clinton or Noël Coward, with the words at his fingertips? Or must he dig for the language to express himself, halting along the way? Is he passionate or private? Or both?"

I had to develop some relatively quick, handy ways to build a character, assuming that most directors would offer me little—and that the shooting would often be rushed. I saw early on that the production rarely rushed the cameramen's work. Directors and cinematographers are engaged in a marriage. Shooting a film is an enormous jigsaw puzzle that director and cinematographer are primarily charged with figuring out. In this process, the actors are like midwives of creativity. Thus, the technicians want to get the performances over with as quickly as possible. In many of my films, acting would eventually become about delivering lines smartly and with as little fuss as possible.

In the 1980s, I met Sol Yurick through my friend Ronnie Dobson. Yurick, a wiry, rabbinical man, had written the great novel *The Warriors* in 1965, which Walter Hill had made into a wonderful film in 1979. Yurick also wrote the novel *Richard A* and the unusual short story "The King of Malaputa." In 1996, my company acquired the rights to Yurick's 1966 novel *Fertig*, and adapted it into a film starring Ben Kingsley, Amy Irving, and me. My friend David Black wrote the script for the film, whose title was changed to *The Confession*, and won the Writers Guild Award for best adapted screenplay the following year. The film tells the story of a man, Harry Fertig (played by Kingsley), who believes that certain hospital staff and administrators are directly responsible for the death of his young son through negligence. In what he sees as a biblical act of revenge, Fertig murders these staff members. He is represented by a conflicted lawyer named Roy Bleakie (played by me), and at trial he insists on pleading guilty and serving out whatever sentence befalls him in memory of his son.

This was the first film I produced, and I found it a difficult undertaking. Securing a budget, a director, a decent crew, the right cast, and appropriate New York locations was a job that ultimately distracted from my work on-screen. Add to that the fact that my part just wasn't written as well as Ben's role. Bleakie's conflicts and inner turmoil didn't come through as clearly as I had imagined, or maybe I just wasn't very good. I began to believe that I didn't have the ability to do both jobs. I certainly lacked the desire. I am continually amazed by and have the deepest amount of respect for someone like Warren Beatty, who has developed great scripts with top writers, then directed those films while starring in them alongside some of the world's greatest actors. For his efforts on *Reds*, he won an Oscar for best director and was nominated for best picture and best actor. You must have abundant talent and drive to do that. Beatty once told me, "Until you take ultimate responsibility for all of it, you're going to end up frustrated." But I lacked the patience to emulate him in that regard. I wanted the right producing partner who could speak for me in all things and protect me so I could just act. But the best producers in the movie business want to work with the actors who bring with them the resources necessary to improve their odds.

Perhaps I was wrong, however. Perhaps expanding my curiosity and responsibilities would have benefited me. Every take in front of the camera is an opportunity. But if acting is the only card you have to play, that can be a lot of pressure. I tried to get to a place where the work was its own reward. I wanted the results to become secondary. Free of the phone calls on Saturday mornings, when agents reported the disappointing news about a particular film, I could enjoy acting more. By the late '90s, I embarked on a string of leading and supporting roles that gained little attention, though each offered its own charms and gratifications. I want to mention a few of those and why I think they were ultimately worthwhile.

> *Thick as Thieves* (1999): In which the wonderful gentleman Scott Sanders directed his own screenplay. I had a ball shooting with Andre Braugher (if talent were the only requirement, he'd be the biggest star in the world), Bruce Greenwood, Michael Jai White, and the nonpareil of independent cinema, Richard Edson.

Notting Hill (1999): Where, for just one day, on a set in London, I got to breathe the same air as the remarkable Julia Roberts.

Outside Providence (1999): A funny script from the Farrelly brothers directed by the very talented Michael Corrente. Jon Abrahams as "Drugs" Delaney steals the movie with the dramatization of his letter to his friend Dunph at boarding school.

Thomas and the Magic Railroad (2000): Britt Allcroft (who adapted the Thomas video series and the film from the post–World War II books by the Reverend Wilbert Awdry) was one of the kindest and loveliest people I've ever worked with. I've often had my eye out for children's programming because of my own kids. Working with Britt was one of the best experiences I've ever had as Britt coaxes the child out of each cast member, which I found sweet and fun. Plus, I got to shoot a movie with Peter Fonda!

Nuremberg (2000): Canadian production rules demanded we use a French-speaking Quebecois crew and director (Yves Simoneau), which added a layer of difficulty to shooting this miniseries for TNT. But the opportunity to be on camera with Chris Plummer and Max von Sydow was enough to make it all worthwhile.

State and Main (2000): Putting together a great ensemble cast is difficult, and on this film, we were very lucky. To get to work every day with the likes of David Paymer, Bill Macy, Philip Seymour Hoffman, and Sarah Jessica Parker was a rare experience for me. Mamet writes great comedy, and this is one of the few of my own movies that I can stand watching.

Pearl Harbor (2001): At three hours, the movie was severely bloated, in my opinion, and Michael Bay reminded me of the G. D. Spradlin character from the movie *North Dallas Forty* to Jerry Bruckheimer's Steve Forrest: two demanding men who expected their stars to leave it all on the field. But Ben Affleck is a prince. And the chance to research my character, Major Jimmy Doolittle, and his career in aviation was a wonderful bonus.

The Royal Tenenbaums (2001): I'm not in this movie; I just provide incidental narration.

But it's so damn good that I like listing it among my credits. Wes Anderson pulled off something amazing here. After Hackman spent the '90s smirking through most of his roles, Anderson somehow got Hackman to stifle that impulse, and the result was one of Hackman's best performances ever. Which is saying a lot.

Path to War (2002): I got a call from my dear friend John Frankenheimer—he of *The Manchurian Candidate*, *Birdman of Alcatraz*, *Seven Days in May*, and *Seconds*, to name a few—for an HBO film about Lyndon Johnson and the escalation of Vietnam. This would be John's last film. What an honor. He was a great director as well as urbane and funny. Again, the research for this film was fascinating, and I owe the late Richard Holbrooke a note of thanks for his insights into my character, Robert McNamara, and his career.

The Cooler (2003): When I read the script and got to the page where my character kicks a pregnant woman in the stomach, I asked my agent, "Don't I have enough troubles?" He told me to keep reading. Eventually, I found that writers

Frank Hannah and Wayne Kramer had a great movie. Kramer, who directed, was prepared, insightful, and fantastic to shoot with. His cinematographer, James Whitaker, shot efficiently and everything looked great. Again, working with Bill Macy, a great actor who keeps you on your toes, is always fun. I was nominated for an Oscar for the role and lost to that fucking Tim Robbins for that fucking *Mystic River* directed by that fucking Clint Eastwood. Just kidding.

Second Nature (2003): My divorce custody case exploded as I boarded the plane for London to shoot this film. A great script by the talented E. Max Frye (who wrote *Something Wild* and, later, *Foxcatcher*) gave us a real opportunity. But the combination of all-day shoots and painful nightly conference calls with my divorce lawyer took its toll on me. My company produced the film, but I couldn't shake the distractions I carried to work. One great memory, however, was meeting Sir John Mills while we filmed in Denham.

The Cat in the Hat (2003): Bo Welch, one of Hollywood's most prolific and admired set designers, made his directorial debut here. I had worked with Bo on *Beetlejuice* and seen why everyone loves him. The film was a disappointment in several ways, but it was nice to shoot on a lot (for a change) and watch them spend a gagillion dollars on costumes, sets, and all things Seussian.

Along Came Polly (2004): The draw here was the writing of John Hamburg, who also directed. This is another of those films in which I played a supporting role to a big-ticket comedy star (Myers or Carrey or, in this case, Stiller), which is never easy, because you're not there to make people laugh—they are. So your scenes are cut. But at least the pressure's not on you.

The Last Shot (2004): Jeff Nathanson, a great writer (*Catch Me If You Can*), made his directing debut on this film. I had always wanted to work with Matthew Broderick, and a bonus was working with Tony Shalhoub, surely one of the most talented men I've worked with. If you want a sample, check out the scene in Tommy Sanz's living room while he watches rugby. Shalhoub's performance as a benched mobster is as dry as sheetrock and incredibly funny.

The Aviator (2004): I couldn't miss the opportunity to work with Scorsese, and to watch Leo at work, however briefly, was just as important. In his film roles, DiCaprio takes full advantage of the opportunities showered on him. He is a great film actor. And although the movie was a tad voluptuous, the fact that Marty lost best picture and best director to *Million Dollar Baby* is another example of Oscar weirdness.

Elizabethtown (2005): Filming this movie was a bit of a blur, as my personal life was beginning to suck the oxygen out of everything else. But Cameron Crowe's writing is so fresh and weird, while he is perhaps the greatest gentleman in the directing business. I'd go anywhere to work with him again.

Mini's First Time (2006): In this indie comedy-drama, my character is having an affair with his stepdaughter. I was forty-seven, and it never occurred to me to ask how old Nikki Reed was. When I found out, just as we finished, that she was seventeen, I flipped out on the producers, who had told me something different. In any case, Nikki is a wonderful actress who has become a steadfast advocate for animal rights, which I admire her for greatly.

The Departed (2006): Scorsese came calling again, and this time my character and dialogue had a bit more crackle. Marty won the Oscar (finally) for this film, and although I'll never play a lead role in a movie directed by someone of his caliber, it was a thrill just to spend those couple of weeks in Boston with that cast. FYI: Bostonians don't approve of your accent even if you grew up in Boston!!

The Good Shepherd (2006): It is not easy to have a director approach you with his notes after a take when that director is Robert De Niro. As I looked into his face and heard that unmistakable voice, I saw an onslaught of movie moments streaming in my mind. The movie itself, I think, suffered from Matt Damon's signature warmth and humanity, which colored his character, the embodiment of American exceptionalism. The role required a screen persona of cascading whiteness who had performed a conscience-ectomy on himself, like William Hurt.

Prior to my divorce, I could name every film I had made and in what order. After 2000, that became impossible. One thing all of these disparate films have in common is that I remember only a few things about each of them. This is a natural consequence of getting older as that list grows longer. But my fight for custody of Ireland was like fighting cancer. It hung over every relationship, holiday, and job. All of my actions, every plan I made, every detail, was completely dictated by the chance of seeing my daughter. Often those plans were jettisoned at the last minute, in complete violation of the court's order. I was separated from Kim in December of 2000. By the end of 2005, I was battered and numb. During this period, a whole host of other ancillary types of jobs started to pop up, work I took just so I could stay home in New York or LA. Voice-overs, sitcoms, guest starring with Jimmy Caan on his show *Las Vegas*, you name it. I didn't want ever to miss a shot to see Ireland because I was in Prague or Sydney. I rearranged everything so I wouldn't lose a single visit.

During my visits with her, Ireland and I would lie on the floor of her bedroom. We'd make a bed out of every blanket we could find and put pillows up against her dresser. We'd watch her favorite shows, *The Fairly OddParents* or *The Powerpuff Girls.* Not a lot was said during these viewings. My job was to simply keep the healthy snacks and watered-down juices coming. Before long, Kim would emerge in the doorway, glaring and tapping her watch to indicate that it was time for Ireland to be bathed and gotten ready for bed. I try to remember, when I'm with my young children now, how precious these moments are. After I was separated, there were times I would have traded anything to be back on the floor of Ireland's bedroom watching *Dexter's Laboratory.*

The love of a parent for a child is ineffable. When I think of all that I missed, of the chances to be a father to my first child and how much of that was stolen from me by some hateful, rapacious lawyers or cowardly judges, I'm overwhelmed by a great loss of faith. I wrote a book about my divorce called *A Promise to Ourselves,* which was the cri de coeur of a father who is alienated not only by his ex but also by the divorce-industrial complex, including the courts themselves. One of the more gratifying experiences of my life was to have fathers, and even some women who had suffered at the hands of that system, thank me for the book. It's something I'm very proud of.

When things did not go my way, when one indignity after another piled up until I couldn't take it another minute, bad things happened, for which I have no one to blame but myself. In 2007, at the height of that battle, I left a very angry voicemail message for my daughter that my ex-wife and her lawyers then released to the media. Like rubbernecking drivers making their way past a serious accident, news and entertainment programs played it over and over again. Commentators like Nancy Grace stated that the tape should affect the outcome of my custody case. Some years later, *Entertainment Tonight* saw fit to dedicate a segment to the "anniversary" of its release. And even though I had been led to believe, by virtue of my employment at the time on *30 Rock*, that I was part of the "NBC Family," Matt Lauer invited Harvey Levin, the intrepid reporter and erstwhile attorney, on to the *Today* show to discuss the release of the tape. The show only contacted me after Levin was done giving his views. I haven't appeared on the *Today* show since.

If the goal of my ex and her lawyers was to damage or ruin my relationship with my daughter, then I certainly gave them the ammunition to do that with. My friends and family, the people closest to me who actually understood the situation, knew that the words on that tape were actually aimed at someone else. But as a therapist later told me, correctly, "If you hadn't left the message, none of this would be happening." In all honesty, my relationship with my daughter was permanently harmed by that episode. And in that sense, my ex-wife and her lawyers succeeded. I fully expected Ireland to move to Paris or London or somewhere else far away to attend school. Or head to India to do relief work the moment she was old enough to get far away from both of her parents who, as she would rightfully believe, had allowed bitter resentments and egos to overwhelm their love for their child.

My relationship with Ireland has healed. But just as something that has been broken is never quite the same, the fragile years of childhood that are battered by high-conflict divorce are irreversibly affected. Divorce itself is child abuse. I tell friends and loved ones now that if they have to split up, to know that any failure to achieve "collaborative divorce" will take a toll that will last forever. I think the worst thing one can do is to put a child in the middle of these battles. That is what I did. And I am reminded of it and I am sorry for it every day.

The voicemail and its aftermath killed a number of activities for me, and my ongoing support for specific issues and particular candidates was one of those casualties. On a beautiful summer afternoon in 2007, Senator Barack Obama was entering the lobby of my Central

Park West apartment just as I was leaving. He was no doubt heading to meet potential Democratic supporters, which my building had in number. It had been only a few months since the voicemail had leaked, and I wasn't feeling like someone you'd want to be standing alongside if you were running for the highest office in the land, but I nodded to Obama and he smiled back. I have the highest admiration for President Obama, and I believe he served his country with an abundance of intelligence and grace. But at that point, I couldn't imagine he or anyone else wanted my support, so I'd stopped offering it. I've often regretted any lost opportunities during Obama's years in the White House, the chance to work with his administration on behalf of the arts or children or the environment. I simply felt that my family life and reputation were in tatters.

I found that the world of independent film was changing underneath my feet as well. Production companies were offering interesting roles to good actors, but the budgets were plummeting and so were the paychecks, unless you ranked among the biggest stars. It appeared that Hollywood had come to heed Katzenberg's prescient admonitions regarding the old, unsustainable economics of the movie business. TV was becoming the only place you could get paid, if getting paid was part of your plan. A great migration was oc-

curring, as TV, and especially cable and then streaming services, gambled on the more complex, darker
material that both film audiences and actors sought.
People spoke of a new "Golden Age of Television," and
I had seen the example of Jimmy Gandolfini, who I had
worked with on *Streetcar* in 1992. By 2006, Jimmy was
heading toward the end of his remarkable run on *The
Sopranos.* He'd won every award, the show had made
him rich, and the role of Tony Soprano put him on the
map as one of the most respected actors in the business.

In early 2006, before the voicemail incident, I
pitched a television pilot, a political drama, to FX,
and their executives sounded inclined to make it. As
we began the most preliminary talks about the project,
Lorne Michaels called me. He said he had a project—a
sitcom—that he was producing for NBC and he wanted
to cast me in the ensemble. Here it was: a job with a
regular schedule that meant I could reliably travel to
LA to see Ireland, who was eleven years old. Lorne, as
you may know, is rather persuasive. And the next thing
I knew, I was drinking an iced coffee on the set of his
latest comedy venture, embarking on a role that would
bring me something I hadn't had in a long while: an
audience.

13

Lemon, There Is a Word

Whenever anyone told me I was funny, I was reminded of when people in high school tell someone that he can hit a fastball or shoot a basketball well. Then he gets to college and everyone is big and fast and strong. After that, if he turns professional, everyone around him seems inhuman. They're the biggest, fastest, and strongest. That's what *SNL* was like for me. The worst idea the writers there came up with was funnier than the best thing I could think up. My definition of funny changed while working with them. If people think I can say a line in a way that gets a laugh, I'll take it. But I'm not funny. The *SNL* writers are funny. Tina Fey is funny. Conan O'Brien is funny. You're only funny if you can write the material. What I do is acting.

The first time I hosted *SNL*, surrounded by some

of the most talented young comedians in the business, I was scared to death. Luckily, it occurred to me that, because I did not have an iconic career in films, because I wasn't Schwarzenegger or Stallone or someone who invited a parody of their work, I was better off trying to just be a member of the company. I would play the soldier, the teacher, the priest, or the NPR guest in the sketch and do my best to just fit in. Once I did that, things got a bit easier. The cast wants the host to succeed, to make the show a good one, so they are very generous and helpful. The first *SNL* cast I worked with included Tim Meadows, Kevin Nealon, Jan Hooks, and the late Phil Hartman. Over the years, I worked with several different *SNL* casts and some of those performers went on to great careers in film and TV. But none was funnier than Hartman, who is perhaps the only person to crack me up during the live show. Phil could channel any kind of character, from smart to dumb to truly insane. He was a wonderful actor. When I heard about his death, I was stunned and sickened.

After the third or fourth time I hosted (I've been given many chances to improve), I started to get the hang of it. Along the way, I had the opportunity to do the show with some of the biggest musical acts in the business. One year I hosted when Whitney Houston was the musical guest. After her dress rehearsal, I was introduced to her backstage. "You truly are the most talented singer out there today," I said, a bit starstruck. She paused and said, "I know, baby," then walked on. In 1993, I hosted the show when Paul McCartney was performing and met the warm and down-to-earth Linda McCartney backstage. We briefly talked about her animal-rights work, since I had been introduced to the issue while living with Kim. Then she asked me, "Have you met Paul?" "No," I told her. "Well, go over and talk with him. He'd like that." The idea that I would approach McCartney like he was any other *SNL* music act was unimaginable to me. The music of the Beatles and McCartney's solo career, along with other Brits like the Rolling Stones, the Who, and Led Zeppelin, made up the bulk of the vinyl and cassettes I collected back in my youth with the precious money I could spare. When I was in high school, a guy in my neighborhood had sold me his Acoustic Research speakers. Normally, they would have been prohibitively expensive, but he said he was desperate financially, and had to unload them. Because I couldn't afford headphones, I would lie on the floor of my bedroom late at night, with the giant ARs framing my head, listening to *Houses of the Holy, Quadrophenia, Got Live If You Want It!,* and *Abbey Road.* Now, the musician who wrote and sang so many of those songs that I played over and over again, sprawled on that floor, was right in front of me. The guy who sang "I Saw Her Standing There," "Blackbird," and "She Came in Through the Bathroom Window," with a range from "Helter Skelter" to "Yesterday," was twenty feet from me, and his wife was telling me, "Go ahead. Go and talk with him." When I finally did approach him, he was as charming as you'd expect. No one in show business has had to manage the feelings of his overwhelmed fans as much as McCartney. I realized then that this is the greatest thing about the business. One day, you're on the floor, moaning, "Aaaaaaahh-hhh, look at all the lonely people." The next, you get to host your favorite comedy variety show and the musical act is Paul McCartney.

Hosting several episodes of *SNL* over the years exposed me to what good comedy writing is, but it didn't make me want to run out and star in a sitcom. I would joke with Lorne about joining the cast, but it wasn't until 2005, when I guest-starred on *Will & Grace*, that I began to think a TV comedy might fit into my ever-changing plan. I had played a part on *Friends* in 2002. I loved working with Lisa Kudrow and thought Jennifer Aniston was a doll. However, we began shooting the episode just a day or two after it was announced that the cast had signed on for season nine at a million dollars per episode for each of the show's stars, and everyone seemed a bit distracted. On the set, I'd barely spoken with the producers, who were naturally focused only on their celebrated ensemble. Later, when I taped *Will & Grace*, the set was looser. The producers, Max Mutchnick and David Kohan, seemed as available to their guests as their stars did. The *Will & Grace* shoot also enabled me to talk with Megan Mullally and pick her brains about the realities of shooting a half-hour sitcom.

I have always been madly in love with Megan Mullally. Some have compared her to Madeline Kahn, and although I hear some echoes, Megan is such an original in terms of her timing, her warmth, and her mixture of insanity and sexiness. Like Megan, Jane Krakowski went on to nail the self-absorbed, horny femme fatale on *30 Rock*. In my mind, there is a line from Marilyn Monroe to Madeline Kahn to Megan to Jane. Scattered in between are a lot of talented female comics and actresses who are scoring in film and TV, of all ethnicities and ages, like Rosie Perez, Wanda Sykes, Sarah Silverman, and Tig Notaro. But with her high-pitched voice and loopy delivery, I've always found Megan irresistible.

One day on the set, she outlined the sitcom schedule for me. In so many words, she said that they started on Mondays and read the latest script for a couple of hours, then went home. On Tuesdays, they rehearsed for a couple of hours, then left while the writers rewrote the script. Wednesdays, they rehearsed and camera-blocked all day, and the same on Thursdays. Thursday nights, they loaded in the audience and taped the show. Then they went home and got a big check. This was no chain gang. The day of the taping, we stumbled our way through a dress rehearsal and then performed one of the few live *Will & Grace* episodes ever produced. Like the *SNL* cast, Sean Hayes, Eric McCormack, and Debra Messing were welcoming and patient with me.

Television moves along. On films, you can sit around interminably. You hope the result is worth it. But you also think about all of the weddings, family gatherings, and overall moments of your life that you miss while shooting. Working with the legendary director Jim Burrows, who oversaw all 194 episodes of *Will & Grace*, made me think of the live, four-camera comedy like a miniplay. We were in the theater, playing to an audience, only we taped it, edited it, and ran it on TV to a few million people. The audience for one night of a hit sitcom is bigger than the entire run of a hit play. Funny people like Megan, the schedule, directors like Burrows—it all started to add up.

When *Will & Grace* was over, I thought about my arrangement with Ireland. I realized I might as well leave open the possibility for sitcom work if it came my way. My life at the time was flying to LA every other Friday. I'd head from the airport to pick up Ireland at school and take her to eat somewhere. Weekends at the time involved shopping, movies, lunches, and dance classes with her friends, while I stood off to the side. Divorce or no, a father is a chauffeur and chancellor of the exchequer to the mother's role of queen. But, as all parents will no doubt acknowledge, we are there for their benefit, not the other way around. I would wait for and gratefully accept whatever crumbs of attention came my way. On Mondays, I would read to Ireland's class through a volunteer program the school offered for available parents. By ten a.m., I was in a car on my way to the airport. I did that every other weekend during the school year. Eighteen times between Labor Day and Memorial Day. I spent more time on planes and in airports than I ever imagined possible, as travel seemed to take over my life. Ireland would sometimes opt out of our weekend early or wouldn't show up at all, but I kept coming. I didn't know what else to do. Like a dumb animal, I had only one thought, one gear. I wanted to see Ireland. To make her laugh, to do for her, to love her.

When I first met Tina Fey—beautiful and brunette, smart and funny, at turns smug and diffident and completely uninterested in me or anything I had to say—I had the same reaction that I'm sure many men and women have: I fell in love. Tina was then the head writer at *Saturday Night Live*, and I was hosting that week's show. The writers and producers were packed, impossibly, into Lorne's satellite office overlooking Studio 8H, where *SNL* is produced. (This was once Toscanini's private office when he directed the NBC orchestra in 8H. The building has quite a history.) When Lorne finished giving his notes after the dress rehearsal, I asked Marci Klein, the show's talent coordinator, if Tina was single. She pointed to a man sitting along the wall. Or maybe he was standing? This was Jeff Richmond, Tina's husband. Jeff is diminutive. Tina describes him as "travel-size." When I saw him, I thought, "What's she doing with him?" With his spools of curly brown hair and oversized eyes, Jeff resembles a Margaret Keane painting. When I ended up working with the two of them years later, I changed that to "What's he doing with her?" Jeff, who was the talented music supervisor on *30 Rock*, is as loose and outgoing as Tina is cautious and dry. "Just remember one thing," Lorne said. "She's German."

30 Rock was a work in progress in its first season, like many hit shows. If you watch a series like *Will & Grace* or *The Sopranos* in their first seasons, the performances are nearly unrecognizable a year later, as the cast slowly perfects their characterizations. The character of Jack Donaghy is a guy from a background much like my own. After attending Princeton, he is drafted by the Dallas Cowboys of the business world, General Electric. GE owned the NBC television network when we started *30 Rock*, so Jack is called upon to apply the expertise that enabled him to dominate the microwave-programming division to the task of TV programming. It's the "Fairfield way," a reference to the company's then Connecticut headquarters. GE would "widgetize" comedy. Turbines, locomotives, comedy shows, it's all the same. Just apply the tenets of Six Sigma, Jack Welch's favorite management tools, and a GE exec will conquer the field.

An ensemble show will thrive only if you have the right ensemble. I know that sounds obvious, but if you change one element, change any role, you may not have the same success. I've read that the Beatles were offered the services of any drummer in London to replace Ringo Starr, who was viewed as the weak link in the band in terms of musicianship. At one point, Starr was called away to honor a previous contract to perform with another group. One of London's top percussionists showed up at the studio to play with the Beatles, who had to finish recording an album. "The guy was the greatest drummer in London," the source said. "And they didn't want him. It had to be Ringo. The band said it had to be those four and no one else."

30 Rock, of course, isn't as culturally relevant as the Beatles. But similarly, I think *30 Rock* had to be Tina, me, Jane, Tracy Morgan, and Jack McBrayer, along with a half dozen others in smaller roles, or it would not have flown. The show was a critical hit, but never a ratings juggernaut. Shows like *Big Bang Theory* and *Modern Family* eclipsed *30 Rock* by wide margins in terms of audience. But *30 Rock*, while taking more than its share of awards over the years, also benefited from being an industry darling. There are shows that people in the business don't watch that are nonetheless huge hits. Then there are shows like *The Larry Sanders Show* or *True Detective*, to name just two, that the people who make TV will follow. If I was at an industry event, often some exec from some media company would come up to me and say, "My son broke his leg skiing. He was in bed for two weeks. We binged every episode of *30 Rock*. Man, that show is funny!" I sometimes wondered if that contributed to keeping us on the air.

Jack McBrayer is a great actor. To play that modern-day Jim Nabors type, but with a twist of Tommy Smothers thrown in, is not easy to do, and I think Jack killed it. Any goodness or heart that an episode required, Jack could be relied upon to deliver it. Jane is an award-winning theater actress who also had her successes on TV, such as *Ally McBeal,* but *30 Rock* was the culmination of a lot of years of good work for Jane. It gave her a reservoir of funny lines and situations, and like any great performer, Jane made the most of them. Whenever I had scenes with Jane, I was excited. She's a wonderful acting partner and can play anything. Tracy Morgan is . . . Tracy Morgan. The persona of the playful, devilish man-child had been nailed by Flip Wilson and other comics, black and white, but many of those were, ultimately, more devil than child. Tracy often sees the world like a little boy. He maintained a sweetness and innocence that could astound me, right up to the next barrage of "motherfuckers" or some sexually graphic imagery that would come flying out of his mouth. But he's an original.

Tina had an enormous level of responsibility on *30 Rock.* The roles of writer, producer, and star are a lot to handle. Over the life of the show, she was honored for all of them. But Tina will tell you she is a writer at heart. Beyond dressing up for red carpets, hosting awards shows, or starring in films, Tina, I believe, is more comfortable in a room full of clever people doing what she does so well. Our characters, Liz and Jack, never consummated their relationship. There was, in place of that, a genuine respect, fondness, and, ultimately, love for a trusted and irreplaceable colleague. For Jack, the only thing better than good sex was a good hire. Over the years, I had bitched and moaned, as only actors can, about being tied to a contract for a show that would never be my own. After season five, I wanted to quit. I came back for season six, had a great time, and was ready to sign for five more years. But a wise decision was made to shoot a tight thirteen episodes and go out head high. As we shot the series finale, on a December night in lower Manhattan, my building rush of nostalgia for the show hit its peak. Freezing my ass off on a boat floating in a marina in Battery Park City, Jack groped his way toward telling Liz he loved her. "Lemon, there is a word, a once special word, that has been tragically co-opted by the romance-industrial complex." That night was tough. The best job I ever had, that I will ever have, was over.

I was lucky to win several awards for *30 Rock*. I think the audience for Tina's writing was more discerning. When people paid a compliment to me about the show, it always began with "I never do this, but . . ." When actors can honestly believe that what they are doing is working, it's a great feeling. *30 Rock* gave me a level of confidence that had been missing in my work for quite some time. I owe that to Tina and the other cast and crew. I owe it to the incomparable Robert Carlock, Tina's right hand. I owe it to the other writers like John Riggi (the most lovable writer in the WGA), Jack Burditt, Matt Hubbard, Kay Cannon, Ron Weiner, Tracey Wigfield, Vali Chandrasekaran, Josh Siegal, and Colleen McGuinness, to name a few. Most of all, I owe it to Lorne. There is a saying in show business, "No one knows anything," an attempt to convey the inscrutability of show business and particularly the key to success. That line should be amended to read "except Lorne." Lorne is wise and discreet. He has walked a path in the industry that has made him one of the rare people I've met whom you would be lucky to know and blessed to receive advice from.

When high school ended, I didn't feel appropriately moved. I wasn't about to break out into a rendition of "Nothing" from *A Chorus Line*, but I didn't feel that this was the end of something important to me. It wasn't important. Same with college. I left GW for NYU, and as I said good-bye in DC to my graduating friends before I headed to New York, I felt detached and anxious. I didn't graduate with my class at NYU either. I went off to work as quickly as possible. But when *30 Rock* ended, all of the feelings one associates with the end of something seminal—feelings that I had missed or squandered earlier, that come from truly investing in an experience—finally came out. That was my graduation. I graduated from the University of Tina. Lutz and Grizz and Kevin and Judah and Katrina and Scott and Keith and Sue and Maulik were my classmates. I wanted to sing "To Sir with Love" to Lorne. Carlock gave me my diploma.

The year 2012 ended with the finale of *30 Rock*. I crossed into 2013 feeling good about myself, my work, and the future for the first time since 2007 and the voicemail issue. I had crawled out of a well and now wanted to enjoy my life in every simple way. *30 Rock* afforded me a lot of creative freedom. I wanted 2013 to be a new year filled with productivity, happiness, and success. And when things didn't go as planned, I could hear the voice of Joe Zarza saying, "Xander Baldwin . . . you're gonna learn everything the hard way."

14
So Long as I Know

When *30 Rock* ended in December of 2012, I was about to turn fifty-five years old. The show had provided me with a much-needed stability, not only in terms of work but also in terms of the goodwill that came with it. The consistency of my schedule became more precious to me as I got older. I had made a few movies between 2006 and 2012, while making *30 Rock*. Some were worthwhile, like *It's Complicated*. Working with Meryl Streep had always seemed like an unattainable wish, almost a dream. When that opportunity came around, I was overjoyed. Meryl is nine years older than me, so when Nancy Meyers offered me the role of Meryl's ex-husband, I thought about that for a bit. But Nancy pointed out that the leading men in Hollywood have no qualms about casting someone much younger as their love interest. Why should it be any different for the greatest actress of her generation? The notion of age didn't matter to me. It became clear, and more so once we began shooting, that my character was a man who was once in love with his ex-wife and who discovered that he was still in love with her. My job was to be in love with Meryl. That is not a difficult thing to do.

I made a movie called *Lymelife* with a wonderful writer-director named Derick Martini. The cast included Jill Hennessy, Cynthia Nixon, and Timothy Hutton, whose career I had long admired in films like Sidney Lumet's *Daniel* (see this movie) and *The Falcon and the Snowman*. The making of the film itself was an ongoing saga, where the cast was told to get ready to go to work, only to have the financing drop out at the last minute. The principal cast, which also included Rory and Kieran Culkin and Emma Roberts, stayed committed to the project through three such rounds of hope and eventual disappointment. When the money finally came through, I realized that this was the direction that much of independent filmmaking was going in. With their dreams of doing the creative work they had set out to do on the line, actors, directors, producers, and writers were calling it a victory simply when the movie got made.

That was no longer enough for me. So much change

was brewing in my life. I had dated my share of people since my divorce. I was with one woman in particular for quite some time. But while Ireland was a child, I convinced myself, rightly or not, that remarrying would have sent my daughter a signal that looked like abandonment. With all that had gone on in my relationship with Ireland, all of the unwanted public scrutiny and shame, I was certain that moving on would have only made it worse. When I ultimately told my girlfriend that I couldn't move forward, that I didn't want to get married again, she changed, dramatically. The relationship was then overwhelmed by mistrust and friction.

But life only moves forward. And, if we are lucky, someone comes along who reminds us of that. What I wanted in terms of romantic partners, before and after my divorce, always confounded me. A lot of push and pull out of fear, jealousy, and doubt. It's almost like I needed a sign. Then, on an unusually mild February evening in 2011, my friend Brendan and I were wandering around downtown with no destination in mind. Sarma Melngailis, the now infamous owner of Pure Food and Wine, was a friend of mine, and eventually, I would puzzle over why Brendan and I went into her restaurant, as I wasn't particularly craving the raw vegan menu. Did God want me to go there, to give me some precious opportunity? Some peace? A cleft in the rock of the world? I don't know. I do know that on very few occasions in my life I have met a truly extraordinary woman, singular in ways beyond the limitations of attraction, who seemed to have a light shining on her. Typically, there was some wall between her and me. Sometimes that woman was already married to someone else. I would hear God say to me, "Not now. Not this woman. You're not ready. Besides, I wouldn't do that to her." (God laughs.) "Perhaps at some point, when the time is right. I simply want you to see what someone truly special looks like. Not someone without faults or without their own past. But unlike anyone you've ever met. Someone who wouldn't hurt someone out of spite. Someone smart, opinionated, funny, caring, kind, evolved." The woman I met on Irving Place on February 18 was all of those things and much more. Suddenly, the idea of avoiding commitment, of not moving forward, seemed misguided. A risk-free life is not worth living.

I believe that things change only when we are truly ready for the change. We come to a situation or event that could be a great turning point in our lives having been prepared by both adversity and hope. And then, if you let it, the future just opens like a flower, becoming more beautiful every day. Hilaria and I moved in together in November and things progressed quite quickly after that. We were married on June 30, sixteen months after meeting. In December of 2012, Hilaria told me she was pregnant with our daughter, Carmen, so as we turned out the lights on *30 Rock*, an entirely new life was unfolding for me. I had embraced so many different activities and passions throughout my career, springing from not only real beliefs but also boredom and loneliness. I didn't have a family to come home to, so why not put on a tux, for the third time this week, and raise money for this group or cut this ribbon or perform a reading at this event? Now, my life with Hilaria and Carmen put me on a road that demanded more of my energy, perhaps all of it. The reality that I couldn't predict, let alone confirm, where I would be in six months became unworkable and foolish. My new family was my commitment, and the primacy of acting was in my rearview mirror.

I probably listen to radio more than any other medium, so I had flirted with doing a radio show for some time. The author Lisa Birnbach was a friend of mine, and after a twenty-minute phone chat with Lisa, I would say to her, "We should be broadcasting these calls." Lisa possesses a quick wit like Tina, and she could dispense an inexhaustible quantity of it. I approached Scott Greenstein from Sirius to find out what the radio market was like for mere mortals like me who, unlike Howard Stern, could not command tens of millions of dollars. I thought that the hours involved, the New York base, and the relatively simple production demands were what I needed. As not all movie opportunities were going to be as exciting as going to Rome with Woody Allen or as interesting as watching Julianne Moore and Cate Blanchett give Oscar-winning performances, radio seemed a viable option even before I had met Hilaria.

I concocted a half-baked Howard Stern–knockoff show, with Lisa and me as hosts. We would have a cast of a couple of comedians, a culture editor, a news anchor, and various guests. I wanted to bring on a young guy we'd call "The Kid." We'd give him a credit card and some cash (a radio-level expense account), then turn him loose on Manhattan nightlife. The object was for The Kid to spend the night doing everything that Lisa and I were too old to do. Openings, exhibits, theater, galleries, movies, parties, clubs, clubs, clubs. I batted this idea around with a couple of friends who, as I remember it, looked at me in a way that said, "Why do you want to do radio?"

I got a call from Kathie Russo, a veteran radio producer and the widow of the actor Spalding Gray. Kathie listened to my idea and essentially talked me out of it (too much production work to write a daily show à la Stern) and talked me into a podcast with me at a microphone interviewing people. Lorne Michaels would often say, "It's like that thing . . ." and then go on to make some comparison, so I considered the title *It's Like That Thing*. I settled on *Here's the Thing*, which everyone says in conversation. We began in 2011. As far as my distributor, WNYC, was concerned, I would use the enormous Show Business Chums directory that I had in my rolltop desk and call all my pals in Hollywood, New York, and London. We did a few test interviews, some by phone. One such "phoner" was with Wyoming senator Alan Simpson. Being unable to see him in person, however, hampered my ability to steer the conversation in any perceptible direction, and Simpson came off like Ross Perot, muttering a lot of non sequitur folksiness. We never did another interview again that wasn't face-to-face. The first show that we posted online was with Michael Douglas, recorded in his New York home. Douglas is a prince whose career I have long admired, not to mention my worship of his dad. Not a bad start.

Right away, I liked doing the show. People ask me why I do it and the answer is that it's storytelling in its own right. I want to tell their stories: Peter Frampton, Herb Alpert, Rosie O'Donnell, George Stephanopoulos . . . If, during our talk, my own experiences overlapped theirs, so be it. I also wanted to interview people in the way that I wanted to be interviewed. I wanted a longer format, not like morning talk shows where the guest is on and off in six minutes after a series of prerehearsed exchanges. I wanted spontaneity. I wanted the guests to share what they wanted to share, without feeling pursued or judged. I had sat in interviews with venues like the *New York Times* where the assumption is always that the *Times* is doing you a favor. You're taught to believe that everyone needs the approval of the *Times*, so you try to win over some smug writer who sits, coiled and unimpressed. Until you don't. (I thought an effective way the *Times* could conquer their recent financial troubles would be to charge people a fee to have their name not mentioned in the paper.)

We recorded nearly all of our guests for an hour. Sometimes longer. No one is interested in my guests more than I am. I am, openly, a fan. I could have listened to Thom Yorke all day. We podcasted an interview with Billy Joel that was, I believe, unedited. Just the two of us, bullshitting, for over an hour. I began to think that bullshitting with the likes of Billy Joel was something I could do full-time. The deal with WNYC wasn't bad. It wasn't great either. I thought about the straightforwardness of the old *Tomorrow* show, with

Tom Snyder. Perhaps I'd have a "ninja" set, like Charlie Rose, with the perimeter blacked out. No audience. Quiet. Real. Not screaming crowds as if we were on a roller coaster. I pitched the idea to Lorne.

While I was shooting *Rock of Ages* in Fort Lauderdale, I was invited to a conference of NBC executives at the Universal theme park in Orlando, Florida. TV executives who are paid a lot of money to run large divisions of broadcast and cable networks have a self-regard normally confined to former presidents. Indeed, their jobs put them in a rarified group. In Orlando, however, it was interesting to watch a gathering of relaxed, confident men talk about the business of television almost entirely devoid of the topic of content. In my brief evening among them, there wasn't a single question about what I wanted to do or why. The concept that nobody knows anything took on a new meaning. How can you fire an exec over content when the subject never comes up? Executives at this level simply hire people to brief them on the creative worthiness of a project. Many of them didn't watch or even like TV. Television programming was just a product sold by companies like Comcast, and as with any other network, they couldn't have cared less what was on TV, to a degree. A time slot was like a piece of real estate. And like retail landlords, they just wanted to collect the highest rent possible.

The proposal was to give me a weekly slot on Friday nights at 12:30. It was explained that every show in the Friday 12:30 slot, on each network, was underperforming in terms of ratings. Once Fallon arrived to replace Leno, and Seth Meyers replaced Jimmy at 12:30, the network would consider giving me a crack at Seth's Friday slot. Or, if Carson Daly returned for another season of his show *Last Call*, I might be given Friday nights at 1:30. None of this transpired, of course, because while NBC Entertainment was, understandably, focused on launching Jimmy Fallon on *The Tonight Show*, I was offered a one-year contract with MSNBC, as a sort of extended pilot series.

Once at MSNBC, I heard some strange and unsettling things about how the place was run. One thing that I think is worth repeating was when a veteran producer, a woman, sat me down to explain how MSNBC actually functioned. I'd been having a tough time communicating to Phil Griffin, the head of MSNBC, and to Jonathan Larsen, the producer Griffin had assigned to my show, about the style of program I had in mind. I didn't want the usual MSNBC look, with their harsh lighting and dreary design. I thought their sets looked like a Soviet interrogation room and told them so.

Larsen had recently been fired from Steve Kornacki's show, and he told me that Griffin sent him to "babysit" me. The news division had different standards than the entertainment division, Larsen highlighted, suggesting I might invite Kathy Griffin to be my cohost. His lack of enthusiasm for me and the show was front and center. He had a contract with MSNBC and he was simply showing up for work.

In the midst of this less-than-wonderful environment, the female producer said, "Look. The people who work here are career, professional newspeople. There are not a lot of good jobs with network salaries out there anymore. Some of us have kids in private schools. We have retirement and insurance to think about. This is a good job compared to what's out there. And, remember, no one is watching." I squinted my "Come again." She paused for effect. "No one is watching. The ratings are awful. But because of cable carriage fees, we're still around. We've got a good thing here. So . . ." She put her finger over her mouth and shushed me. "Stop complaining."

One day, Phil Griffin introduced me to Ronan Farrow. It wouldn't be long before I was wondering how I could get some of what Ronan had, as he managed to remain on the air even as his ratings plummeted to 11,000 viewers among the desired demographic. My show, entitled *Up Late with Alec Baldwin*, pulled in low ratings in the demo as well, but our numbers were more than ten times Farrow's, who was given a year to develop on the air. My show was dropped after five episodes. If the ratings were all of it, I'd understand. But they weren't.

The MSNBC situation was souring, and my simultaneous efforts to make a peaceful home for my wife and new family were consuming me. In August of 2013, my wife had just given birth to our daughter, Carmen. As Hilaria tried to embrace this remarkable time in her life, a period now filled with an intrusiveness she had never experienced, several tabloid reporters and photographers started to collect around our apartment building. In past exchanges with these people, some of them played by the rules, as I see them. Others walked a line between what they argue is journalism and what I label as harassment. When that line is crossed, sometimes I let it go. Sometimes I don't. I make the call. I remember the curse Joe Zarza put on me, about learning everything the hard way, whenever I think about November 14, the afternoon Harvey Levin, always prompting my own chronic hatred of the tabloid press, came back to pay me a visit.

When I left that terrible voicemail message for my daughter Ireland in 2007, there was no mistaking what was said and who the recipient was. I spent the subsequent months either in a state of suicidal depression or wanting to find Harvey Levin and my ex-wife's lawyers and beat them to death. Afterward, I was careful to make a vital distinction between an excuse and an explanation in terms of my behavior. There was no excuse for what I did. But my explanation was that I was completely outmaneuvered by my ex-wife in the gamesmanship of divorce custody. Kim's attorneys were the most contemptible people I had ever met. I suppose I never had a hope of prevailing in any of the rigged contests that California family law insists you participate in if you simply want to see your child. I had wanted to be a father to Ireland. There had never been a complaint, publicly or privately, about my parenting before my divorce. Everyone knew how much I loved Ireland. Ireland knew, too. That essential fact is dismissed in divorce court, allowing the legal fees to flow. Certainly, protecting innocent children from the shrapnel of divorce combat is an important task. But it is not the only task. Fathers' rights are among the lowest of priorities in these cases, making it easier for judges to take a side and simplify the matter and, thus, move things along. With the voicemail, I provided the court with the tool it needed in order to disassemble that relationship: the incontrovertible proof that I deserved to lose the custody decision.

In Westwood, California, in 1983, I pulled up next to a pump at a gas station and got out of my car. Back then, you still had to "pay inside," and as I walked toward the garage, I heard a man shouting. I turned and saw that a thirty-something white guy was actually shouting at me. A bald and bullet-headed bantam of a guy, a less-interesting-looking Ed Harris, was complaining that I had cut him off at the pump. (Actually, he appeared to be at a different pump and attempted to back into the space I was in line for.) He rushed up to me and was basically spitting as he yelled, now right in my ear. I was, for all intents and purposes, still the Berner High School football team's Billy Pilgrim when it came to physical confrontation. I entered the store and squared up to the counter, where two short, very powerfully built Iranian guys who ran the place prepared to ring me up. I continued to ignore Typical Southern California White Dude as he said something like, "Why don't you go back to fucking UCLA, man!" I didn't actually register that as offensive, but then he put his right hand on my left shoulder and started to spin me around. "You hear me, man?"

he shouted. And, in the briefest moment in time, I changed.

I cracked this guy right on the chin. I only weighed 190 then, but he went flying backwards, his arms windmilling, and crashed into a metal rack of candy and gum. The Iranian bodybuilders were right on me, lifting me nearly off the ground and shouting "No to be fighting in zee store" as they escorted me out. The voices of my high school coaches may or may not have been sounding in my head, like in some Alan Sillitoe short story. The last time I experienced that was when, during my college years, Eugene Valentine put fireworks in my mom's garbage can, waking her up one evening. Eugene, very drunk, virtually walked into four or five punches, and it was over. I was always someone who hated that kind of situation. But it was the LA paparazzi who really turned me.

Walking through the terminal at LAX with Kim and, later, with Ireland, we had a bodyguard/driver, the great Jeff Welles, who would peel off and put Kim and Ireland in the waiting car while I went for the baggage. One day, as we separated, a photographer began his taunting spiel. "What happened to you, Alec? You used to be such a nice guy. Then you met that crazy fucking bitch and—" Bang! I hit him. Another time a guy, walking in front of Jeff, lunged over his shoulder and, single-handed, tried to snap Kim's picture, his long lens nearly hitting Kim in the face. Bang! I hit him. The day we took Ireland home from the hospital, a photographer named Alan Zanger followed us. In the driveway, Kim was sobbing, asking me to get rid of the guy so he couldn't get a picture of her with the baby. As I approached him to wave off his camera, he said, "Let me get the picture and I'll go," as if we were bargaining. Then he cocked his arm back as if to hit me with the camera. Bang! Zanger had me arrested. That evening, on the local CBS affiliate, their legal correspondent railed against me for my assault of Zanger. The correspondent was a lawyer named Harvey Levin.

On the Internet there are many pictures of me wrestling a paparazzo named Paul Adao. In August of 2013, immediately after the birth of Carmen, Adao was around every lamppost and awning on our block. The pattern was typical. I don't bother with photographers who keep their distance. Adao not only did not keep his distance; he literally tripped, fell, and sat on a baby in a stroller as he walked backwards, shooting film, on a residential street in Manhattan. The thought that my neighbors now had to contend with the excesses of the tabloid media since I had moved onto their block saddened me. Just a few months later, the tabloids wanted to hound me about a stalker who tried to rush her way into our lobby and, eventually, up to our apartment, insisting she was my jilted girlfriend and had to either explain something to my wife or attack her. (The woman was found guilty at trial and literally chose to accept a sentence of six months at Rikers Island rather than enroll in court-supervised therapy.)

Whenever these eruptions occur, sanctimonious tabloid types get on some bullshit show like *Nancy Grace* and scoff at celebrities who insist on some degree of privacy, especially for their children. On November 14, in the wake of a verdict in the stalking case, the swarm of bees got close again. I yelled for them to get away from my wife, our car, our lives. And as I turned away, you can hear everything I say quite clearly, every word up until I say "cocksucking . . ." something. In a moment such as that, I don't jump into a car and write down the dialogue. On subsequent broadcasts of the videotape of the event, viewers also can hear every single word I say—except that word. Harvey Levin, of course, wanted to make sure you didn't miss a thing. So, on his broadcast, he put a title across the screen, which was the word "faggot." That was on a Thursday. By Monday, I was fired by MSNBC.

In the wake of that, I wasn't attacked only by the likes of a CBS affiliate legal correspondent or some screechy hen like Nancy Grace. On CNN, Anderson

Cooper, joined by blogger Andrew Sullivan, sounded off about the need for me to be "vilified." I was condemned by GLAAD spokesperson Rich Ferraro. The response from every corner of the gay community was one of either judgment, condemnation, or a good deal of free psychoanalysis. Over time, I have come to understand the role certain people play inside of the gay community. There is no larger platform and no wider audience for their pontifications than when a famous person is "outed" as a homophobe. It's the form of outing that they love, the outing that's right and necessary. The rest of the time, Cooper and Sullivan make due with relatively modest audiences. Unless, in Cooper's case, it's New Year's Eve. Ferraro, no doubt, is on a vigilant watch for the next homophobic outburst that GLAAD can raise money on. And if you're wondering if I've ever used the word "faggot," I call my gay friends that all the time.

In subsequent litigation (contractually stipulated mediation, actually, which I am prevented from getting into too great a detail about), MSNBC's lawyers opened up with the *TMZ* video. I had assumed that a news organization such as NBC would have enlisted an "acoustician" (a word I picked up while at these meetings) to provide incontrovertible evidence that I had said the offending word. That didn't happen. Their lead attor-

ney, poured into his conservative suit like melted wax
and resembling Jabba the Hutt, smirked and sighed
at my every utterance. Those years in divorce court
with Kim, however, had paid off. Not even this guy's
douchebaggery could distract me. My lawyer Ed Hern-
stadt was sharp and helpful. Typical exchanges went
like this:

> Hernstadt: "Did you fire my client because he said
> 'faggot'?"
> Jabba: "'Cocksucker' is a homophobic slur as well."
> Hernstadt: "Just to be clear, which word is he being
> fired for?"

NBC has a "human resources" problem. When it
came time to dismiss or ease into retirement names
like Jay Leno, Conan O'Brien, Ann Curry, David
Gregory, and, eventually, Brian Williams and Billy
Bush, NBC's owners, during the GE and Comcast
eras, did not view their stars as people who required
or deserved any special treatment as they were being
fired. Perhaps especially as they were being fired.
They were employees, like in any of their other businesses. MSNBC eventually settled on a portion of
the unpaid balance of my contract. I believe they did
that because they could not prove I said the offending

word. The reason they couldn't prove that is because I didn't say it.

(When I subsequently offered, online, the word "fathead," I was joking. Ineffectively.) So long as I know, that is all I have to hold on to. Such battles with the press, tabloid or otherwise, can have lasting and toxifying results. When you lose all perspective, you run the risk of getting in touch with your inner Nixon, a condition marked by a romanticized paranoia, teeming resentments, and a limitless appetite for settling scores.

On an episode of the PBS television program *American Masters* devoted to the life and career of Woody Allen, the subject of Allen's personal tribulations and tabloid scandals is touched on. Allen responds with an aplomb I only wish I had, saying: "Everybody had an opinion about my private life, which I felt they were all free to have. And free to respond in any way that made them happy. They could sympathize with me, not sympathize with me. They could dislike me, they could like me. It could have no effect on whether they saw my films. They could never see my films again. None of that mattered to me."

I wasn't that self-possessed.

That same year, a photographer from the *New York Post*, accompanying a *Post* reporter who attempted to interview me outside my apartment, later told the paper that I had called him a "coon." Aside from the fact that I wasn't in the habit of using such racist language, let alone words more commonly found in the Deep South in the 1950s, I thought "Where's the proof?" The *Post* is published and edited by people who don't let the truth stand in the way of a successful smear campaign. But, if the photographer is like every other one I encounter, his camera records video as well as shoots digital pictures. Where was the recording?

Walking down East 9th Street near 5th Avenue one evening, within days of the claims of the *Post* (whose photographer turned out to be an ex–police officer) I passed by an older couple, a black man and woman. He was dressed in a suit and tie and camel overcoat. This distinguished man looked up at me and, unmistakably, recognized who I was. His face completely changed as he shook his head slightly from side to side. "Et tu, Alec?" was the message I picked up from him. How I wanted to appeal to him, right then and there. "I went to Florida in '96 to do voter registration work in black communities!" "You don't believe what you read in the *Post*, do you?" Whatever work I had done on behalf of progressive causes over the past thirty years was washed away in one act of the nullification that News Corp outlets and their operatives crave. My heart broke.

The memory of that man's expression was tattooed on me right up until I visited the Hate Crimes office of the Manhattan District Attorney. In the interview they conducted, I asked, point blank, "Is there a video?" The woman running the interview with four others from her staff paused and stared at me, as if to indicate that she was hoping I might incriminate myself in spite of the existence of the video. "There is a video," she replied, after a long pause. "Let's play it," I said. On the video, at no time whatsoever do I use the word "coon" or any other racial epithet. As the photographer rejoins the young reporter, she asks, "What did he say?" He replies, "I think he called me a coon or something." Of course, that claim, with no substantiation, is enough for the *Post*.

That day on East 9th Street, as the elegant man in the camel coat came closer and made out who I was, I could have sworn I heard a disgusted "Mmmm" emanate from him, that low sound coming from a shock or disappointment you didn't see coming.

I wondered how many more African-Americans believed that about me. I had been embraced by many fans in the black community. How many now thought I'd let them down, or worse? Similarly, how many young people who are gay thought that I was judging them or condemning how they lived? I would never be the same after that. It's remarkable what a few trips to the dunk tank of American media can do for your soul.

A couple of months later, I was approached by the writer Joe Hagan to do a piece for *New York* magazine. I once loved the magazine, in the days of Nick Pileggi and Robert Sam Anson. I had little use for it once Murdoch took over in the '80s. But people told me Hagan was a square guy. I was in Madrid in January of 2014 shooting a film and I didn't have much free time. Hagan interviewed me and, in the style we discussed, sent me a piece that was essentially a transcription. When I got his initial draft, it was an incoherent mess. I wasn't interested in writing the piece in the first person, but I had no choice. In the article, I speak of being finished with public life. What I should have written was that I was finished with expecting to find any fun or joy out of public life again. And by "public life," I mean cooperating with the media in any attempt to communicate with an audience. The press is something you develop a relationship with that is, hopefully, polite. It can be pleasant, even playful. But a tabloid mentality seems to have overwhelmed nearly all of that, and the resultant trouble is something you shrink from in order to protect your family.

When I first logged on to Twitter, I thought it was a brilliant means of bypassing the media to speak with your audience directly. Eventually, that idea was crushed by the Internet's right-wing marauders, who level scorching personal attacks while shielding their identities. The majority of the public you want to communicate with are not on Twitter, though some on Twitter are worth the trouble. It can be an excellent news aggregator, so long as you consider the source. But after a year of unfair charges of racism and homophobia; of hearing that Bill de Blasio had condemned me for the *TMZ* incident in his never-ending quest to be the most politically correct politician in America; after watching cable news anchors, regardless of their sexuality, take me down based on the testimony of someone like Harvey Levin, I knew that we had entered a new era in terms of the effect the press was having on the country and vice versa.

On social media, people called me a drunk. They said I was abusive toward my daughter. I was a "libtard." I was a wife beater. I was washed up. Irrelevant. I should stay out of politics. I was un-American. The profiles of these people almost always featured words like "Support the Troops," "Christian," "Military," "I support law enforcement," "Make America Great Again." A tsunami of such raw bile, excreted by those Americans with a boundless suspicion of or abject hatred for anything unlike themselves, propelled Donald Trump to be elected president of the United States. Even as I write that, I stare at those words in disbelief.

Throughout my life, I have embraced a lot of causes that I believed in. Eventually I formed a foundation to channel certain sources of my income toward supporting the arts, the environment, and education, to name but a few. Some of the greatest satisfactions of my life have derived from my work with the New York Philharmonic, the Hamptons International Film Festival, and the East Hampton Library. But whatever I have done involving politics, regarding both candidacies and issues, has come at a real cost. The *New York Post* is not evenhanded in how they treat celebrities, and those labeled as liberals suffer the most by way of the Murdoch machinery. The cauterization of progressive thought, progressive achievement, and progressive history is what fuels the Breitbart–Murdoch–Koch brothers– Roger "Drop Your Pants" Ailes–Sheldon Adelson– Richard Mellon Scaife version of the news. Their goal is the destruction of any emergent leadership that they view as an obstacle to their accumulation of greater wealth and power. I've been told, over the years, that my politics have negatively affected my career. Maybe some didn't realize that speaking out about what was best for the country was also my career. I only wish it were more so.

15

The Interests of the Great Mass

If I ran for president of the United States, you'd be lucky. Just as if you ran for president, I would be lucky. This country needs to see some new faces in that arena. American politics needs some new blood, because the problem in our country today is one of choice. We don't have enough men and women who would make good public servants who are willing to run for elective office as well as submerge themselves in the immorality of our current campaign system. You really do have to sell your soul, or a significant portion of it, to corporations, super PACs, and rich donors in order to win most statewide elections today. And that transaction is a big part of what is killing this country.

I learned a good deal about campaign financing and proposed reforms to it from a man named Burt Neuborne, a professor and the legal director of the Brennan Center for Justice at NYU Law School. I met Burt, and his colleague Josh Rosenkranz, through my association with The Creative Coalition (TCC), which I served as president of beginning in 1995. TCC was founded by the actor Ron Silver. Silver had the ego of an Argentinean polo player. When we traveled together to Albany on an Amtrak train in 1990, Silver masticated every syllable while expertly coaching our group for a meeting with Governor Mario Cuomo about the pending New York State Environmental Quality Bond Act. Silver was there again in 1997, when we gave testimony before Congress regarding the federal funding of the National Endowment for the Arts. Silver drilled us with the opposition's talking points and anticipated questions. He taught us about "cover"—the response we'd have ready when our opponents made the inflammatory remark we hoped they would make—which often served as the counterpunch that won the argument for our side. It was the political education of a lifetime. Silver, who had played Alan Dershowitz in the film *Reversal of Fortune*, possessed the mind of a lawyer beyond anyone I had ever met who didn't actually hold a law degree, as well as a political acumen that easily could have put him in office. In fact, several people I've met while on the TCC advocacy path were among the most informed and dedicated of activist-artists. Richard Masur, a TCC member and onetime president of the Screen Actors Guild, knew more about health insurance, in terms of both policy and politics, than anyone I'd met. The same goes for Mike Farrell of *M*A*S*H* regarding the death penalty.

My own political education began in the den of my childhood home as I sat with my father watching the events of the late 1960s, particularly the Vietnam War, unfold on network television news. By the time I was ten, my political consciousness was already nearly concretized. In that regard, I'm no different from people who are raised in a home that is pro or anti any of the issues of the day: the NRA, immigration, gay marriage, abortion, or Obamacare. Politicization starts at home. My politics are my dad's politics, based on the simple idea that, as the richest nation on Earth, America has a greater obligation to reach out and help those who have not realized even a modicum of what we take for granted here. The standard of living, the freedoms, the educational opportunities, and the hopes for a better life, if only for our children, are either elusive or completely out of reach for an exploding number. This is also true here at home, and it's unconscionable.

On the cold afternoon of November 22, 1963, my friends and I played in a neighbor's yard while our mothers huddled around a television watching the news following the assassination of President Kennedy. This was the first political event I recall. I was five years old. My father deeply admired the Kennedy family's blend of intelligence, wit, and, above all, idealism, so JFK's death hit him very hard. He drove down to Washington to experience the president's funeral, standing among the large crowd on Pennsylvania Avenue to view the cortege.

A mere five years later, Robert Kennedy was murdered in Los Angeles, an act that would dramatically change my father's life, as well as the fate of the country. The hope that the United States would leave Vietnam and end the insanity there, for both countries, died in the Ambassador Hotel as well. Bobby Kennedy's funeral would be different for my dad. He took my sister Beth, my brother Daniel, and me into Manhattan, where we stood in the incredibly long line filing north up Park Avenue from what was then the Pan Am building. The line turned left onto 51st Street, and the mourners were ushered into the northern entrance of St. Patrick's Cathedral. As I was about to enter, a reporter for WOR radio approached me with a microphone, and asked, "Are you going to pray for Senator

Kennedy?" I was stunned and silent, but the reporter persisted as my father just shrugged, as if to say, "Well, answer him!" "Are you here to pray for the senator?" the reporter asked again. "Yes," I replied sheepishly. "What are you going to say?" he asked. "A Hail Mary," I said. "How does that go?" he asked. On June 8, 1968, at the 51st Street entrance to St. Patrick's, I recited the Hail Mary at Robert Kennedy's funeral for a New York radio audience. After that, politically speaking, what other future could I possibly have?

After my unsuccessful run for class president at George Washington, I started to become more jaded. The election opened my eyes to the kinds of people who envision themselves in leadership roles. When I'd arrived for freshman orientation at GW, I unpacked my bags in a six-man suite where four of my five roommates had already declared themselves political science majors, and two of those four stated that they were planning to run for president of the United States one day. (The one guy not studying poli-sci moved out after one semester, as he wanted to live with other pre-meds, or "anyone who knew what they were talking about.") At school, I interned for the congressman from my home district, Jerome Ambro. Right away, I was given an assignment working with the organization No Greater Love, a veterans group that wanted each of the country's 435 members of Congress to help recognize a Vietnam vet from their district who had successfully reacclimated upon returning home. After a couple of days' worth of research, I recommended Ron Kovic.

Kovic, a Massapequa native who had been taught by my father in high school, was the author of the memoir *Born on the Fourth of July*, which was later made into a hit film by Oliver Stone starring Tom Cruise. Ambro's chief of staff and district director went slightly nuts at my suggestion. They brought me in to meet the congressman, who thanked me for my efforts and then explained how Kovic's antiwar positions made him precisely the wrong vet for the program. I spent the rest of the semester reassigned to "constituent services," which usually meant helping track down some type of missing government benefit for a voter from the district. The rest of the time, I would join the other interns at receptions all over the Hill, where we drank, ate as many hors d'oeuvres as possible, and lied, expanding the scope of our internship's responsibilities as much as possible.

When I went to New York to attend NYU and then started my acting career, I put politics on the shelf. Ronald Reagan had been elected president in 1980, and as unhappy as I was about that, I was consumed with getting my bearings in the business. The period between 1979 and 1987 was largely one of political dormancy for me, but when Reagan was reelected in 1984 (and I was near the peak of my drug addiction and alcoholism), I made the exception of a brief and odd little stopover in the office of Tom Hayden. I contacted the California assemblyman's Santa Monica office and explained that I wanted to volunteer for him. Some of the women in the office watched *Knots Landing* and asked me what I was doing answering Hayden's mail. I explained that I had been bound for law school before I picked up acting and that, once in LA, I had a lot of time on my hands. A guy who worked there, unsure of what I was after, gave me a job in, you guessed it, constituent services. This time, my task was usually getting to the bottom of an overcharge on a water or power bill.

In 1985, Hayden invited me to his home for an event he was hosting with his wife, Jane Fonda. All of a sudden, I was sitting in one of the premier salons of political Hollywood. The biggest film and music stars of their day, representing different generations, were gathered in Jane and Tom's backyard to listen to a speech by Nobel Prize winner Desmond Tutu. At any given moment, I fully expected someone to ask me to put on a white jacket and start serving canapés. I thought to myself, "What the hell am I doing here?" But Hayden, in addition to being an incredibly bright and dedicated political fighter, was completely unpretentious. His attitude was, "If you care, if you're engaged in the fight, and if you want to learn, you're welcome here." We stayed in touch, and in 1988, Hayden put me on the list for a party in honor of his latest book, *Reunion*, to be held at the home of Courtney Kennedy Ruhe, one of Bobby Kennedy's daughters. There, I came face-to-face for the first time with Ethel Kennedy. Though her husband had been gone twenty years, to me it might as well have been a month. I spared her my recollection of the ten-year-old me at St. Patrick's, but to say that I was overwhelmed when I met her is an understatement. After a brief moment of small talk, Mrs. Kennedy did what all Kennedys do: she changed the subject, charging into some issue of the day.

In July 1988, my connection with Hayden got me invited to the Democratic convention in Atlanta as a guest of the California delegation. The group I was with included Ally Sheedy, Sarah Jessica Parker, my brother Billy, Judd Nelson, and Rob Lowe. Dukakis was the nominee, and although I had my doubts about his electability, I was ardently opposed to Vice President Bush as president, if only because he had been director of the CIA. (I believed then, and I believe now, that having been the head of any secret intelligence agency in this country disqualifies one from being president.) In October of that year, Ethel invited me to her home in Hyannis Port. With my sister Beth in tow, we watched Lloyd Bentsen wither Dan Quayle during their debate with the famous line "Senator, you're no Jack Kennedy." Sitting with Ethel, one wall going up a staircase covered with Kennedy family photos, my sister Beth and I looked at each other, both giddy, in a way that clearly said, "Do you think Dad can see us?"

Not all of the Kennedys are created equal in terms of the ineffable quality that distinguishes them in American political life. The blend of charisma, the ability to articulate the facts, and the high level of passion are rare in politics these days. For me, Bobby Jr., his late brother Michael Kennedy, and his sisters Kathleen and Kerry are examples of how the best of the Kennedy genetics resurfaced in the next generation. But no one can top Ethel for her sheer life force. She is sharp, indefatigable, funny, intense, and well practiced (as all Kennedys must be) at granting strangers a chance to experience the Kennedy zeitgeist. I could not begin to imagine where she found the personal courage she had accessed in order to carry on with her life. A few years later, after Bill Clinton—who carries some of that Kennedy spirit—had moved into the White House, I was invited to a party there featuring a screening of Ron

Howard's film *The Paper*. To my delight, I was seated next to Ethel. At one point in the movie, a gun went off and Ethel grabbed my arm. To see the look on her face, all those years later, showed me that though she is tough, that moment is still there.

My romantic feelings for nearly all things Kennedy aside, the fall of 1988 was also when another invitation arrived, and with it, one of the greatest political contacts I'd ever make. While shooting *Miami Blues* in south Florida that year, I was invited to attend a Dukakis fund-raiser at the Los Angeles home of Norman Lear. I wondered if flying across the country while I was shooting, to feel out of place among a pack of powerful Hollywood celebrities again, was the best idea, but a friend told me I'd be crazy to pass up such the chance.

At Norman's home, a line snaked its way through the property to reach Michael Dukakis, perhaps the last Democratic candidate to win the nomination with such a deficit of charisma. Like Humphrey, McGovern, Carter, and Mondale immediately before him, Dukakis was old school: an earnest and ultimately uninspiring candidate, the kind that one assumed Reagan had knocked off for good. The Massachusetts governor was a decent enough guy, yet he made priggish Vice President Bush seem downright affable. When I turned from Dukakis to shake Norman's hand, my excitement spiked. "Now, this guy ought to be running for president," I thought. Norman proved to be more than a powerful political eminence; he became a mentor. The organization he founded, People for the American Way (PFAW), focused my political activities in a way for which I will always be grateful, both to Norman and to the group as a whole. Lear is a hero and a legend in the community of artist-activists I count myself among.

Over the course of the next decade, from 1988 to 1998, I tried to navigate the ups and downs of my career, but speaking on behalf of The Creative Coalition and PFAW and attending countless events, both issue-oriented and on behalf of individual candidates, became like a second job. I crisscrossed the country incessantly. On a few occasions, I landed in LA, forgetting that I had an event in New York within the coming forty-eight hours, and hopped on a plane to turn right around (something I could only do in my thirties!). The one thing I maintain about that period of intense political advocacy, and beyond, is that I never appeared on behalf of any cause in order to line my own pockets. The work I did never enriched me in any way. I think that has confused or frustrated some people, like some Republicans and conservatives for whom politics must always involve some form of profit taking. It's as if my political opposites were saying to me, "You've made a little money. Why don't you play eighteen holes, kick back, have a beer? Relax! The spotted owls and the poor people and hybrid cars, they're all gonna take care of themselves." My response to that is, "Convince me. Teach me. Show me how to be like you and not worry about all the things you don't worry about." I'm still waiting for a persuasive response.

I fought voter suppression in Florida after the 2000 election. I wanted to secure federal support for the arts in every state in the country, particularly for those communities that are not as culturally abundant as New York, Boston, Chicago, and San Francisco. I argued for saner gun control laws and protested the death penalty not only as cruel and unusual but also as fiscally impractical. I fought for a woman to have control over her own reproductive choices. But my favorite issue was to urge both federal and state governments to take money out of politics. Burt Neuborne and Josh Rosenkranz lectured our TCC gatherings about *Buckley v. Valeo*, the case that they believe was rushed into the Supreme Court with the hope that its cleansing effects might impact the 1976 election. But the ruling proved to be porous in many ways. Since then, the systematic assault on campaign finance reform by elitist hacks like John Roberts or originalist fanatics like the late Antonin

Scalia has only served to keep the White House, and a great many other offices in this country, in the hands of rich, white, corporate-leaning Christian men or those who will do their bidding. Campaign finance reform is the linchpin of nearly every problem we face as a nation, just as our oil-based economy is the linchpin of our issues abroad. If the first issue is not addressed, we will continue to see the US electoral system gamed by insiders who put forth enormous amounts of money on behalf of any candidate who will read from their script in order to get the role of a lifetime. Even if that candidate is a foppish casino operator who had heretofore shown no interest in national politics.

In 1994, the chance to serve the Kennedys came again. Senator Edward Kennedy was running for reelection in Massachusetts in a tough race with Mitt Romney. I met Michael Kennedy, Ted's nephew, in Hyannis while we were (what else?) playing football on the front lawn. I knew Michael was full-on Kennedy when he climbed up onto the hood of a car to catch a touchdown pass, claiming the front end of the car was in bounds. We spoke about how I might help Ted. In the critical month of October, I traveled to western Massachusetts (as it was assumed Teddy had Boston sewn up) for four consecutive four-day weekends, most of them with Michael. We went to VFW halls, community colleges, and Democratic clubs, where I spoke in front of groups as big as a thousand people and as small as twenty. We made around seventy stops during that month, fueling ourselves with pretzels and Snapple. On October 25, Ted was set to debate Romney. Michael told me that in spite of the polls, Ted needed a good showing, especially in the first and more-watched debate, in order to nullify the issue of his age. Romney was now the fair-haired leading man, but Ted came out prepared, robust, combative. Everyone scored the first, pivotal round for Ted. On October 23, just before that first debate, as I was driving with Michael to Boston to catch my flight home, Ted called his nephew, who then handed me the phone. All of a sudden, I was reminded of driving around western Massachusetts (oddly enough) back in 1992, while shooting *Malice*, when the news came on the radio that Bill Clinton had defeated Bush. I choked up at that moment, thinking that there really was hope for this country. When I took the phone from Michael, I choked up again as Senator Kennedy thanked me and said, "If I win this thing, I really couldn't have done it without your help." And although I knew that was hyperbole, I felt that Ted's 1994 campaign was one where I really had made a contribution. I thought, "If I can get people to vote for Ted, is there someone else I could get them to vote for? Could it be me?"

In 1997, *New York* magazine put me on the cover with the title "See Alec Run." The mostly positive piece teased my aspirations to some state political office, but my allergy to campaign fund-raising told me I wasn't ready. To run for office meant I would have to give up the work I loved (for the most part) on the stage and screen to play a part I didn't want to play: a politician raising money. As fast as those rumors came, they went, and stories about me running for the Senate or Congress, for governor or mayor, were treated with a more dismissive tone, as in, "Yeah, we've heard all that before." A year after the *New York* cover story, Bill Clinton came to East Hampton, the first sitting president to travel to the East End to attend a political event since FDR. My new home had yet to be remodeled, so the DNC stepped in to stage the event. A local builder who was my friend spruced up our house and put together some furniture. Then Kim and I hosted Bill and Hillary at our house with a concert by Hootie and the Blowfish for around a thousand people. That night, the Secret Service wanted a dedicated bathroom in the house for the president, so we had designated a powder room in the hallway and marked it as off-limits. When the president was eventually escorted to it, he found it was locked. The Secret Service men knocked on the door crisply, and a muffled reply came from inside, and after what felt like an eternity, the door opened and revealed my mother standing there. I moaned the most theatrical "Moooooooom" you could imagine. The president of the United States put his arm on my shoulder and said, "Don't worry, Alec. I understand. I've got a mother, too."

After the event at our home, a group repaired to Turtle Crossing, a ribs joint on the highway in East Hampton, where every celebrity who had a home in the area—including Steven Spielberg and his wife Kate, Kathleen Turner, Roy Scheider, Lauren Bacall, Chevy Chase, Sidney Lumet, and Christie Brinkley, among others—was seated at picnic-style tables, eating chicken, ribs, coleslaw, and corn bread with the president and First Lady. At one point, Clinton sat in a corner with Kim and me, where he spoke intently about the brewing Lewinsky scandal. Eventually, he leveled his eyes at us, his long, thin fingers pressed into his breast in a plaintive pose. "Even if I did do it," he said, "don't I deserve to be forgiven?" Just then, someone pulled up next to the president and snatched him away. Kim spun toward me and squealed, "I think he just told us he did it!"

Whatever Clinton did or didn't do, none of it warranted the despicable and offensive nonsense that followed. I watched the impeachment proceedings while in South Africa with Kim, who was making a film there. On satellite television, some British Sky channels came in and I was able to see the news reports of what the Republicans were attempting to do. The whole sordid story about this witch Linda Tripp setting up Lewinsky to get the president made me sick. I agreed with Hillary Clinton's assertion that many of their troubles were the result of a vast right-wing conspiracy, and I detested Kenneth Starr (whom Pepperdine University disgraced itself by hiring, no matter its right-wing leanings) and Henry Hyde's hypocrisy, and those feelings would eventually prove impossible to shake.

When I returned home, I appeared on Conan O'Brien's show in what I thought was obviously a parody of the McCarthyite mentality Hyde had fostered. On *Conan*, I called for Hyde to be "stoned to death" as I rose out of my chair, shaking my fist and plainly overacting. Plainly, that is, to everyone except the media and the Republicans, who both seemed to think that I was actually serious about the threat. The Democrats have their hacks, too, so Jack Valenti piled on, voicing his disapproval, stating, "It's not something you parody." Looking back, I still believe that Hyde disgraced his office with his actions against Clinton. The GOP, with an Ahab-like obsession, would stop at nothing to settle the score over Nixon and nullify Clinton. And now, nearly two decades later, that's still all that the modern GOP stands for, nullifying election results and settling scores, old and new.

In that vein, the 2000 election dealt me a devastating blow. PFAW had sent volunteers down to Florida as part of its "Election Protection" effort, and I traveled there to work on the Arrive with 5 program, whereby we helped register tens of thousands of new voters. However, many of those we registered were turned away or their votes were ultimately not counted. It was painful to watch Jeb Bush seem to rig an election on behalf of his less-competent brother, as I believed then and still do that George W. Bush was simply a variant of Ronald Reagan. But Reagan was a front man who brought to the table an indisputable electability, then turned the whole thing over to his handlers while he essentially performed the role of president. He did not, however, steal an election. Both parties are guilty of some rather brass-knuckled electoral tactics, but nothing compares to the 2000 election (until, of course, we learned about Russian hacking). Once Bush won, 9/11 presented his crew with what they were after: a war for oil during which they destroyed an entire civilization, then handed the rebuilding over to their friends in investment banking and multinational construction, often with no-bid contracts. How much money do you think Bush Family and Friends Inc. made in the wake of 9/11 and the subsequent invasion of Iraq in the ensuing seven years and beyond? Along the way, the administration also squandered all of the goodwill we were poised to reap in the wake of the 9/11 tragedy.

During America's forays into the Middle East since the 2003 invasion of Iraq, we've all seen photos of men and women either holding or standing over their dead child, the parent's face a mask of suffering. Such images lead me to wonder what we can honestly expect from the people of these regions in terms of their feelings toward us? Even if the actions of the United States are well-intentioned, how much blood of innocent civilians is on our hands? I know that Americans live very sheltered lives in terms of the consequences of our foreign policy and that whoever is president must work to end that suffering.

After eight years of Bush, I wasn't sure what the country was ready for. When Obama won, I sat in the kitchen of my New York apartment and cried. What a great day for democracy. When he was reelected, it was even sweeter. I think Obama was a good president, and

I was sad to see him go. Those who believe that Obama has betrayed his promises about things such as closing Guantanamo or questioned his policy on an accelerated drone program are missing something, I believe. The military, the CIA, and the NSA have their own agenda. The president is the one official elected by all Americans, and yet he does not call the shots. When presidents come into office believing they are actually in charge, that's how you get to Dallas in 1963 and people get killed. Then, maybe, his brother wishes to pick up where he left off and is killed as well.

I became complacent when Obama won, which is more a sign of my age than anything else. Our guy was in, so we were covered. Politics was also boring the hell out of me. I wondered who could right this ship after eight years of Cheney as puppeteer. Again, I thought of running for office myself. In 2013, some Democratic leaders from different corners of New York politics approached me, and we had a serious talk about me running for mayor, but my wife and I were expecting our daughter, Carmen, that summer, and we agreed that it wasn't the time for an all-consuming race like that. What else would I run for? I believed that running for president, even building my way there by winning some other office, was impractical because the country remained stuck in the idea that the highest office should be someone inside of the current system. Also, I believed Hillary would win easily in 2016.

As Election Day approached, a couple of friends, both New York media execs, asked me if I wanted to join them at celebratory events they were producing to mark Hillary's pending victory. The Donald Trump we had been presenting on *Saturday Night Live* seemed to delight nearly everyone in the People's Republic of Manhattan, so I had many such invitations. The *SNL* Trump sketches prompted people to approach me, thank me, and beseech me to "keep going" more than any other portrayal or piece I have performed. It was ironic, to say the least. In 2013, Harvey Levin wanted the public to believe I was a hate-filled homophobe. The *Post* said I was a racist. Suddenly, liberal downtown types were coming up to me everywhere I went, all day, every day, urging me to continue with this funny way to channel all of their not-so-funny fears, as well as their hatred of the suddenly viable Trump candidacy. And then this god-awful nightmare descended.

There is no point in dissecting Hillary Clinton's loss here. Enough analysis of that exists to last us all ten lifetimes. I had always admired Secretary Clinton's mind, her courage, her self-control under painfully difficult circumstances, and her tenacity. Trump, of course, exploited the fact that voters across the country would accept him as the sharp, no-nonsense, can-do executive he portrays on television. And he knew that they would not consider the fact that in New York, his hometown and base of operations, Trump is endured, at best. I will not go so far as to say he is a punch line, because in New York, making a lot of money counts for something, and according to him at least, Trump has made a lot of money. But Trump was never an admired New Yorker, a sought-after speaker, or dinner guest. He has never shown an appetite for the Great Political Imperative that New York politicians must manifest in order to be a real leader: empathizing with the day-to-day hustle and bustle of working-class New Yorkers. In fact, he has actually been an enemy of the working class, refusing to pay many of his contractors and using undocumented workers on job sites going back to the 1980s. Trump has abused power at every station stop of his life. Now he has the most powerful position in the world. Some people make a lot of money, but it does not fundamentally change who they are. Others become rich while choosing to never honestly reflect on the role luck played in their good fortune, electing to tune out the cries and complaints of those who can only truly be helped by reforming the system that enriches the Donald Trumps of this world.

I could go on. In another book, perhaps, I might go into greater detail about what the president of the United States ought to do and who that person ought to be. We have so many problems in the modern world, and we can no longer plead ignorance of any of them. Prioritizing those problems, knowing what order we must proceed in, like triage, is essential. Foreign policy, education, war-making, jobs, environmental regulation, disease control, infrastructure, criminal justice and incarceration, climate change, a fair tax policy, immigration, and, yes, a government role in curating our diverse cultural heritage: all of these, and more, must be on the table. The presidential candidate who defeats Trump in 2020 must present a clear, transparent plan for what he or she will do and when. The thing that is clearest now is that Trump must go, either in 2020 or sooner. It is imperative that we replace those who think they own this country with those who built it.

On May 8, 1962, John Kennedy addressed the United Auto Workers in Atlantic City on the subject of the responsibility of both organized labor and auto executives to control inflation. This excerpt from that speech says it all. When we read it today, Kennedy exhorts us to raise the bar, increase our expectations, seek a man or woman who will at least attempt to work for all Americans and do as much good for as many of them as possible. As he put it:

> Now I know there are some people who say that this isn't the business of the President of the United States, who believe that the President of the United States should be an honorary chairman of a great fraternal organization and confine himself to ceremonial functions. But that is not what the Constitution says. And I did not run for President of the United States to fulfill that Office in that way.
>
> Harry Truman once said there are 14 or 15 million Americans who have the resources to have representatives in Washington to protect their interests, and that the interests of the great mass of other people, the hundred and fifty or sixty million, is the responsibility of the President of the United States. And I propose to fulfill it.

I believe America is a great country, but we are never greater than when we actually do great things: World War II, the moon landings, the Peace Corps, the billions upon billions of dollars we gift every year to a world in need. At times, we've also elected some truly great leaders. One thing we ought to do, however, is shore up the integrity of our electoral system. Because it isn't really a democracy if you can't honestly count the votes.

16

Doubt Thou the Stars Are Fire

I love second chances. I love the concept of renewal. I love to see people come back from some adversity, self-inflicted or not, and untangle themselves from a difficult situation. They may correct some perceived mistake they've made. Make amends, if you will. Consequently, they prove to themselves and to others what they're capable of, what they're made of. You can call it redemption, or choose another word, but most important, they find some real degree of peace, even happiness.

I'm always nudged by the phrase "Life, liberty, and the pursuit of happiness." I understand the basic impulse to live, to survive. I've witnessed how countless people around the world have suffered and died in pursuit of their liberty. It's the last part, however, that always pokes at me. When was I happy? Truly happy?

Back during my grass-cutting career, my brother Stephen and I would go to a Chinese restaurant near our house and order fried rice. We'd sit on the curb in the strip mall parking lot, eating out of the containers. It was our very own fine dining experience. I never ate better in my life. Those pickup football games at dusk, the testosterone and ego galloping up and down the field that we carved out within the golf course. I can feel that air around me now. We were so focused and present. No cell phones. No streaming TV. There was nowhere else we wanted to be, no one else we wanted to be with. When I close my eyes and think back to that time, that feeling runs through my heart again. What I wouldn't give to go back and see us then. Just to look at us, at my young self, and say, "Do you realize that you have everything you could want right here?"

I had nothing then, especially not pretension. At GW, my well-heeled friends would talk of going to dinner at one of their favorite DC restaurants, Lonny Swa's. "The guy's name is Lonny Swa?" I asked. "What kind of name is that?" After cracking up at my expense, they headed over to La Niçoise. No eating fried rice on the curb of the strip mall for this crowd. A few years later, when I was sitting with David O'Brien and his coterie at the East Five Three, someone would make a crack that everyone was in on but me. While they were all chuckling, O'Brien would turn to me and quietly explain what a codpiece was. So funny and kind, a rare combination. I loved him. I was in love with him. I was never sexually attracted to men, but who knows? If I was braver, less hung up by what I was raised to believe about sex. "Just be yourself," he seemed to say. I remember him like it was yesterday.

Before Ireland was born, I would lie on the floor of a house in the San Fernando Valley, assuming that my first marriage was over, sleeping on the floor by the fire with ten dogs. Ten little dogs who became my friends and who gave me some of the only real love I had in my life then. I had some of the best nights of sleep in my life with those dogs on that floor. I had learned to love animals by Kim's example. I learned to love them even more when she pulled away.

When Beth and I sat in Ethel Kennedy's living room on the Cape watching the 1988 debate, my dad was another man whose spirit was in that house, if only for one night, twenty years after our trip to St. Pat's. My dad did everything he could to make me happy. Will I ever see him again? Do some parents seek their children beyond this life? That bond, that cord, that bloodline that pulls and pushes. Where did he go? What has he been doing with himself all of this time? Can he see and hear me?

When I met Tony Hopkins, Meryl, Gregory Peck, Julie Andrews, De Niro, Pacino, Peter Shaffer, and Scorsese, those moments made me happy because I was meeting Hannibal Lecter, Karen Blixen, Atticus Finch, Mary Poppins, Jake La Motta, Michael Corleone, and the man who wrote *Amadeus*. And the man who made *Raging Bull*. I was a fan. I still am. That never goes away.

I want to end this book contemplating happiness and renewal. In my life, I have seen a number of people get a second chance. My mother has had that wonderful opportunity, and I'm extremely proud of what she's done with it. After my father died, my mother sold our home to my sister Beth, who proceeded to move in and begin raising her family, which would grow to six children. Eventually, my mom and that whole gang packed up and moved to Syracuse in search of cleaner air, less density, and lower costs. After a while, they found a very pretty area that I love to visit. In Syracuse, you are never more than a twenty minutes' drive from the farm belt, with its open land and silos and cows. We call it "Sibera-cuse" because of all the snow, but I love it there.

But before they moved up north, my mother was approached by a coalition of Long Island breast cancer support groups to spearhead a project at the State University of New York at Stony Brook, not too far from where we grew up. Long Island is often the focus of intense debates about breast cancer statistics. One group there is named 1 in 9, based on the assertion that, statistically, one in nine women on Long Island will be diagnosed with the disease over the course of her life. My mother, who was diagnosed with breast cancer in 1990, had been working with the Susan G. Komen organization, and in 1996, doctors and administrators from SUNY Stony Brook asked her to lend her name, and her children, to a breast cancer research facility.

The Carol M. Baldwin Breast Cancer Research Fund was dedicated in 1996, with a ribbon cutting attended by SUNY and New York–area elected officials and my mother and siblings. Shirley Strum Kenny, the president at SUNY Stony Brook at the time, was overwhelmingly supportive of my mother's organization and their fund-raising. The ongoing goal is to raise money so that the SUNY medical team can find a cure. Among all the talk about numbers and statistics, however, I focused in on one thing. My mother was transformed.

The SUNY facility and the eventual opening of an upstate chapter, once my mother and sister had relocated to Syracuse, were not things I would have envisioned in my mother's future. Born in 1929, raised in

Syracuse during World War II, she gave up her early work as a teacher to have a family. She struggled for much of her adult life with the burden of raising six kids with no money. There were times she was, literally, about to go insane. Then, when she was fifty and her children were out the door—either in school, playing ball, or getting into some manageable degree of trouble—she went to work. Her job as a supervisor of a marketing research firm, operating on the floor of a local shopping mall, was just right.

But while my father's death in 1983 floored my mother, it also freed her. Gone from her life, permanently, were the haunting questions of what would become of them, as a couple, and of her as a woman in middle age if their marriage finally died. Instead, it was he who died. And with him went the fear, the mystery, and the fantasy of her own future. In the years after his death, my brothers and I had some success, and that certainly helped launch my mother's fund, as it was understood that we would share certain duties to raise money for my mom. My sister Beth has made the quest for a breast cancer cure her life's work as well. Over the years, we began to joke about how my mother had become a bigger celebrity than any of her sons. We joked that she'd push any of us off a cliff for a photo op, now that she was the "celebrity."

Over the years, the fund has matured. My brothers and I are middle-aged men ourselves now. Perhaps, up in Syracuse, we can still pull in a crowd to the charity's banquet or golf match, but my family's name, in terms of its celebrity quotient on Long Island, has waned. However, the Carol M. Baldwin Breast Cancer Research Fund is, to me, a great second act. Although my mother appreciated not only my father's role as a pillar of our community but also his place in the hearts of his children, I think that she wanted something to be remembered for, too, just as we had dedicated the Massapequa High School auditorium for my dad. I am close to shedding tears as I write this: he never could have done all that he did if it weren't for her. Never. None of her children could have achieved what they achieved without her contribution as well. All men want some degree of accomplishment. Women do, too.

The tense relationship I had with my mother throughout much of my childhood cast a shadow over many of my relationships over the years. But since my father's death and the organization of "The Fund," as we call it, I have enjoyed a far better rapport with her. She wanted to be on an equal footing with him in the eyes of her children. Once that was realized, she actually became happy again. And seeing her change, watching her become so purposeful and fulfilled, made me very happy as well. I love you, Mom. And I am so proud of you.

My professional life has been, ostensibly, immersed in culture. But at the end of a film or TV project, the word that describes how I feel is not necessarily "renewed." The most fulfilling experiences I've had as an actor have been in the theater, the only medium I could count on for a reliably satisfying artistic result. It was the only place I could bring what I had to offer and believe that it mattered. Often in filmmaking, the people in charge don't even understand what you do, let alone appreciate it. Movies and TV are, primarily, commercial enterprises. And although the theater (Broadway in particular) is not without its commercial imperatives, the work there is more thoughtful and deliberate. More important, it is where you have the chance to grow in some meaningful way.

Performing onstage in *Prelude to a Kiss* was the first time I ever believed that I had any talent for acting. Working with people as smart and nurturing as Norman René and Craig Lucas, as well as the incredibly talented cast, was a classroom, especially coming off the shoot for *Hunt*, which was a different sort of education. That growth continued in *Streetcar* three years later. Performing a role as iconic as Stanley,

I truly believed that the result, the critical reception, didn't matter. Just to play those scenes, say those lines, and rehearse with Greg Mosher could only help me grow. On closing night, tears rolled down my cheeks at the curtain call, as I knew I would never play that role again. To the young actor I say take those chances. Fall on your ass. Fail. It will only benefit you.

By the time we closed *Macbeth* at the Public Theater in 1998, I had learned a great lesson about keeping my focus on my own work by watching Angela Bassett, who played Lady M. Trained at Yale, where she received her undergrad and master's degrees, Angela was intense, kind, and intelligent. But above all, she was prepared and this was instructive. She reminded me that acting is work. It's unique work. It can be enjoyable. But it requires an effort and precision that can't be faked or bypassed with good looks and charm. Just as I did with *Loot* and the likes of Joe Maher, Charlie Keating, and Zeljko Ivanek, I usually found something to learn from the people I worked with onstage, some of whom had decades of experience performing the theater's greatest roles.

Unlike working in film and TV, which nearly always requires complex scheduling, with everyone coming and going, in the theater there is a chance to share an experience like no other. As I got older, I wanted to pass on whatever I had to share by making myself available onstage and off, in both rehearsal and performance. Quite often, however, the younger cast members had longer résumés than mine and didn't need my advice. In fact, I welcomed any they had for me! I also had one or two situations in which someone in the company was eager to take me on. In the movies, I was never a bankable star. That alone can make you feel a tad illegitimate. Similarly, in the theater, there was the occasional actor or director who wanted to test me, confront me, as they thought I wasn't his or her equal onstage. When I performed in the Broadway production of *Orphans* in 2013, Dan Sullivan, a director I had looked forward to working with, appeared to be uninterested and it seemed as though there were other places, other rehearsal rooms, where he'd rather be. The production was a nightmare. And yet I learned a few things on *Orphans*. I learned that once you ascertain what the play is really about, you want to know the director's relationship to that theme. *Orphans* was, for my character, about parenting, about being a father. Sullivan, it turned out, seemed like he didn't want to do a play about fatherhood. But fortunately, those situations are rare. Rehearsing with someone like Walter Bobbie (*Twentieth Century*) and Scott Ellis (*Entertaining Mr. Sloane*) is the norm, and that is heaven.

The scheduling for me to work onstage has been tricky, and I've had to pick and choose those engagements carefully. Telling people in film and television that you are either unavailable or unwilling to come at their call is never easy. The guiding principle seemed to be to pick plays and playwrights whose words I would never tire of saying (that means a strong reliance on revivals), and to accept the risk that I might never get it right. Each night that we did *Equus*, in 2010, my goal was to embrace the nougaty text of Shaffer's play, line by line, in an effort to understand Dysart, the psychiatrist, and the anesthetization of his own sexuality. I literally never said all of Shaffer's lines properly. During the Sunday afternoon matinee that was our final performance, I transposed two lines and crashed my final run at a perfect show, in terms of the text. But what a mountain to ski down!

Other choices were made purely based on the hope of having fun. When I performed *Twentieth Century* with Anne Heche, it was an opportunity to enjoy Hecht and MacArthur's great comedy, which required as much energy, timing, and focus as anything I've ever done. Audiences loved the show. And what a cast. So many great veteran actors, for whom Hecht and MacArthur were a staple, came to see the show and visited backstage afterward to say the kindest things to me.

They included Mel Brooks and Anne Bancroft, Paul Newman and Joanne Woodward, and Chris Plummer. When Shirley MacLaine materialized at my dressing room door, my castmate Stephen DeRosa practically hyperventilated.

I've always had a special love for Joe Orton's writing. Ever since I dreamed of filling in for Maxwell Caulfield in the 1981 production of *Entertaining Mr. Sloane*, I couldn't wait to get onstage and shake hands with Orton's brand of anarchic wit. When the chance came to do *Sloane* at the Laura Pels for the Roundabout, twenty-five years after Max's run at the Cherry Lane, I was elated. The production had its ups and downs. And judging from the fact that some of my favorite Orton lines elicited a quieter response than I had anticipated, I think the New York audience for this playwright may have waned a bit. But what other playwright has a character, in the course of admonishing a young man to steer clear of his sister, say the line, "Give me your word that you're not vaginalatrous!"?

I haven't been onstage as often as I would have liked, but my fondest memories live there. And the importance of the theater and the people I've worked with there always seems to lead back to the very beginning, to Tuck and to the cast of *The Doctors* and what they passed on to me. Learning to act while in the spotlight is difficult. The theater is where you learn. (At times, I tell myself the theater is all one needs to counterbalance a five-year run of a campaign advertising a credit card.) What a gift to work with directors like Max Stafford-Clark (*Serious Money*), Tony Walton (*Equus*), Steve Hamilton (*Gross Points, All My Sons*), Greg Mosher (*Streetcar*), Walter Bobbie (*Twentieth Century*), and Scott Ellis (*Entertaining Mr. Sloane*), and with actors like Michael Wincott, Julie Halston, Jennifer Van Dyke, Laurie Metcalf, and Richard Easton.

In light of some of the highly dubious commercial endeavors I've undertaken, either to fund my charitable foundation or keep the lights on or both, I've subsequently yearned to embrace projects that, like the theater, are good for the soul. Renewal doesn't have to mean an escape from the business altogether. It can mean simply trying something different. I've sung a duet with Barbra Streisand, hosted a radio podcast, worn a coconut bra playing Luther Billis in a concert performance of *South Pacific* at Carnegie Hall. I've produced webisodes in which I gave romantic advice to strangers in the backseat of a car. I've hosted a game show. But the most rewarding of all of those excursions may be my job as the radio announcer for the New York Philharmonic.

In 2009, I attended a concert at Carnegie Hall featuring Christoph Eschenbach and the Philadelphia Orchestra. Seated in the box next to me were Matías Tarnopolsky, the vice president of artistic planning for the New York Philharmonic, and the one and only Zarin Mehta, president and executive director of the Phil, brother of Zubin Mehta, and gentleman without equal. "What are *you* doing here?" Tarnopolsky blurted out. After I explained that years of being trapped in a car in another life had made me a classical music fan, Matías and Zarin exchanged a look; then Zarin said, "Come see me." Soon after that, I was hired as the announcer for the New York Philharmonic's weekly radio broadcast. What a great honor, education, and joy that has been.

In the '80s, I would drive around LA, listening to KUSC, KFAC, and other, now lost FM classical stations. As I'd approach the gates of Warner or Paramount to head into an appointment, the symphony on my radio was still unfolding. I'd call the stations' programming directors, whose numbers I kept on speed dial on my Motorola car phone (yes, you'd dial and they would pick up the phone), to find out all of the details of the piece: composer, ensemble, conductor, recording label. Then I'd hustle over to Tower Classical on Sunset and order the discs. There was no ArkivMusic back then, no Amazon, so I would have to drive back to West Hollywood to pick up the order two weeks later. But it was so worthwhile. Before the advent of digital downloads, I collected a lot of music. I concentrated on that battery between conductor and ensemble that produced much of the more acclaimed classical recordings, back when many of the majors were recording more frequently: Charles Dutoit with the Montreal Symphony, Leonard Slatkin with the St. Louis, George Szell with the Cleveland, Georg Solti with the Chicago, Bernstein with the New York Phil, Levine in Boston, Previn in London, Zubin Mehta in Los Angeles, Eschenbach, Barenboim, Gergiev, Dudamel, Tilson Thomas, Maazel, Haitink, Masur, Salonen, Dohnányi, Abbado, Boulez, Karajan, van Zweden, Boult, Muti.

Classical music renewed me. Like painting and literature, it put me in a grounded place of peace. So much so that if I did it all over again, I'd learn to play the piano and become a conductor. Oh, God, would I ever. Go online and watch Charlie Dutoit conduct. Dutoit, the most elegant of them all. What I wouldn't give to be him for a year. These men (and a few women, like Marin Alsop) float on a cloud made of God-given genius and intense hard work. In the audience, I have been disappointed countless times at the movies, less often at the theater, but never at the symphony, where the orchestra brings to bear the remarkable talents of men and women who exist in their own aerie atop the performing arts. With all my heart, I urge you to visit the symphony in your town or nearby. Afterward, you just might be renewed.

My taste runs toward the lush, the romantic, the sonorous. I've been compiling the list of the recordings I want played at my funeral for some time:

Mahler's Ninth Symphony, fourth movement, Lorin Maazel conducting the New York Philharmonic.

Chopin's Nocturne in B-flat Minor, op. 9, no. 1, performed by Yundi Li.

Mahler's Fourth Symphony, third movement, George Szell conducting the Cleveland Orchestra.

Ravel's *Ma Mère l'Oye* (the *Mother Goose* Suite), Charles Dutoit conducting the Montreal Symphony Orchestra.

Rachmaninov's Symphony no. 2 in E Minor, third movement, André Previn conducting the London Symphony Orchestra.

Chopin's Nocturne in D-flat Major, op. 27, no. 2, performed by Lang Lang.

Ralph Vaughan Williams's *Serenade to Music*, Sir Adrian Boult conducting the London Philharmonic Orchestra.

Tchaikovsky's Symphony no. 6 (*Pathétique*), fourth movement, Valery Gergiev conducting the Orchestra of the Kirov Opera.

I know, I know. It's a long playlist. But come to my funeral, if only for the music. For those of you who are classical fans, I know I'm laying up on the fairway here, going for par. But, hey, at that point I'll be dead. Allow me this last indulgence.

As an actor, you are called upon to make the public private. You're asked to say lines that express the deepest of feelings and, hopefully, imbue them with a veneer of reality. You'd think it would be easy for someone who does that for a living to express publicly how they feel about someone, but the words that come always feel inadequate. Because you handle words with such facility, manipulate emotions so freely, the reality of love becomes complicated. How do you even know when you're acting?

During the period after my divorce, I only dated people who didn't ask for much, as I didn't have much to give. If they wanted the relationship to progress in some way, after a while it sputtered and died. There were a couple of women who saw the worst of me then, as I'd suddenly pull my car over, get out, and scream at my lawyer for fifteen minutes. I was incapable of trusting anyone and therefore also incapable of making any plans. (And who would want to make plans with me during that period?) I was getting older and resigned myself to a life of "compartmentalized intimacy." I fantasized that I would go about my work, spend whatever time with Ireland I could get, and have a very compartmentalized love life. I joked with my friends about going on an annual "sex cruise," where I would find someone with a similar desire to indulge herself like a camel consumes water. One long drink that carries you through, for a very long time, till the next opportunity. An honest, basic transaction. The only things missing were risk and any sense of the restless passion that I'd normally equate with love.

One day, at the lowest point of my custody battle, I lay on the floor of my house in a ball, sobbing. The loss and loneliness were simply crushing me. Everything I had done came to nothing. I never gained any ground. I was more like an uncle in the life of my daughter than a father. I swore to Almighty God that if, one day, I had another chance to meet someone and have a family, to make a home that had what was good about my childhood home while fixing what was wrong, I would give anything in return.

I met Hilaria a couple of months after I'd sworn to my closest friends that I was done looking, finished with hoping. And that time, I actually meant it more than the scores of other times I had sworn that. But when I met Hilaria, I knew there was something unique about her. Hilaria is one of those rarest of people. When you meet her, you know who she is. You don't suspect; you know. Like her remarkable beauty, her intelligence, honesty, and decency are plain. And rather than just inventory my feelings for her, which are many and deep, let me tell you about her and why I am so lucky.

Beyond her spirit and her system of beliefs regarding health, fitness, and nutrition, Hilaria is the most emotionally mature person I've ever met. "*Somos un buen equipo,*" she had engraved inside of our wedding rings, which means, "We are a good team." You'd be lucky to be on a team with someone like this. Grounded, tough, and always prepared to argue her position thoughtfully and effectively (that's a good thing, right?), Hilaria is, most importantly, willing to press every ounce of her being into the service of her friends, family, and those she loves. You couldn't have a better friend. Professionally, you couldn't have a better coach or instructor if your goal is healthier living. Since she had to conquer her own period of unhealthy living, her advice, gained through experience, is simple and practical. When we met, I was bloated, unfit, and careening toward a diagnosis of diabetes. I believe that Hilaria saw me for what I once was and, with her help and example, could be again. To live with someone that fit and healthy, in both mind and body, can be frustrating. At my age, I wondered how much change, how much progress, I could honestly be expected to make. But Hilaria, more patient and kind than any ten people I've ever met, leads by example only. This woman has never uttered an unkind or derogatory word toward me, ever. Not once. (Can you imagine being able to hold your tongue in that way?) She suggests. She recommends. She offers materials to read about nutrition and exercise. And then, the rest is up to you. I have not hit some of my goals these past few years, but I can only imagine where I'd be today if I had not met her. In terms of marrying a real partner in this life, I am the luckiest man on earth.

When I met Hilaria, I was nearly fifty-three and she was twenty-seven, a quarter of a century difference in age (as some on the Internet are eager to remind me every day). Hilaria was raised between Boston and Spain, and aside from our difference in age and upbringing (I've always found it interesting to meet, let alone fall in love with, someone who doesn't know Ed Sullivan, subway tokens, or Howard Johnson's restaurants), Hilaria has had to make some serious adjustments in order to make our life together. The glare of the kind of attention we deal with can be unnerving. Of course, she deals with it better than I do. After we married, we proceeded to have three children in slightly over three years. That plan has offered its own form of renewal. (As I'm rounding the corner toward sixty with three children aged three and under, some days a cruise, any kind of cruise, but especially a sleep cruise, doesn't sound so bad.) But my home is everything I expected and wanted it to be. Hilaria and I do talk about some things other than our children. We also disagree about some things. Thankfully, those are minor. But this is what we both wanted. I wanted Hilaria. I wanted the life we have together. I could never have met anyone, in five hundred lifetimes, who is a better mother. My children are the luckiest children on Earth.

My other child is twenty-one now. It must be odd

for Ireland to look at the other children, in diapers or toddling around our home, either in person or on Face-Time, and say to herself that these are her siblings. But Carmen is so aware of Ireland, often pointing to an airplane in the sky and asking, "Is that Ireland coming?" Ireland, in spite of it all, is loving and funny. God, Ireland is funny. If she wants an acting career, she has more of the necessary elements, perhaps, than anyone in my family. Yes, she is clever and beautiful. She's eclectic and funny. But most important of all, she is in no hurry for you to know her. Which compels you to come to her. In acting, that may be the most important quality of all.

It's easy for two people to lose each other while fulfilling their obligations to their children. (We now have three: Carmen, Rafael, and Leonardo.) There were times I watched my own parents move around our house as if the other person weren't there. I remember when it was just the two of us, when I had Hilaria, this remarkable woman, all to myself. As a mother, she has limitless room in her heart for her children, and even a little bit more to spare. I will take what I can get. I try to remember that my job is to care for her as she cares for our family, to support her in whatever way I can. To deliver whatever stability and certainty I can. When I think of my wife, I'm reminded of *Hamlet*:

Doubt thou the stars are fire;
Doubt that the sun doth move;
Doubt truth to be a liar;
But never doubt I love.

A few moments before our wedding ceremony, which took place on a warm and beautiful day, Hilaria's friend Yoel came to me bearing a wrapped package, inside of which was a small decorative box in antique silver. I opened it to find a piece of paper on which Hilaria had written the most beautiful and meaningful words ever meant for me. That box sits next to my bed, and from time to time, I take out the piece of paper to remind myself of who this woman is and how lucky I truly am. In return, I say, "*Te quiero, mi vida. Te quiero con todo mi corazón.*"

17

Nevertheless

There are so many stories and anecdotes that I have left to tell. There's so much advice I've received that's worth passing on. But this book is what I thought represented the best cross-section of what I've seen, what I've learned, and who I am.

While we were shooting *Path to War* with John Frankenheimer, the great Michael Gambon told me my favorite joke of all time. Be forewarned that is does contain an ugly misogynistic epithet that the Brits tend to throw around in a less gendered way. I'll probably mangle this. But here's my version:

Lord So-and-So, an English tragedian in the mold of Donald Wolfit, upon whom Ronald Harwood based the character of Sir in his play

The Dresser, is touring the provinces, performing Antony and Cleopatra. One evening, he takes
the stage to make an announcement.

ENTER SO-AND-SO (to applause).

SO-AND-SO *(quieting the audience)*:

"I regret to inform you that tonight the role of
Cleopatra shall not be portrayed by Lady Margaret Thornbush *(a murmur in the crowd)*, but
instead shall be assayed by my wife, Emily
Treadwell."

SPECTATOR *(from the back of the house and
shrill)*:

"Your wife's a fucking cunt!"

SO-AND-SO *(after a pause)*:

"Nevertheless."

I used to discount any observations about surviving in
show business. Or any business, for that matter. That

was, of course, when I was young. (Am I getting ready to play Shelley Levene? Willy Loman? King Lear!!) It feels like it's harder than ever to survive in the entertainment business. God knows, I have made many mistakes in my career. Nevertheless, I have more work than I can handle.

I made my share of mistakes raising my daughter Ireland. Nevertheless, I love Ireland with all my soul and I believe she knows that. And that she loves me, too.

It has taken me a lot longer than I thought it would to get my life in order so that someone might want to share it with me. Nevertheless, my wife and our kids are *un sueño hecho realidad*.

I have talked and talked and talked about politics and public policy, and some of it has been effective and worthwhile. Some of it, not so much. Nevertheless, my passion for justice is still easily stirred and my desire to comfort the afflicted is undiminished, regardless of the cost. Even in these almost incomprehensibly cynical times, I still have hope that our country can find its way to liberty and justice . . . for all.

And, finally, I have neither the time nor the talent to write a book. Nevertheless, I wrote this book in my

own words and, such as it is, I offer it to you to enter-
tain, to motivate, to inspire, and to learn. Not so much
for you to learn about me, but for me to learn about me.
I have learned so much while piecing this together. My
thanks to you for reading it.

The Actors Index

I never had many actors as friends. I suppose that's because the days at work are usually long and work is often play, so it's a different kind of friendship. But I have loved so many actors. Their wit, charm, and style. Their vanity, insanity, and courage. So, knowing I will forget more than a few, let me attempt to distill that affection into this simple index:

A is for Julie Andrews, the most elegant movie star of them all. And Woody Allen, the funniest screenwriter of them all. For Abbott and Costello. And for Jean Arthur in movies like *Shane* and *Mr. Deeds Goes to Town*.

B is for Burstyn and Blanchett, Beatty and Bening. For Banderas. For Javier Bardem, Peter Boyle, and Richard

354 · ALEC BALDWIN

Burton. For Kevin Bacon, Gabriel Byrne, and the Bridges clan (how I enjoyed working with Lloyd!). B is for Kathy Bates and Anne Bancroft. And B is for Brando—and I'll watch it all, the good, the bad, and the great. B is for Ingrid Bergman. For Bogart and Bacall. What I would have given to work with Bogart.

C is for Cagney and his athleticism, passion, and tenderness. It's for Joan Crawford. For Sean Connery, Jimmy Caan, and Michael Caine. C is most definitely for Tom Cruise. For Don Cheadle. For Montgomery Clift and John Cazale. For Lee J. Cobb and Tony Curtis. For two Chaneys and a Chaplin. And Gary Cooper.

D is for Bette Davis. To hell with flawless skin and symmetrical features and a swimsuit body. It's the force of her acting (like Nicholson's) that develops the film while it's still in the camera. It's for Depardieu, Deneuve, and de Havilland. For Daniel Day-Lewis and Willem Dafoe. For two Matts, Dillon (because I love *Drugstore Cowboy*) and Damon (because we both died in *Team America*). For De Niro, D'Onofrio, Del Toro, and DiCaprio. Faye Dunaway, Marlene Dietrich, and James Dean. Douglas, *père et fils*. And for Duvall, one of the rare originals in Hollywood.

E is for Emilio Estevez (that's two E's). And for Clint Eastwood, the Bill Belichick of Hollywood. He'll make movies after he's gone. ("You'll find the shot list in the brown folder in my office.")

F is for Firth and Fiennes, for Glenn Ford and Albert Finney. And Errol Flynn. For Laurence Fishburne. It's for all the Fondas. (What a family. And wasn't Henry Fonda great in *Fail Safe*? Tied with Fredric March in *Seven Days in May* for Best Portrayal of the President.) For Mia Farrow.

G is for Jimmy Gandolfini, whose great talent got me to watch TV again. For Mel Gibson. And Andy Garcia, Scott Glenn, and Gielgud. And Andy Griffith. For John Goodman and Ryan Gosling. It's for Cary Grant, Ava Gardner, and Clark Gable. (Don't miss Gable in *The Misfits*.) G is for Alec Guinness. And Garbo. And John Garfield. And Judy Garland.

H is big. Two Hepburns (Katharine and Audrey), two Hunts (Helen and Linda) and a Hunter (Holly). Two Hoffmans (Dustin and Philip Seymour) and a Huffman (Felicity). Hackman and Hanks. H is for Anjelica Huston, Goldie Hawn, and Salma Hayek. Ed Harris and Woody Harrelson. Heston and Holden. Dennis Hopper, Anne Heche, and John Hurt. It's for Timothy Hutton and Rock Hudson. And Julie Harris. (For Julie's memorial, I wrote that her voice was like rain.) And my dear, dear Anthony Hopkins.

I is for Jeremy Irons and Amy Irving and the talented Michael Imperioli.

J is for Samuel L. Jackson. And the Jones gang, as in Dean, Cherry, and James Earl. And Derek Jacobi.

K is for three Keatons, Diane, Michael, and Buster. For Boris Karloff and Ben Kingsley. For Grace Kelly and Gene Kelly. For Keitel and Kidman. It's for Kevin Kline. And Deborah Kerr.

L is for Patti LuPone, that funny, crazy, raging hurricane of talent. It's for two Leighs (Vivien and Janet) and a Jason Leigh (Jennifer), Ray Liotta and Nathan Lane. It's for Jessica Lange and Sophia Loren. For Bela Lugosi, Peter Lorre, Alan Ladd, and Burt Lancaster. For Angela Lansbury and Martin Landau. For Carole Lombard. And Jack Lemmon.

M is for Robert Mitchum, Ray Milland, and Walter Matthau. For Malkovich and McKellen, Rita Moreno and Liza Minnelli. Demi Moore and Julianne Moore. For

Steve Martin and Bill Macy and Malcolm McDowell. Zero Mostel, Eddie Murphy, and the Marx brothers. For Barry Miller and Viggo Mortensen. For Elizabeth McGovern, Frances McDormand, Helen Mirren, and Bette Midler. For Anna Magnani. M is for Paul Muni, Fredric March, and James Mason. For Marilyn Monroe, Steve McQueen, and Shirley MacLaine. And Mastroianni.

N is for Paul Newman and Liam Neeson and Nick Nolte. For Patricia Neal. For Edward Norton and Sam Neill and David Niven. But for so many reasons, for so many moments, N is for Nicholson. Nicholson. Good God, what an actor.

O is for Olivier and Peter O'Toole and Maureen O'Hara. And for Carroll O'Connor and Edmond O'Brien. And O belongs to Gary Oldman, who is, in my opinion, the greatest film actor of his generation.

P is for William Powell. For Chris Plummer and Sean Penn. For Mary-Louise Parker, Gerry Page, Bernadette Peters, and Joan Plowright. And Estelle Parsons. For David Hyde Pierce and Mandy Patinkin. Most of all, P is for Gregory Peck. And Poitier. And Pacino. If you watch the films of these last three alone, you'll learn everything you need to know about acting.

Q means I'm holding two pair: a pair of Quinns and a pair of Quaids (Anthony and Aidan, Randy and Dennis).

R is for the great Basil Rathbone. I must have watched that Sherlock Holmes serial with Rathbone and Nigel Bruce dozens of times. It's for Christopher Reeve and Chris Rock, Mark Ruffalo and Mickey Rourke. For Meg Ryan, Molly Ringwald, and Gilda Radner. For Ray Romano (whose TV show made me laugh out loud on airplanes). For George Raft, Claude Rains, Edward G. Robinson, and Ginger Rogers. Isabella Rossellini and Gena Rowlands. R is for two Redgraves (Vanessa and Lynn) and a Richardson (Natasha). For Burt Reynolds and Tony Randall, both of whom were dedicated to the theater. It's for Jean Reno, one of the most interesting leading men of the last fifty years. R is for Julia Roberts and Debbie Reynolds and Redford.

S is for Woody Strode. For Dean Stockwell and Harry Dean Stanton. For Spacey and Spader and Sutherland, father and son. For Jerry Stiller. And Maggie Smith, Susan Sarandon, and Jean Simmons. For George C. Scott and Campbell Scott, Paul Scofield and John Savage. It's for Gloria Swanson. For Kim Stanley, Eva Marie Saint, and Sissy Spacek. For two Stapletons (Jean and Maureen) and a Swank. For two Sheens (Martin and Charlie) and a

Shandling. For Roy Scheider. For Tom Selleck and William Shatner. For Will Smith and Gary Sinise. Rod Steiger. For Maggie Smith. And Omar Sharif, Barbara Stanwyck, and James Stewart. For Peter Sellers, Elaine Stritch, and Meryl Streep. For Sinatra. And Streisand.

T is for Spencer Tracy. It's for two Turners (Kathleen and Lana) and a Tomei. For Gene Tierney, Kristin Scott Thomas, and Emma Thompson (don't you love Emma Thompson?). For Aida Turturro and John Turturro. Rip Torn and Jessica Tandy. Two men who danced their way to movie stardom, Russ Tamblyn and John Travolta. It's for three Taylors: Robert, Rod, and of course the biggest movie star of them all, Elizabeth.

U is for Ustinov. And Blair Underwood. And, believe it or not, a pair of Ullman(n)s, Tracey and Liv.

V is for von Sydow and Jon Voight, both among my favorites. How I love Jon Voight in *Deliverance*.

W is for the incomparable Debra Winger. And Billy Dee Williams. For Sam Waterston and Chris Walken and Treat Williams. For Owen Wilson and Forest Whitaker. W is for two Watsons (Emma and Emily) and a Weaver (Sigourney). For Rachel Ward and Natalie Wood. It's for

Gene Wilder, Robert Wagner, Eli Wallach, Richard Widmark, and Jonathan Winters. For Winfrey, Witherspoon, and Winslet. Denzel Washington and Robin Williams. For Mare Winningham and Alfre Woodard. For the remarkable Shelley Winters. And Teresa Wright. For John Wayne. And Joanne Woodward. And Orson Welles.

X is a rating we all try to avoid.

Y is for Michael York and Chow Yun-Fat. For Loretta Young.

Z is for Zellwegger and Zeta-Jones. And Anthony Zerbe. (Zerbe, in *Papillon*: "How did you know that I have dry leprosy? That it isn't contagious?" McQueen: "I didn't.")

I'm exhausted. But there you are. Not a bad list. And so many I left out! Maybe even on purpose? That could be a whole other book!

Acknowledgments

I wish to thank Karen Gantz, my literary agent, for her encouragement during the process of writing my first book and during this one as well. Karen's intellect, generous spirit, and thoroughness cannot go unmarked.

My thanks to Jonathan Burnham and Emily Griffin at HarperCollins.

I am grateful to Mark Tabb, my collaborator on my first book, whose lessons stayed with me and surely helped my writing in *Nevertheless*.

Special thanks to David O'Brien, J. Michael Bloom, Arnie Herman, Elaine Aiken, Jane Shatz, Vicki Green, Monsignor George Deas, and any other kind, caring soul who helped me through the difficult times.

Thanks to my mother, my siblings, and to their families for many of the memories that fuel this book.

Particularly Beth, with whom I will always have a special bond.

Thank you to all of the writers of books, screenplays, journalism, and speeches I have come across in my life and have attempted to steal from as inoffensively as possible.

Thank you to my theatrical agents, Matt DelPiano and George Lane, for performing the miracle of maintaining my career.

Thank you to my wife, Hilaria, who listened to me complain and moan about writing this book and supported me in so many ways, including suggestions regarding the writing itself. Her help has been invaluable.

About the Author

ALEC BALDWIN is a multiple Emmy, Golden Globe, and Screen Actors Guild Award–winning actor, producer, comedian, and philanthropist. He also has been nominated for an Oscar and a Tony Award, and is the author of the *New York Times* bestseller *A Promise to Ourselves*. He lives in New York City with his wife, Hilaria, and their three children.

THE NEW LUXURY IN READING

We hope you enjoyed reading
our new, comfortable print size and found it
an experience you would like to repeat.

Well – you're in luck!

HarperLuxe offers the finest in fiction and
nonfiction books in this same larger print size and
paperback format. Light and easy to read, HarperLuxe
paperbacks are for book lovers who want to see
what they are reading without the strain.

For a full listing of titles and
new releases to come, please visit our website:

www.HarperLuxe.com